Global Conflict and Security since 1945

Editors: Professor Saki R. Dockrill, King's College London and Dr. William Rosenau, RAND

Palgrave Macmillan's new book series *Global Conflict and Security since 1945* seeks fresh historical perspectives to promote the empirical understanding of global conflict and security issues arising from international law, leadership, politics, multilateral operations, weapons systems and technology, intelligence, civil-military relations and societies. The series welcomes original and innovative approaches to the subject by new and established scholars. Possible topics include terrorism, nationalism, civil wars, the Cold War, military and humanitarian interventions, nation-building, pre-emptive attacks, the role of the United Nations and other non-governmental organisations (NGOs), and the national security and defence policies of major states. Events in the world since September 11th 2001 remind us that differences of ideology, religion and values and beliefs held by a group of societies or people affect the security of ordinary peoples and different societies often without warning. The series is designed to deepen our understanding of the recent past and seeks to make a significant contribution to the debates on conflict and security in the major world capitals.

Advisory Board Members:

Professor Mats Berdal, Chair of Security and Development, King's College London

Ambassador James Dobbins, Director International Security and Defence Policy Center, RAND

Professor Sir Lawrence Freedman, Vice Principal (Research), King's College London

Professor Bruce Hoffman, Georgetown University and former Director of RAND's Washington Office

Titles in the series include:

Vesselin Dimitrov
STALIN'S COLD WAR: SOVIET FOREIGN POLICY, DEMOCRACY AND COMMUNISM IN BULGARIA 1941–48

James Ellison
UNITED STATES, BRITAIN AND THE TRANSATLANTIC CRISIS
Rising to the Gaullist Challenge, 1963–1968

Jon Roper
THE UNITED STATES AND THE LEGACY OF THE VIETNAM WAR

T. O. Smith
BRITAIN AND THE ORIGINS OF THE VIETNAM WAR
UK policy in Indo-China, 1943–50

Forthcoming titles:

Peter Lowe
CONTENDING WITH NATIONALISM AND COMMUNISM
British policy towards South-East Asia, 1945–65

Ken Young
WEAPONS SYSTEMS AND THE POLITICS OF INTERDEPENDENCE

Global Conflict and Security since 1945
Series Standing Order ISBN 978–0–230–52123–0 hardcover
(*outside North America only*)

You can receive future titles in this series as they are published by placing a standing order. Please contact your bookseller or, in case of difficulty, write to us at the address below with your name and address, the title of the series and one of the ISBNs quoted above.

Customer Services Department, Macmillan Distribution Ltd, Houndmills, Basingstoke, Hampshire RG21 6XS, England

The United States and the Legacy of the Vietnam War

Edited by

Jon Roper

First published 2007 by
PALGRAVE MACMILLAN
Houndmills, Basingstoke, Hampshire RG21 6XS and
175 Fifth Avenue, New York, N.Y. 10010
Companies and representatives throughout the world

PALGRAVE MACMILLAN is the global academic imprint of the Palgrave
Macmillan division of St. Martin's Press, LLC and of Palgrave Macmillan Ltd.
Macmillan® is a registered trademark in the United States, United Kingdom
and other countries. Palgrave is a registered trademark in the European
Union and other countries.

ISBN-13: 978–0–230–50042–6 hardback
ISBN-10: 0–230–50042–0 hardback

This book is printed on paper suitable for recycling and made from fully
managed and sustained forest sources. Logging, pulping and manufacturing
processes are expected to conform to the environmental regulations of the
country of origin.

A catalogue record for this book is available from the British Library.

A catalog record for this book is available from the Library of Congress.

10   9   8   7   6   5   4   3   2   1
16   15   14   13   12   11   10   09   08   07

Printed and bound in Great Britain by
Antony Rowe Ltd, Chippenham and Eastbourne

Cariad, N. C. A. J.

Contents

Acknowledgements

In May 2005 a colloquium, 'Thirty Years On: The United States and the Legacy of the Vietnam War 1975–2005', was held at the British Academy in London. I would like to thank Lawrence Freedman, FBA, and Saki Dockrill for their help and advice in organizing this event, together with Michael Reade, assistant secretary for public events, and his colleagues at the Academy who made it possible. The colloquium was the catalyst for this book.

It has been a pleasure to have the opportunity to work with all the contributors, and I am grateful for the support they have given me in the course of this project. Three chapters – from Jonathan Schell, H. Bruce Franklin, and Phil Melling – are based on the presentations they first gave at the British Academy Colloquium. In inviting further contributions to this book, I was able to draw on the work of long-standing colleagues and friends of the Department of American Studies at Swansea University. Indeed, in 1988, Bill Ehrhart, John Hellmann, and Walter Hölbling came to the conference on 'Vietnam and the West' which Phil Melling and I organised there. Subsequently, in 1991, John spent time as a visiting professor and from 1997 onwards, Bill became a visiting (now honorary) research fellow in the Department.

I first met Subarno Chattarji when he took advantage of Bill Ehrhart's presence in Wales to visit and to talk with him as part of his research into the poetry of the Vietnam War, undertaken for his doctoral degree at Oxford University. I would like to add my thanks to his in acknowledging John Baky's help at the Imaginative Representations of the Vietnam War Collection at La Salle University in Philadelphia, where Subarno was able to present the research on which his chapter is based.

Michael Strang and Ruth Ireland have offered advice and encouragement throughout the production of this book, and I have appreciated their assistance together with that of their colleagues at

Palgrave Macmillan. The Department of American Studies and the School of Humanities at Swansea have continued to provide a congenial environment in which to work.

Jon Roper
Swansea

Contributors

Subarno Chattarji is lecturer in the Department of American Studies at Swansea University. He was formerly Visiting Professor in American and British Literature, at Miyazaki International College, Miyazaki, Japan. His publications include *Memories of a Lost War: American Poetic Responses to the Vietnam War* (2001).

W. D. Ehrhart holds a PhD in American Studies from the University of Wales at Swansea, and teaches English and History at the Haverford School in suburban Philadelphia, Pennsylvania. Ehrhart enlisted in the US Marine Corps in 1966 at age 17. He fought in Vietnam with 1st Battalion, 1st Marine Regiment, receiving the Purple Heart Medal, the Navy Combat Action Ribbon, and two Presidential Unit Citations, and achieving the rank of sergeant. The author of 14 books of prose and poetry, as well as 10 chapbooks of poetry, and editor or co-editor of four anthologies, Ehrhart's most recent collection is *Sleeping with the Dead* (2006).

H. Bruce Franklin is the author or editor of 19 books on American history and culture, including 4 about the Vietnam War. He flew for three years as a navigator and intelligence officer in the Strategic Air Command, and in 1966 resigned his commission in protest against the war. He is currently the John Cotton Dana Professor of English and American Studies at Rutgers University, Newark.

John Hellmann is Professor of English at the Ohio State University. He is the author of *Fables of Fact: The New Journalism as New Fiction* (1981), *American Myth and the Legacy of Vietnam* (1986), and *The Kennedy Obsession: The American Myth of JFK* (1997). He served as a Senior Fulbright Lecturer at the University of Antwerp in Belgium in 1985 and again at the University of Bonn in Germany during 1992–93.

Walter W. Hölbling is Professor of US literature and culture at the University of Graz. Among his recent publications are *What is American? New Identities in US Culture* (2004) and *Nature's Nation Revisited: American Concepts of Nature from Wonder to Ecological Crisis*

(2003). He has also written on the subjects of American Studies in Europe, US postcolonial fiction, and affinities between American literature and political rhetoric.

Philip H. Melling is Professor of American Literature and Cultural Studies in the Department of American Studies at Swansea University. He has published monographs on the literature of the Vietnam War and contemporary Fundamentalism. From 1993–2002 he was general editor of the journal *Borderlines* and during that period published widely on the American novel and film. His most recent research is on Hemingway and Cuba and an article of his on Hemingway and Afro-Cuban Religion recently appeared in *The Hemingway Review*.

Jon Roper is Professor and Head of the Department of American Studies at Swansea University. His research interests encompass American political ideas, the American Presidency and the impact of war on American politics, culture and society. He is the author of *Democracy and Its Critics* (1989), *The American Presidents: Heroic Leadership from Kennedy to Clinton* (2000), and *The Contours of American Politics* (2002). Other edited books include (with John Baylis) *The United States and Europe: Beyond the Neoconservative Divide* (2006).

Jonathan Schell is *The Nation*'s peace and disarmament correspondent, and the Harold Willens Peace Fellow at the Nation Institute. In 2005, he was Distinguished Visiting Fellow at the Center for the Study of Globalization at Yale. His numerous publications include *The Real War* (1988), *The Unconquerable World: Power, Nonviolence, and the Will of the People* (2003), and *A Hole in the World: A Story of War, Protest and the New American Order* (2004). A collection of his essays was published as *The Jonathan Schell Reader* (2005).

1
Over Thirty Years

Jon Roper

Over thirty years ago most Americans who had remained after the achievement of what their then President had called in 1973, a 'Peace with Honor,' together with those Vietnamese who scrambled to go with them, left hurriedly as South Vietnam was invaded from the North and re-unified as one country. Among the Vietnamese who remained in what was swiftly re-named Ho Chi Minh City was Pham Xuan An, who throughout the war had worked as a reporter for US media organizations – principally for *Time* magazine – but who, as a Viet Cong colonel, had passed military secrets to the North. As *The Washington Post* noted in his obituary – he died in September 2006 aged 79:

> Although his job as a spy was to uncover and report the plans of the South Vietnamese and U.S. military, he was so good at collecting and analyzing information that he was considered the best Vietnamese reporter in the press corps. He said he did not lie, tilt the news or spread disinformation in the stories he filed.

His wife and family left the country, yet Pham Xuan An stayed in Vietnam after the invasion. It was, he subsequently admitted, 'the stupidest thing I ever did.'[1] However in many ways his is a story that encapsulates the complexities and contradictions that characterize the war in Vietnam.

In 1975, as helicopters clattered away from the roof of its embassy in Saigon, and military equipment was unceremoniously dumped in the South China Sea, the Vietnam War, the origins of which stretched back another thirty years, finally ended. Since that time, for over thirty years, the consequences of America's military involvement in Southeast Asia has caused deep and enduring divisions within the United States, not least among those liberals who had initially seen it as a necessary part of the strategy of containment. If America entered Vietnam when there was a broad ideological agreement upon both the aims and the direction of the nation's foreign policy and its use of military power overseas, its prosecution of the war there led many liberals to question whether its moral compass had gone awry. Vietnam undermined the architecture of American foreign policy, with political aftershocks that are still evident today.

Liberal realism and the reality of war

As Lawrence Freedman points out in *Kennedy's Wars* (2000), 'Cold War liberalism had a distinctive framework of its own.' It was articulated by those such as Arthur Schlesinger Jr, who, in *The Vital Center* (1949), emphasized the need to maintain the liberal-conservative alliance that as a result of World War II had successfully overcome the totalitarian threat from the right – fascism – but which now faced an equal, if not more dangerous challenge from the totalitarian left in the form of what was perceived as a virulent and expansive international communism. This was not simply an argument for ideological consensus in the face of such a prospect. Military action might also be necessary. Freedman cites Schlesinger's observation 'that while it might be the case that ideas cannot be fought with guns, "it is equally true that you cannot fight guns with ideas alone." '[2] Within two decades, however, such liberal realism was encountering the reality of war in Vietnam.

Garry Dorrien charts the fate of what he refers to as the ' "Vital Center" liberalism that claimed the mainstream of American politics in the late 1940s and 1950s' through the changing attitudes of Rheinhold Neibhur – whom Freedman identifies as 'the great philosopher of liberal realism.'[3] Niebhur initially supported Lyndon Johnson and the Vietnam War, and in 1965 was awarded the Medal of Freedom by the President, who in the citation accompanying the award described the theologian as having 'invoked the ancient insights of Christianity to illuminate the experience and fortify the will of the modern age.'[4] Yet as Dorrien observes:

the Niebuhr-quoting realists in the Kennedy and Johnson administrations created a disaster in Vietnam, and the Vital Center
exploded, hurtling Niebuhrians to the right and left. To his sad
surprise, Niebuhr tacked to the left, joining the antiwar movement.
By 1966 he lamented that America had turned the Vietnamese
civil war into an American imperial war: 'We are making South
Vietnam into an American colony....We are physically ruining
an unhappy nation in the process of 'saving it'. By 1967 he called
for an American withdrawal from Vietnam and a public outcry
'against these horrendous policies.'5

For Schlesinger, writing in 1966 in an attempt to stir American public
opinion against Lyndon B. Johnson's prosecution of the war, 'the
Vietnam story is a tragedy without villains.'6 But it was not without
its political casualties. Niebuhr and Schlesinger contributed to the
prevailing climate of opinion that persuaded the President not to
run for a second full term in office in 1968: because of Vietnam, LBJ
effectively resigned from office albeit in less spectacular fashion than
did his successor, Richard Nixon, six years later. Schlesinger would
subsequently describe both of them as psychologically disturbed, as
the 'Imperial Presidency' was consumed in the political fire-storms of
Vietnam and Watergate.7

Each of their successors, moreover, has felt in different ways and
with varying intensities the long shadow of the war in Vietnam.
Gerald Ford, during whose short administration the North's invasion
took place, and Jimmy Carter during four troubled years in the White
House, both wrestled with the complexities of the immediate post-
Vietnam erosion of national self-belief. Thereafter, the legacy of the
war impacted upon Ronald Reagan, whose actions in the Iran-Contra
scandal were attributable to his inability to persuade the public to
support his interventionist ambitions overseas. Its aftershocks fell
upon George Bush, whose conviction that he had laid to rest the
memory of failure in Vietnam by swift military victory in the Gulf in
1991 proved mistaken and upon Bill Clinton, whose conduct during
the time he was eligible to be drafted to Vietnam came back to haunt
his campaign for the White House in the following year. And now,
George W. Bush's pursuit of the 'war on terror' in Iraq has raised very
real fears among his critics of another debacle of similar proportions
to that which took place in Southeast Asia.

Looking back two decades after the war, Robert McNamara believed that 'we made an error not of values and intentions but of judgment and capabilities' in committing military forces to Vietnam.[8] The decision to fight in Southeast Asia was the product of the ideology that underpinned America's strategic and tactical thinking during the Cold War. It was a perspective on the world that intellectuals such as Schlesinger and Neibuhr helped to shape, and which public servants like McNamara did much to implement. In *Kennedy's Wars*, Lawrence Freedman shows how the crises that confronted the Kennedy administration, in Berlin, Cuba, Laos, and Vietnam were not only linked, but also framed within the context of an ever-present fear that they might escalate to nuclear conflict. Kennedy's approach: cautious, measured, maintaining options rather than fore-closing on them worked particularly effectively in the defining weeks of his Presidency, as he found a resolution to the Cuban Missile Crisis. However, the resulting conviction that ways could be found to manage other potential Cold War-flashpoints was influential in persuading members of his administration that successful intervention in Vietnam was possible.

It was only after Kennedy's death that Vietnam fractured America's political consensus and there was a growing realization that military activism in support of ideas of containment and the threat of countries falling like dominoes to Communist influence might be misplaced. Kennedy did not have to deal with that changing reality. His successors – Johnson and Nixon – did. The 'credibility gap' that emerged was not simply that which opened up between what the President said about Vietnam and what people came to believe was the reality of the situation there. It was also the result of a fundamental questioning of the ideological assumptions upon which Cold War policies had been predicated. Just as McCarthyism had threatened the civil liberties which anti-communism claimed to wish to preserve, so America's conduct of the war in South Vietnam seemed to do little to win 'hearts and minds' there or at home. By 1967, when Jonathan Schell was told by an American soldier that it 'was necessary to destroy the village in order to save it,' the extent to which America's reasons for being in Vietnam were being compromised by its actions there was underlined. It was what they saw as this loss of direction in the nation's moral compass in the prosecution of the war that helped turn many liberals against it.

Whatever his hindsight, at the time even McNamara himself was not immune from such doubts. Like Schlesinger and Niebuhr he became skeptical about what America was bringing about in Southeast Asia. In May 1967, as Neil Sheehan points out, the Secretary of Defense gave Johnson 'a memorandum saying that the president could not win the war in Vietnam and ought to negotiate an unfavorable peace.' In June, he authorized the compilation of the *Pentagon Papers*, and later that year, following a meeting with Schell, asked him to dictate his account of the destruction that he had witnessed taking place in Quang Ngai province, lending him an office and allowing him canteen privileges in the Pentagon while he did so. After three days a copy of the resulting report was left at the Department of Defense while subsequently Schell submitted his manuscript to *The New Yorker*.[9]

Toward the end of his life, Reinhold Neibuhr had wondered whether, in the light of America's actions in Vietnam, 'perhaps there is not so much to choose between Communist and anti-Communist fanaticism.' As Garry Dorrien observes:

> thus did the Cold War liberals back away from the ravages of anticommunist containment in Vietnam; a long succession of Kennedy and Johnson administration officials followed Niebuhr in repenting of imperial overstretch.

Yet while some liberal realists reacted against the reality of Vietnam, others became concerned at the impact of the failure of America's intervention upon its capacity to exercise military power overseas. This, as Dorrien argues, 'was the political context that gave birth to neoconservatism.'[10] Following America's withdrawal of its forces from Vietnam, moreover, the legacy of this polarization between those liberal realists who turned against the war and those who migrated to the right of the ideological spectrum influenced the subsequent historiography of the war.

Advocacy history

Interpretations of the Vietnam War can thus be seen as an example of the contemporary style of – in Carl Degler's words – 'advocacy history' on either side of the ideological divide.[11] Soon after American

involvement had ended, in 1977, Norman Podhoretz, editor of
Commentary and a leading neoconservative charged that 'the same
liberals who had run the Vietnam War under Kennedy and Johnson
were atoning for their sins by keeping America at home.'[12] In *Why
We Were in Vietnam* (1982) he was convinced that by the time that
Vietnam was re-unified in 1975, the argument over the war had
'already been settled in favor of the moral and political position of
the antiwar movement.'[13] If Vietnam came to be seen as an enduring
symbol of the folly of military intervention overseas, then neoconservatives like Podhoretz were concerned that America's future capacity
to use military power in support of its perceived strategic interests
would be undermined. In this context, the challenge was to rebut the
antiwar perspective and to present a revisionist account of what had
happened in Southeast Asia.

There were attempts to accommodate competing ideological interpretations within what were presented as dispassionate historical
narratives tracing America's military involvement in Southeast Asia,
but the difficulties inherent in such an approach were, on closer
examination of their arguments, self-evident. In 1983, for example, in
association with the PBS television series, Stanley Karnow published
Vietnam: A History. It won a Pulitzer Prize and rapidly established itself
as one of the most popular books on the war, described by reviewers as
'extraordinarily objective' and 'a seminal work.' Consider, however,
its opening vignette of the Vietnam War Memorial in Washington
DC. The names on it, Karnow suggests,

> Represent a sacrifice to a failed crusade, however noble or illusory
> its motives. They bear witness to the end of America's absolute
> confidence in its moral exclusivity, its military invincibility, its
> manifest destiny. They are the price, paid in blood and sorrow,
> for America's awakening to maturity, to the recognition of its
> limitations. With the young men who died in Vietnam died the
> dream of an 'American Century.'[14]

At that time, it was possible to be cavalier with the use of the
word 'crusade,' but the rest of Karnow's language is also revealing.
America's altruistic 'sacrifice' is described in terms – 'noble or
illusory' – that resonate with neoconservatives and liberals alike.
America's casualties become silent witnesses to the nation's newly

found 'maturity': Vietnam is seen as its childhood folly or adolescent adventure. This explanation of the meaning of the war is one from which American readers of *Vietnam* might take some comfort. The nation has grown up, moved on: failure and defeat were aberrations in the broader sweep of America's history. Later, Karnow quotes Clark Clifford: 'we made an honest mistake. I feel no sense of shame . . . We felt that we were doing what was necessary. It proved to be unsound.'[15] It was surely preferable to feel unencumbered by historical embarrassment rather than to remain haunted by the past. From this perspective, the Vietnam War can be seen as an episode in American history that can be understood, explained, and rationalized as a discrete event: a failed attempt to follow a policy motivated by good intentions in the context of the perceived ideological framework of Cold War foreign policy.

Like Podhoretz, commentators such as Harry Summers complained that early works saw America's action as 'patently illegal, immoral, and unjust.' Those who argued against this anti-war orthodoxy were intimidated by this 'tyranny of fashion' – 'woe betide anyone who had the audacity to challenge this received truth.' During the 1980s, however, the rising tide of revisionism shaped the historiography of the war in another direction. By 1985, Summers wrote approvingly, there had been a 'significant improvement' in the literature. 'Once dominated by emotional, one-sided, and in some cases deliberately distorted accounts, now at long last evenhanded and objective works are finding their way into publication.'[16] Indeed, by the end of the decade, different interpretations of the war became part of what had become characterized as the 'Vietnam Debate.' Anthologies presented both sides of the 'argument' about why America had become involved in Vietnam, how the war had been fought, why it had ended in failure and defeat, and what lessons might be drawn from such opposing viewpoints. An objective analysis was assumed to emerge from a synthesis of the different perspectives presented.

For Leslie Gelb, who worked in both the Department of Defense and the State Department during the Johnson and Carter administrations, and who became head of the Council on Foreign Relations, the 'irony of Vietnam' in the title of the book he wrote with Richard Betts was that 'the system worked.' Until Congress had refused to fund the South Vietnamese government, they argued, America had managed to maintain its objective of a non-communist government there.

William Sullivan, US ambassador to the Philippines and then Iran, went further in identifying the 'positive consequences' of America's involvement in Southeast Asia. He suggested that the 'Vietnam operation' had been 'one of the master strategic strokes of the century' which had resulted in 'an equilibrium in the Pacific which is probably the best that has prevailed there since the sixteenth century.'[17]

In 1990, the introduction to a book which promised 'a fresh look at the arguments' over Vietnam was adamant that 'the United States entered the war in Indochina with the highest of moral objectives: to protect the right of self-determination of the people of the republic of Viet Nam (RVN) and to maintain world order by deterring aggression.' This was revisionism, revitalized in the year after the Berlin Wall had been torn down. It reclaimed the moral high ground for Cold War American foreign policy as well as pointing out that the failure to contain communism in Vietnam had proven the domino theory correct since: 'no amount of historical reexamination or introspection will alter the high moral purpose of the United States or the reality that North Vietnam has militarily conquered South Vietnam and subjugated Cambodia and Laos.'[18] These ideological divisions that continue to shape the historiography of the war are also reflected in other spheres: notably in the ways in which the war was represented in popular culture, by Hollywood in particular and also in the growing body of literature written by those who witnessed it at first hand.

War films and the literature of war

For Richard Slotkin: 'Cultural crisis is the mother of myth/ideological invention, and the Vietnam War is a particularly appropriate symbol of the catastrophe that overtook the liberal consensus and the New Frontier.'[19] The three major Hollywood films that sought to present America's experience in Vietnam to its movie-going public that were released prior to Ronald Reagan winning the Presidency in 1980, *Coming Home* and *The Deer Hunter* (1978), and *Apocalypse Now* (1979), reflect the issues that confronted liberal realists during the 1960s. These films questioned the morality of the war while examining its impact upon the soldiers who had fought it and the communities they had left behind. The latter two in particular offered complex interpretations of the war through allegorical references and attempted to place America's experience in historical and literary contexts.

For Slotkin, therefore, *The Deer Hunter* 'interprets the Vietnam War as an enactment of fundamental American values by drawing on motifs from *The Searchers* and Cooper's Leatherstocking Tales.'[20] In it, the central character, Michael, played by Robert de Niro, returns from Vietnam no longer able to appreciate, as he had prior to his experience there, the challenge of hunting and killing a deer with the aesthetically satisfying 'one shot.' The metaphor is extended when, returning to Vietnam to bring Nick (Christopher Walken) home, he witnesses his traumatized friend gambling his life away in a game of Russian roulette. In the closing scene, members of the close-knit immigrant community to which Michael and Nick belonged sing 'God Bless America.' It is left to the audience to decide whether this is an ironic commentary on the war or a defiant patriotism that endures despite the impact Vietnam has had on them, personally and collectively, or indeed neither, for as John Hellmann has argued, 'Michael and the other characters make a half-conscious call for grace, a parallel to the Puritan settlers' anxious renewal of their special covenant with God, the compact which in secular form has been central to the idea of America.'[21]

In *Apocalypse Now*, the central mission undertaken by Willard (Martin Sheen) is not against the Vietnamese, but aims to root out and destroy a renegade American. The film not only approaches Vietnam through a reworking of the themes explored in Joseph Conrad's *Heart of Darkness* (1902), but also, as Phil Melling has pointed out, again re-examines American cultural impulses that were prevalent in colonial times in Puritan New England. Puritans thought of settlements in terms of 'good' and 'bad' enclaves. For Melling: 'Colonel Kurtz is menacing precisely because he has established a bad enclave and has incorporated into that enclave too many of the nativist features the American military associate with the enemy.' Kurtz (Marlon Brando) has rejected America's way of fighting the war and has instead privatized it, disappearing into the jungle to organize the natives in pursuit of his own purposes and objectives:

> Kurtz's encampment is remote and camouflaged; it is redolent with wilderness energies and pagan ritual; it flourishes in spite of orthodox political and military belief; it pays no heed to

the conventions of the garrison; and it disputes the compelling commission from God to build a visible city on a hill. The encampment, therefore, is a threat to Puritan order and stability.[22]

The film established in the popular mind iconic symbols of the war: the ubiquitous helicopters and the rock-and-roll soundtrack become the backdrop that defines America's dominating presence in the jungles of Vietnam.

By the mid-1980s, however, more straightforward revisionist questions were being asked in movies about the war. In *Rambo, First Blood Part 2* (1985) the hero (Sylvester Stallone) only had to enquire 'do we get to win this time?' and then fight his celluloid war to a successful conclusion. Of the films released during Ronald Reagan's presidency, however, it was Oliver Stone's Oscar winning *Platoon* (1986) that provided a commentary on the collapse of America's Cold War liberal consensus. Vietnam becomes a war between disillusioned liberal realists who see it as immoral, and those who believe that power should take precedence over morality. Stone's hero, Chris Taylor (Charlie Sheen), is an idealistic volunteer, but his experiences in Vietnam rapidly lead him to question America's mission and purpose there. The film is a morality play in which Taylor eventually makes the – for liberals – right moral choice in siding with the 'good' Sergeant Elias rather than the pragmatic but 'bad' Sergeant Barnes. He leaves Vietnam having concluded that the real enemy he had battled there was his conscience: 'I think now, looking back, we did not fight the enemy, we fought ourselves and the enemy was in us.' In its graphic and apparently authentic depiction of the experience of those who fought in Vietnam – Stone had served in America's forces there – the film also reflected a growing preference among conservatives to concentrate on the qualities of the ordinary GIs caught up in the conflict rather than to analyze the significance of the event. In that sense, *Platoon* is able to satisfy opposing ideological constituencies even as it illustrates the divide between them.

Literary representations of the war reflect a similar diversity, not simply in the ideological outlooks of their authors. Michael Herr, for example, offers new journalism's account as an observer of and participant in what to him becomes America's dexadrine-fuelled rock-and-roll experience in Southeast Asia. In *Dispatches* (1977), for the increasing number of deracinated draftees, the drugs, the music, and the war are inseparable. In an early vignette, along with Tim Page and Sean Flynn, Herr is mistakenly thought to be with the morale-boosting United Services Organizations (USO):

'Aw, we thought you was . . . ' cause your hair's so long.' Page took the kid's picture, I got the words down and Flynn laughed and told him we were the Rolling Stones.[23]

In between the opening and concluding chapters, 'Breathing In' and 'Breathing Out,' Herr's Vietnam is revealed in all its postmodern confusion. Hitching rides on military helicopters, Herr explores the theatre of war as though writing scenes from a film: indeed he later contributed to the screenplay of *Apocalypse Now*. While inhaling and exhaling, moreover, he provides the accompanying soundtrack: sprinkling his narrative with lyrics from, among others, the Rolling Stones, Frank Zappa, and Jimi Hendrix. Back in America:

Out on the street I couldn't tell the Vietnam veterans from the rock and roll veterans. The Sixties had made so many casualties, its war and its music had run power off the same circuit for so long they didn't even have to fuse. . . . What I'd thought of as two obsessions were really only one . . .

The concluding observation: 'Vietnam Vietnam, Vietnam, we've all been there' suggests that the war should be seen as a defining and common cultural experience, but what Herr presents is a simulacrum of a war that others describe in different terms.[24] Indeed, as John Hellmann suggests, *Dispatches* is 'an intensely fragmented, self-absorbed work' which 'is less a book about Herr's journey in Vietnam than about his subsequent exploration of that experience.'[25]

Among the many other autobiographical accounts of those who experienced the war, another widely cited work, Philip Caputo's *A Rumor of War* (1977), was published in the same year as *Dispatches*. Caputo was among the first American combat troops sent to Southeast Asia in 1965, and also, as a journalist, was among those Americans evacuated from Saigon a decade later. During his time serving with the Marines near Da Nang, he, like Jonathan Schell in Quang Ngai, witnessed the increasing intensity of the conflict.

There was another side to the war, about which no songs were sung, no jokes made. The fighting had not only become more intense but more vicious. Both we and the Viet Cong began to make a habit of atrocities.[26]

Caputo realizes the dilemmas that he faces in trying to distinguish between enemies and non-combatants – as Herr too had observed, 'trying to read the faces of the Vietnamese, . . . was like trying to read the wind.'[27] Charged with two counts of the pre-meditated murders of Vietnamese civilians, he concludes that:

> The deaths of Le Dung and Le Du could not be divorced from the nature and conduct of the war. . . .As I had come to see it, America could not intervene in a people's war without killing some of the people. But to raise those points in explanation or extenuation would be to raise a host of ambiguous moral questions. It could even raise the question of the morality of American intervention in Vietnam.

Eventually the charges against him were dropped, but Caputo faced the same problem that disillusioned liberal realists confronted in Vietnam. Like them, he could regard himself as 'a moral casualty' of the war.[28]

In an epilogue to the book, describing the fall of Saigon, he remembers 'back a decade, to that day we had marched into Vietnam, swaggering, confident, and full of idealism. We had believed we were there for a high moral purpose. But somehow our idealism was lost, our morals corrupted and the purpose forgotten.'[29] Caputo does not attempt to explain how these things occurred: they just 'somehow' happened. Rather than human agency being involved, the implication is that it is the war itself that is to blame for the decay of honest intentions. With both sides becoming habituated to atrocities, the reality of the conflict was such that it could be regarded as neither 'good' nor 'just.' America's failure is inevitable. Forced into a fight where there is no moral high-ground to be taken, the war for the 'hearts and minds' of both the Vietnamese and those Americans who turned against their country's intervention could not be won. For Caputo, that is the meaning and significance of Vietnam.

In contrast, a constant refrain among the characters in John Del Vecchio's novel, *The 13th Valley* (1982), is that 'it don't mean nothing.' In characterizing the war as meaningless, Del Vecchio deconstructs America's intervention in Southeast Asia as not so much an immoral as a nihilistic war. Such Nietszchean sentiments, moreover, make his work reminiscent of Norman Mailer's World War II novel, *The Naked and the Dead* (1948), the narrative structure of which it also resembles. Toward the end of Del Vecchio's novel, Chelini (Cherry), psychologically traumatized through his experience of war, tells Brooks, his commanding officer, that 'God created man in his own image. Then God became man. Do you know why? It's because Man is God.' Mailer's protagonists reached a similar conclusion. In *The Naked and the Dead*, Lieutenant Hearn poses the rhetorical question, 'Man's deepest urge is omnipotence?' As Major General Cumings argues in reply, he concludes that 'the only morality of the future is a power morality, and a man who cannot find his adjustment to it is doomed.' In this restatement of Nietzsche's idea that 'the will to power' transcends all moral codes, Mailer effectively predicts the outcome that Del Vecchio chronicles in Vietnam.[30]

As this brief survey shows, the legacy of the Vietnam War in American society and culture is seen not simply in the fragmented consensus which influences the historiography and the movies made about the war, but also in the range and diversity of writing from those with personal experience of it. Some of the veterans who volunteered to fight America's war in Vietnam were inspired to do so by the soaring rhetoric of Kennedy's inaugural. They anticipated experience of combat to be similar to that which they had seen in any number of John Wayne movies. Those who went to Vietnam, either as observers or participants in the fighting, and who shared the liberal realists' sense of disillusionment were among the many who subsequently have written of their experiences, either as reportage, autobiography or fiction. Among veterans, however, there are distinctions: between those whose opposition to the war was a result of what they witnessed there and those who doubted its legitimacy before they went, yet who still participated in it. There are still others, writing from a different ideological perspective and from a variety of vantage points, who do not share the widespread antipathy toward America's involvement in Southeast Asia.

The United States and the legacy of Vietnam

The contributions to this book thus focus on the legacy of the Vietnam War with an awareness both of its continuing relevance as a cultural and political reference point, and the enduring controversy that it generates. In Chapter 2, Jonathan Schell considers the competing ideological interpretations of the significance of the war outlined in this introduction. For some, it illustrated the fact that military power is not sufficient to overcome the political will of a people intent on achieving national self-determination and independence. The collapse of the Soviet Union in the wake of such events as the growth of the Solidarity movement in Poland was further evidence of this proposition. For others, the crisis of self-confidence that came with America's defeat in Vietnam meant that it was necessary to refashion the criteria by which military power might be used successfully: the so-called Weinberger and Powell Doctrines of the 1980s. Schell examines these competing 'lessons' drawn from the Vietnam War and discusses how, after the rhetorical revisionism of Reagan's presidency, the re-assertion of American military power in the Gulf War of 1991 and in the contemporary conflict in Iraq once more focuses attention on the arguments as to how the failure of America's Cold War mission in Southeast Asia should be interpreted.

In Chapter 3, H. Bruce Franklin argues that the realities of the Vietnam War and its aftermath have been submerged under the weight of a cultural construct that Americans now call 'Vietnam,' but which is made up of a collection of fantasies fuelled by representations in Hollywood movies and other productions of popular culture. This theme is explored through an examination of the roles of the twin iconic figures of American myth in relation to Vietnam – the spat-upon veteran and the abandoned POW – in the context of events such as the war against Iraq in 1991, the 1992 defeat of President George H. W. Bush, and the unsuccessful Presidential campaign of John Kerry in 2004. Discussing representations of the war in movies such as *The Deer Hunter*, the chapter shows how this collection of American fantasies now functions in contemporary American culture, psychology, and politics as a substitute for the reality of Vietnam and the history of the war.

Hollywood, therefore, has been a powerful influence in shaping perceptions of Vietnam. In Chapter 4, John Hellmann focuses on *Apocalypse Now Redux* (2001), Francis Ford Coppola's re-edited, re-mastered, and significantly expanded version of his 1979 surrealist epic. The re-release gave newspaper and magazine reviewers an opportunity to acknowledge that the original *Apocalypse Now* had survived earlier critical ambivalence and resistance to achieve canonical status as the most important cinematic statement on the American experience in Vietnam. With a particular focus on the added forty-nine minutes of footage, the chapter demonstrates how *Apocalypse Now Redux* may be seen as a secondary revision of its initial representation of the Vietnam War as a revelatory cul-de-sac of American mythic history.

Tim O'Brien is an author whose literary reputation was established as a result of his writings on the Vietnam War. In Chapter 5, Subarno Chattarji provides a forensic analysis of O'Brien's critically acclaimed work, *The Things They Carried* (1990). He considers how O'Brien synthesizes reality and fiction, obfuscating the distinction between these different modes of representation in order to recover the experience of war for his contemporary audience. The chapter also discusses how O'Brien's writing can be understood with reference not only to the work of others who wrote of their experience of war – Stephen Crane, Ernest Hemingway, and Norman Mailer – but also through a consideration of the themes addressed by Mark Twain in his novel, *Huckleberry Finn* (1884).

In his contribution to the book (Chapter 6), Walter Hölbling provides a broader contextualization of literary responses to the Vietnam War. He argues that, more so than in other genres and fictions, war stories embody representative cultural concepts and self-images of the society in which they are produced. The chapter demonstrates how American war stories have reflected certain enduring myths. These include ideas of providential mission, just war, exceptionalism, and racial warfare, all of which are embodied in the captivity narratives produced during and after the Indian wars that took place in colonial times.

In Chapter 7, Phil Melling also looks back to colonial times to provide an historical context in considering America's approach to Vietnam and its similarities with the way in which the nation is conducting its contemporary 'war on terror.' He suggests that when Donald Rumsfeld described the war in Iraq as one in which the insurgents existed in 'swamps,' it was an invitation to make the historical connection with American's sense of its original Puritan purpose. That 'errand into the wilderness' also animated the nation's intervention in Vietnam. The 'war on terror' thus re-imagines in Iraq both the Indian conflicts of the late seventeenth century, in particular their culminating horror, 'The Great Swamp Fight,' and the Vietnam War. The chapter also suggests that Rumsfeld's reference to the need to 'drain the swamp' endorses the idea that the 'war on terror' is a war against environment. The rhetoric that celebrates the post-colonial history of New England, when the swamps that offered the Indian sanctuary were drained, becomes an affirmation of the virtue of ecological imperialism as a basis for imposing military control.

In Chapter 8, Jon Roper discusses the political and cultural legacy of the Vietnam War in a different historical context: the aftermath of the Civil War. Until Vietnam, the 'war between the states' was the most divisive war in American history. After the South's capitulation at Appomattox, the Confederacy recovered its sense of military honor through emphasizing the heroic endeavor of its troops, rather than reflecting on the reasons why the war was fought. Presidential rhetoric, from Ulysses S. Grant to Woodrow Wilson, focused on re-establishing national unity instead of advancing the cause of racial equality. It was not until Lyndon Johnson's administration, as the nation's involvement in Vietnam deepened, that the President recognized the need to progress the agenda of civil rights that the abolition of slavery had foreshadowed. The chapter examines how re-interpretations of the South's defeat in the Civil War as the 'lost cause' are redolent of and related to the re-assessment of the nation's defeat in the Vietnam War as a 'noble cause,' and how this has impacted upon the political and cultural dynamics shaping American presidential politics and contemporary foreign policy.

The 'credibility gap' that emerged during the Vietnam War was indelibly widened during the Tet offensive in 1968. The concluding chapter of the book, an essay written by Bill Ehrhart, recalls that time when, in Hue City, he and his fellow marine, Kazunori Takenaga, were wounded by a North Vietnamese sniper. He recounts how he lost touch with 'Kenny,' a Japanese-American who had been drafted to fight in the war, for over thirty years. Having eventually re-established contact with one another, they resumed their friendship and spent time together in the US and in Japan. It is a reminder that those who fought and survived the war still share a common experience and an indelible bond.

Conclusion: The problem of insurgency

The contested legacy of Vietnam, and the argument over its significance between apostate liberal realists on the one hand and neoconservatives on the other, has been thrown into sharp relief by contemporary events. The issue is simple. Is the 'Vietnam Syndrome' – the attitude of those liberal realists traumatized by the war who claim that the American public will not support further military action abroad – to be a prohibition or an inhibition on the Executive's freedom of political action?

For neoconservatives who regard the 'Syndrome' as something to be 'overcome,' the answer is clear: presidential power – and by extension America's power in the world – is undermined to the extent that military options are foreclosed. Neoconservative fears that the experience of Vietnam sapped America's will to act in support of what they perceived to be its strategic interests in the world were not assuaged by the collapse of the Soviet Union and the end of the Cold War. Indeed, in their view, America's passivity since Vietnam, which resulted initially in an emboldened Soviet expansionism – notably in Afghanistan – also encouraged Islamic terrorists to believe that the United States was a soft target. The apparent recovery of military morale as a result of the successful prosecution of the Gulf War in 1991 was not at that time matched with a resurgent political will to commit American forces to a prolonged conflict in Iraq. For neoconservatives an opportunity had been squandered and the nation had made itself more vulnerable to acts of terrorism.

So neoconservatives trace the attacks of September 11, 2001, back to the path that disillusioned liberal realists, who opposed further military interventions, had taken out of Vietnam. Neoconservatives traveled another road. While others questioned the morality of power, they, like Sergeant Barnes in Oliver Stone's *Platoon* and Major General Cumings in Mailer's *The Naked and the Dead*, pragmatically adjusted to what they saw as the power morality of international relations. After September 11, they acted first in Afghanistan and then in Iraq. The use of American military power, punitively and pre-emptively, was, they argued, the best way of ensuring homeland security. The 'war on terror' is thus a product of one side of the ideological divide in contemporary American politics that was an outcome of the impact of the Vietnam War on its society and culture. Yet its continued prosecution now raises similar questions to those that the nation confronted over thirty years ago during its military intervention in Southeast Asia.

Paul Kattenburg worked for the State Department in Vietnam during the 1950s. Early on he recognized the potential military disaster that the US faced there. In 1963, after a trip to Southeast Asia he became convinced that, in David Halberstam's words, 'Vietnam was poison, and it would poison everything it touched.' Kattenburg argued that even the language that Americans then used to describe their enemy was contributing to their problems. Lawrence Freedman thus points out that in his book, *The Vietnam Trauma in American Foreign Policy, 1945–75* (1980), which traced thirty years of American involvement there, Kattenburg 'observed that the very description of opponents as "insurgents" rather than revolutionaries or rebels was disingenuous. It denied the possibility that they might be champions of a popular movement.'[31] The 'insurgency' in Vietnam continued. Thirty years later, in its 'war on terror,' the US now faces what it regards as two insurgencies, one in Afghanistan and the other in Iraq.

Can such wars be won? Consider the view, tempered by the experience of Vietnam, expressed by a leading American politician in 1967, the year before he died:

> no military effort can be successful against a deeply rooted insurgency with any degree of popular support. Still less can any amount of force redeem political failures, or win the allegiance of the people to a government that does not earn that loyalty.

Robert Kennedy thought then that Americans should seek a newer world.[32] The search continues.

Notes

1. 'Pham Xuan An, 79; Reporter for *Time*, Spy for Viet Cong,' *The Washington Post*, 21 September 2006. See Larry Berman, *Perfect Spy: The Incredible Double Life of Pham Xuan An, Time Reporter and Vietnamese*

Communist Agent (Washington DC: Smithsonian Institution Press/ HarperCollins, 2007).

2. Lawrence Freedman, *Kennedy's Wars* (Oxford: Oxford University Press, 2000), pp. 13, 15.
3. Gary Dorrien, *Imperial Designs: Neoconservatism and the New Pax Americana* (New York: Routledge, 2004), p. 21; Freedman, *Kennedy's Wars*, p. 15.
4. *Public Papers of the Presidents of the United States: Lyndon B. Johnson* (Washington DC: Government Printing Office, 1965), 1963–64, Book II, p. 1065.
5. Dorrien, *Imperial Designs*, p. 21.
6. Arthur Schlesinger Jr, *The Bitter Heritage: Vietnam and American Democracy, 1941–1966* (Greenwich: Fawcett, 1968 edition), pp. 58–9.
7. For a discussion of this see Jon Roper, 'The Politics of Sanity: Vietnam, Watergate and the Psychological Afflictions of Presidents,' *Euramerica*, Vol. 30, No. 2, June 2000, pp. 31–68.
8. Robert McNamara, *In Retrospect: The Tragedy and Lessons of Vietnam* (New York: Random House, 1995), p. xvi.
9. Neil Sheehan, *A Bright Shining Lie* (London: Jonathan Cape, 1989), pp. 684, 686–7. Schell's accounts of Vietnam were published as two books, *The Village of Ben Suc* (New York: Knopf, 1967) and *The Military Half* (New York: Knopf, 1968) and in one volume as *The Real War* (New York: Random House, 1988).
10. Dorrien, *Imperial Designs*, p. 22.
11. Carl Degler, 'Remaking American History,' *Journal of American History*, Vol. 67, No. 1, pp. 7–25, p. 15.
12. Podhoretz quoted in Dorrien, *Imperial Designs*, p. 10.
13. Norman Podhoretz, *Why We Were in Vietnam* (New York: Simon & Schuster, 1982), p. 14. The title of Podhoretz's book is a direct riposte to his former friend, Norman Mailer's novel, *Why are We in Vietnam?* (London: Weidenfeld and Nicolson, 1969).
14. Stanley Karnow, *Vietnam: A History* (Harmondsworth: Penguin, 1991 edition), p. 9.
15. Ibid., p. 25.
16. Harry Summers, 'Palmer, Karnow and Harrington: A Review of Recent Vietnam War Histories,' in L. Matthews & D. Brown, eds, *Assessing the Vietnam War* (Washington DC: Pergamon Group, 1987), pp. 4, 9–10.
17. L. Gelb and R. Betts, *The Irony of Vietnam: The System Worked* (Washington DC: The Brookings Institution, 1979). Sullivan quoted in R. McMahon, ed., *Major Problems in the History of the Vietnam War* (Lexington, MA: D.C. Heath & Co., 1990), pp. 604–5.
18. R. Friedman and J. Moore, 'Introduction,' in J. Moore, ed., *The Vietnam Debate: A Fresh Look at the Arguments* (Maryland: University Press of America, 1990), p. xii Other more recent revisionist accounts of the war include Michael Lind, *Vietnam: The Necessary War* (New York: Free Press, 1999).

19. Richard Slotkin, *Gunfighter Nation* (New York: Harper Perennial, 1993), p. 636.
20. Ibid., p. 637.
21. John Hellmann, *American Myth and the Legacy of Vietnam* (New York: Columbia University Press, 1986), p. 187.
22. P. H. Melling, *Vietnam in American Literature* (Boston: Twayne Publishers, 1990), p. 22.
23. Michael Herr, *Dispatches* (London: Pan Books, 1978), p. 14.
24. Ibid., pp. 206, 207.
25. Hellmann, *American Myth*, p. 151.
26. Philip Caputo, *A Rumor of War* (London: Arrow edition, 1978) p. 228.
27. Herr, *Dispatches*, p. 11.
28. Caputo, *A Rumor of War*, pp. 323, 332.
29. Ibid., p. 345.
30. John Del Vecchio, *The 13th Valley* (New York: Bantam Books, 1982), p. 501. Norman Mailer, *The Naked and the Dead* (New York: Holt, Reinhart & Wilson, 1948), p. 282.
31. David Halberstam, *The Best and the Brightest* (London: Pan Books Ltd, 1973), p. 789, Freedman, *Kennedy's Wars*, p. 291.
32. Robert Kennedy, *To Seek a Newer World* (London: Michael Joseph, 1967), p. 177.

2
The Long Shadow of Vietnam

Jonathan Schell

A war in the mind

The year 2005 was a time for commemorations. We had the fiftieth anniversaries of V-E day and V-J day but I have not heard of anyone providing a nickname for the end of the Vietnam War thirty years ago. Maybe it should be D-V day, which would be Defeat in Vietnam day. And which country commemorates its defeats? Nonetheless, there seems to be something almost everlasting about the Vietnam War in American memory. Perhaps the effort to consciously forget paradoxically adds to the staying power of defeats, which, forced into mental shadows, thrive there and spring out again into the light of day unexpectedly. Freud had something like this in mind when he spoke of the return of the repressed.

Vietnam indeed was not supposed to be a war at all – just an advisory operation, and a secret one at that, starting in the early 1960s. You might say that the 'forgetting' began before the war had even happened. And then when it did become a war, and then was lost, and the soldiers stopped fighting, it went on to become a half-hidden war in the mind – perhaps a fitting destiny for a war that many believe turned in the first place on hearts and minds.

Indeed, this mental or psychological character of Vietnam seems to have been central to every aspect of the war. You will recall, for instance, that a central reason that the United States continued the war so long was to maintain American 'credibility' – credibility being the nuclear-age version of what Britain, in its imperial days, used to call prestige. Credibility, or prestige, is of course an intangible quality, a mere impression made on the minds of some people by the actions of others. Thus it was fitting that the defeat in war was succeeded by the war over the lessons of the war, the meaning of the war, and that is the debate to which these remarks are addressed. At the heart of that question of course is whether those lessons were salutary wisdom about how the world works now, or, on the contrary, a 'syndrome,' a sickness, for which a cure should be sought.

The first lesson

I will begin by telling you a little about what I learned in the war, and then reflect more generally on the debate for American policy since. What I know about Vietnam begins with personal experience, so I will be a little bit autobiographical. When I arrived in Vietnam, in December of 1966, at age 23, I was just about as close to a genuine *tabula rasa* in regard to the war as it is possible for a human being to be. I had been rather apolitical as a college student. Then I spent a year-and-a-half in Japan, where I pretended to be a graduate student. The thing about Japan is that they speak Japanese there, and what is worse they write it. So although I did eventually learn to speak the language, I could not read the papers, and I missed out on a year-and-a-half of news, whether of Vietnam or anywhere else. But being young and reckless, and on top of that ignorant, I got myself to Vietnam on a tourist visa, imagining I might write something about it – a preposterous ambition in retrospect. In order to bone up on the subject a little, I bought the only book on the war I could get my hands on: *The Two Vietnams* (1963), by the great French reporter and writer Bernard Fall, whose books to this day remain some of the most invaluable on the war. I also did have one phone number in my pocket, that of François Soulis, also a French reporter, then working for *Newsweek*. I called him up, and he cheerily invited me over. When I arrived at the *Newsweek* office, there was also another gentleman in the office, and seeing a book under my arm, he asked me what I was reading. I answered that it was *The Two Vietnams*. He asked if he could see it, I gave it to him, and he signed it. And that was Bernard Fall.

I was the definition of a pest – a wholly uninformed, fake graduate student who thought he might like to write something – yet those two high-spirited, ebullient, generous, brave, superbly knowledgeable

Frenchmen, both of whom later lost their lives in the war, saw fit to take me under their wing. Soon, with their help, I was out in the thick of the war, first in an operation called Cedar Falls, which was the largest American military operation to date. Indeed it turned out to be the largest operation of the entire war, the reason being that it was such a failure that the US military did not care to repeat the experience.

What I saw on the ground was a policy that obviously was a failure in its own terms. No views on the geopolitical situation were required to see this. No analysis of the domino theory or even reading of *The Two Vietnams* was necessary to understand it. First, the United States was supposed to be winning the loyalty of the South Vietnamese but was in fact inspiring icy hatred in them. That deepening contradiction was at the centre of the whole issue of hearts and minds. Nor did you have to do any investigative reporting to encounter this reality. The hatred was visible in the eyes of the people you met within ten minutes of accompanying American forces on a search and destroy operation, and the impression did not change thereafter. It took the form of a stony, expressionless stare, a murderous-seeming impassivity, as if to say, I dare not move, but the first thing I would do if I could would be to kill you. Second, the United States was supposed to be *helping* the South Vietnamese military, but when the fighting began, that army ran away. Third, the United States was – in the most grossly obvious contradiction of them all – supposed to be building up South Vietnam but was in fact literally and physically tearing it to pieces. Again, no subtle investigations were required to see this. The flames of the burning villages were leaping to the sky; the gigantic areas of forest denuded by Agent Orange rolled on mile after mile outside one's plane window. Finally, the United States was supposed to be Vietnamizing the war, but the Vietnamese did not seem to want any assistance in becoming Vietnamese. That policy – a *de facto* one in 1966, and a declaratory one after Richard Nixon became President – raised a question that is still with us: how many American troops does it take to turn a country into itself? Maybe we will find the answer in Iraq, though I doubt it.

Later, when I did do some research on the war, I came to a conclusion that most of a generation would reach. The battle that mattered in Vietnam was the political one, that is, for those 'hearts and minds.' Hearts and minds were key for a very simple reason that somehow had not been factored into policy. One day the United States was going to leave Vietnam. It might be in five years or in twenty-five years, but it was going to happen. The imperial tide was running out at that moment in global history, and old-style hundred or two hundred year occupations were a thing of the past. When the US left, the Vietnamese were going to run their country, and so it was what *they* thought and wanted that was going to be decisive at the end of the day.

The National Liberation Front and the North Vietnamese understood these things. They often stated that the decisive factor was politics. Let me quote:

> Politics forms the actual strength of the revolution: politics is the root and war is the continuation of politics.
>
> Resolution of the Central Committee of the National
> Liberation Front

> Our political struggle is the manifestation of our absolute political superiority and of the enemy's basic weakness.
>
> Captured National Liberation Front document, 1963

The politics in question were above all those of independence and nationalism. But the struggle to represent those longings had almost certainly been won by first the Viet Minh and then the North Vietnamese Government and the National Liberation Front in the South long before the first American soldier ever appeared in Vietnam, indeed before the first French soldier appeared after the Second World War to reconquer the country. At the very least, the political story had reached its conclusion with French defeat at Dien Bien Phu in 1954 – or maybe even earlier, with the expulsion of the Japanese in 1945. The American war was probably lost before it started.

If I am right, then there is even something subtly wrong about the word 'defeat' when applied to the war in Vietnam. Certainly, *something* did not go right in Vietnam, and I may be splitting hairs, but if you get tired of a venture, yet all your military power is still intact, and may have even increased in the meantime, have you been defeated? Is that the right word to use? It may indeed be that *nothing* the United States did in its decade-and-a-half in Vietnam either helped or hurt the outcome, though it prolonged its arrival and imposed a hideous cost in the meantime. In this sense, the American war emerges as a kind of irrelevancy, the superimposition of a grotesquely one-sided military battle on a struggle that in fact was of a very different character.

The feeling of irrelevancy increases when you consider the aftermath. The war was fought in Vietnam to halt Chinese expansionism. But as it became immediately apparent (and was clear to astute observers even at the time), the Vietnamese feared the Chinese, their historical enemy, more than they feared the United States, and in 1979, China attacked Vietnam in order to 'teach it a lesson' after it had invaded Cambodia and thrown out the regime of Pol Pot. The proud Vietnamese, too, bested the Chinese.

The lessons I have just outlined were indeed learned by, among so many others, the American military, which, in response, came up first with Weinberger doctrine, named after President Reagan's Secretary of Defense, Caspar Weinberger, which then was transmuted into the Powell doctrine, named after the then Chairman of the Joint Chiefs of Staff and subsequently Secretary of State, Colin Powell. Under these doctrines, the military demanded that it be sent to accomplish military tasks, not political or social ones. Military forces, it said, were not set up to do social work. And it demanded an 'exit strategy,' so that it would not be stuck in new quagmires for a couple of decades.

The implications of the defeat – let me revert to that word – were radical, especially for superpowers. Vietnam reinforced a lesson that was being taught in virtually all of the colonized territories. It seemed that there was some other power, some alternative force that could overmatch hugely superior military resources.

The experience suggested, further, that a different relationship might obtain between force and political power than had previously been thought. And *that* lesson, too, as it turned out was by no means confined to Vietnam. The next time I became interested in an anti-imperial rebellion was when I met some Polish people in the United States who were helping out some former high school friends in what looked like utterly quixotic protests against the communist authorities. They were sending packages of mimeographed materials and even food to their comrades. Arrayed against them was the Polish dictatorship, itself backed by all the instruments of violence, propaganda, and bribery at the command of the Soviet empire. And yet as I watched my friends and their friends in Poland – one was the now legendary activist Adam Michnik, another was Jacek Kuron – it seemed that Polish history, and then the history of the whole Soviet Union, and finally of the world's were pivoting around those mimeographed sheets and packages of crackers and cheese. For soon the Solidarity movement arose, ten million strong, heralding the end, this time almost without any violence at all, of the Soviet empire and union and with them the Cold War.

Of course the Poles' protest was something far different from the conflict fought by the Vietnamese communists, who after all waged a bloody people's war and went on to found one-party state. The Poles fought without guns and established a constitutional democracy. Yet in one respect the two movements were alike: both wielded what in essence was political power against a seemingly overwhelming force of arms and armed repression. This experience, still connected in my mind, for all the differences between the two situations, to my experience in Vietnam, led on to a still broader lesson, which I will summarize in just a few words. Surely, one of the most notable facts of the twentieth century is that all of its empires – with the arguable exception of the one of which I am a citizen – have gone under the waves of history. This includes not only the British, the French, the Soviet, the Japanese, but also the ones we scarcely think of any more, such as the Portuguese and the Dutch.

There is something in this world that does not love an empire. And that something has to do with the aroused will of local peoples, who may be weak in relationship to the outside world, but, if steadfast and resolved, are superpowers within their own borders. And it is these mini-superpowers, wielding inferior violence but superior political will, that have, in the second half of the twentieth century, changed the political face of the earth more than the two superpowers, one of which indeed evaporated like the morning dew round about 1989.

All of that, teaching the sharp limitations on the effectiveness of external force in local struggles, was *one* of the lessons, that I, and, of course, millions of others learned from the Vietnam War.

The second lesson

There was another scarcely less important lesson. At just the time that the United States began to intervene in Vietnam, American policy-makers were getting acquainted with a different sort of limitation on the use of force. We must recall that in the strategic thinking of the day the war in Vietnam was a so-called 'limited war.' Limited by comparison to what? Well, to what was then called 'general war' – and that meant nuclear war. Limited war strategy and nuclear war strategy were a pair. I mentioned before that upholding the credibility of American power become an *idée fixe* of American policy makers, both Democrat and Republican. Henry Kissinger's middle initial should be 'C.' for 'credibility,' so passionately interested has he been in this quantity in international affairs. He was one of the American strategists who awakened early to a paradox at the heart of nuclear weapons, namely that although they were fine for making threats, they were of little or no use for actual military employment, because that would bring you to the famous mutual assured destruction – hardly a desirable destination. In his words, 'Power has never been greater; it has also never been less useful.' That was a lesson of nuclear deterrence. If a threat could not in fact be carried out by a rational person, then what use was it? And how 'credible' was it? One remedy was to fain madness, and indeed the strategists did in all soberness recommend this. Nixon, for one, at several junctures wanted to convey to the North Vietnamese that he was a little bit off his rocker. So reported his Chief of Staff, H. R. (Bob) Haldeman. Indeed, in the fall of 1969, Kissinger and Nixon secretly put the nuclear forces of the United States on alert, hoping to menace the Soviet Union into helping out in restraining North Vietnam. But the Soviets did not comply.

Another solution to nuclear paralysis – and Kissinger was one of those who came up with this too – was limited war. The good thing about limited wars, at least by comparison to nuclear wars, was that you *could* actually fight them. You could not just threaten; you could carry out the threat. In Kissinger's words in 1958, 'A strategy of limited war would seek to escape the inconsistency of relying on a policy of deterrence whose major sanction involves national catastrophe.' And Kennedy said to the columnist James Reston after taking a verbal beating from Khrushchev in their summit meeting of 1961 and on the eve of the third Berlin crisis, 'Now we have a problem in trying to make our power credible, and Vietnam looks like the place.'

Such were the strategic roots of the Vietnam War, and they had important consequences. If you threw the burden of shoring up credibility on limited war, it became impossible to withdraw without supposedly undermining the entire edifice of American power. And that was of course the teaching of the domino theory. Thus, the doctrine of credibility first helped push the US into Vietnam and then prevented it from extricating itself.

The relationship of the Vietnam War to Cold War nuclear strategy – a relationship that turned military operations into chiefly psychological exercises, as I mentioned – is one of the most fascinating as well as complicated subjects of the period, and I will not pursue it further. The point for the present purposes is only to observe that if discovery of the incredible power of the aroused political will of local peoples was one severe limitation on the traditional usefulness of force, the nuclear revolution was another. The two lessons of Vietnam converged at a point: they were chiefly about power, especially military power, and more particularly the relationship of military power to political power. It was fine to possess a large mountain of arms, but extracting a political benefit from it was another matter altogether. You were just as likely to hurt yourself as well as others, not to mention the possibility of mutual assured destruction.

What others learned

Others learned lessons from Vietnam quite opposed to the ones just set forth. One of these other lessons was that the soldiers won the war in Vietnam but the press and the politicians threw victory away. In the *New York Times*, the argument was made again on the thirtieth anniversary of the end of the war. Stephen J. Morris claimed that 'In 1974–75 the United States snatched defeat from the jaws of victory.' The reason was a false interpretation of the war foisted upon the country first by journalists and later by historians. As Dean Rusk later said, when asked by Nixon how the war was lost, 'It was lost in the editorial rooms of this country.' There is truth in Rusk's claim but not the truth he meant. The defeat came, not because the press misrepresented victory as defeat but rather because the press and the public came to understand that not all the military victory in the world could save the United States from the defeat that political failure made inevitable. More battles, no matter how successful, were wasted blood.

The scene was admittedly confusing. The curious fact was that the American soldiers *did* win. They won and they won and they won – until they lost. That is, they won their battles. It was the war they could not win. In the words of Marine General Victor ('Brute') Krulak, the big-unit battles with the National Liberation Front and the North Vietnamese 'could move to another planet today, and we would still not have won the war' because 'the Vietnamese people are the prize.'

Yet for those who believed the stab-in-back theory, in which the press and politicians betrayed the soldiers, then the lesson had to be that the war was lost because American will gave out at home. In this version, the lessons I have drawn above become war-losing lessons. My lessons become the 'Vietnam syndrome,' a sickness of the will, and a patriot's obligation is to rebut and overcome them. I become the reason the US lost the war.

In April of 1979, Richard Nixon expressed his fear that the United States would become a 'pitiful helpless giant.' A similar anxiety was once expressed by Kennedy's Secretary of State, Dean Rusk, who said, 'We are the greatest military power in the world if only we act like it.' Of course, acting as great powers had done in the past – that is, using the military force available to them to the hilt – is exactly what the United States could not do in the nuclear age. And that was the dilemma.

Let us look at how the competing lessons have fared since the war. I would summarize by saying that at first, the lessons that I and Weinberger and Powell learned from it were accepted by the public. That is, two-thirds of the public agreed not only that the war was a mistake but that the venture was 'immoral.' And yet over time, the lessons were lost, especially in the political arena. The pattern appears early, in the landslide defeat of George McGovern in 1972. Americans agreed with him that the war was wrong, but they would not put him in office. And indeed, the Democratic Party has felt that it had to work to recover from the taint of McGovernism ever since. Any taint of dovishness, they concluded had to be removed. The defeat of Walter Mondale in 1984 and of Michael Dukakis in 1988 drove that point home with a vengeance.

Meanwhile, of course, Ronald Reagan and George Bush were winning office with the opposite lesson. Reagan said of the American military in Vietnam, 'They came home without a victory not because they were defeated but because they were denied a chance to win.' And after the American victory in the first Gulf War, George Bush said 'By God, we've kicked the Vietnam syndrome once and for all.' Clinton then sought to overcome the political curse of dovishness by vigorously and deliberately moving the Democratic Party into the center on military affairs. It is a process that had its counterpart in the similar operation by Tony Blair in the United Kingdom, with fateful results when it came to decide whether to join in the second Iraq war. That the political cost of appearing 'soft' on something or other, and unwilling, in some general way, to use force, is still operating was shown by the damage that was done to John Kerry in the 2004 presidential election by the attacks on his patriotism by the Swift Boat Veterans. Indeed I would say that American politics since Vietnam has been one long process not of forgetting the lessons of Vietnam but of actively purging them from political consciousness.

That purgation set the stage for the American response to September 11, 2001. The lesson that there are sharp limitations in modern times on the usefulness of military power is hardly one that the leaders of a country styling itself the sole superpower, or even global hegemon, care to hear. And so we see the revival of an old pattern. On the one hand, the Republican party championing the use of force, now on a scale never contemplated even by Johnson or Nixon, and on the other a Democratic party that clearly believes otherwise but does not dare to say so, since it fears the political consequences. The vacillation of John Kerry regarding the Iraq war, which he supported as a senator but then criticized as a candidate in the 2004 presidential race, is the very picture of this confusion and of its political results.

By now, the debate is not so much about one war or another but rather whether, as a general proposition, the United States possesses sufficient will to use force. An example is an article by Peter Beinart, the editor of the *New Republic*, a publication that supported the Vietnam War and later regretted it. It is curious for lack of detail. He distinguishes between 'hard' and 'soft' Democrats, holding up certain 'top Kerry foreign policy advisers, such as Richard Holbrooke and Joseph Biden,' for whom 'Bosnia and Kosovo seemed like models for a new post-Vietnam liberalism that embraced US power.' He goes on, 'And September 11 validated the transformation. Democratic foreign policy wonks not only supported the war in Afghanistan, they generally felt it didn't go far enough – urging a larger NATO force capable of securing the entire country.' But he warns 'The danger is that, in the wake of Iraq, liberals will turn inward, as many did after Vietnam. They will abandon the belief that US power can positively change the Muslim world and instead argue that the United States should merely aggravate it less while killing terrorists where we can.' The discussion remains largely abstract regarding 'the use of force,' whether to be 'hard' or 'soft' whether to 'withdraw' or 'expand America's role in the world.'

And indeed so much of the debate over policy in the United States is like this: not about any particular action but about the United States itself. But is not this exactly what the Vietnam War itself was? Did not the war almost immediately transcend any discussion of events in that long, thin, poor nation, and become a discussion of 'credibility' and America's prestige in the world?

Looking at this lengthy record, it seems to me that, notwithstanding the end of the Cold War, the rise of globalization, and other revolutionary events in global affairs, there seems to emerge a remarkable consistency in the shape of American debates about foreign policy. The United States seems always to be involved in a debate with itself – not so much about Vietnam, or Iraq, or Europe, or South America – but about its own might and role in the world. It is almost as if the United States has been engaged in a several decades long meditation on the nature of power, punctuated by wars that serve as much as teaching aids for the discussion as for any concrete purposes. That may be why mere facts – for instance the lack of weapons of mass destruction in Iraq – seem so strangely unimportant to the policy makers. Finding these weapons, although no doubt desired, was perhaps never at the top of the agenda. What was at the top of the agenda was the assertion of American power on a historically unprecedented scale.

However it is clear that it is simply wrong to suppose that the United States is a new Rome. To claim so is to mistake *hardware* for power. The two are very different. Rome could truly subjugate almost all of the world known to it. The United States today cannot. Even poor, anarchic Iraq is too much. It is still not clear how things will turn out in that land, but it is a remarkable revelation about the capacity of American military power, that the occupation of just one country has absorbed almost the entire available ground forces of the United States. For the great limitations on the usefulness of military power are still present: at the apex of the system, nuclear arms, now in more hands than ever, and at the base, the aroused will of peoples, now just as active as ever.

Are all these thoughts perhaps the product of a mind that has contracted a particularly bad case of the Vietnam syndrome? I do not think so. I feel quite well, thank you, and think that the sickness, if there is one, resides in other minds.

Note

This is a revised and updated version of the Keynote Address given in May 2005 at the British Academy Colloquium marking the thirtieth anniversary of the ending of the Vietnam War.

3
'Vietnam' in the New American Century

H. Bruce Franklin

In 2005, we commemorated what was called 'the thirtieth anniversary of the end of the Vietnam War.' Yes, it was thirty years since the last US military forces were evicted from Vietnam. But anybody who thinks that the Vietnam War ended for America more than three decades ago did not live through the presidential election campaign of 2004, when John Kerry's campaign ship, all festooned with Vietnam War-hero flags and banners, was torpedoed by the 'Swift Boat Veterans,' who succeeded in convincing millions that Kerry was a coward who had aided the Vietnamese enemy and committed the ultimate sin, betrayal of our POWs. The black-and-white POW/MIA flags still flutter all across America, as decreed by law in each and every one of the fifty states. With its image of the heroic American warrior, imprisoned and tortured by Vietnam, it remains the only flag, other than the Star-Spangled Banner, ever to fly, as it does annually, over the White House. On permanent display in the Rotunda of our nation's Capitol, draped in a huge banner over the New York Stock Exchange, and adorning the bumpers of hundreds of thousands of cars, SUVs (sports utility vehicle), pick-ups, and big diesel rigs, the POW/MIA flag projects one of America's favorite images of itself as victim of Vietnam.

And has the war ever ended for Vietnam? Subjected to the most intense bombing and chemical warfare in human history, the land has still not recovered and people may never be free from the genetic damage deeply embedded in their gene pool. Although the US government has grudgingly recognized some of the diseases caused by Agent Orange in American veterans who were briefly exposed (including non-Hodgkin's lymphoma and chronic lymphocytic leukemia), it still refuses to acknowledge any of the effects of Agent Orange, not to mention Agents White, Blue, Pink, and Purple, on the Vietnamese people who have been exposed for decades. In 2002, at the conclusion of the Joint Vietnam-US Scientific Conference on Human Health and Environmental Effects of Agent Orange/Dioxin, the United States formally agreed to support continuing scientific investigation of the health and environmental effects of dioxin in Vietnam. But in February 2005, the US National Institute of Environmental Health Services unilaterally revoked this agreement three days before a court hearing of a class-action suit against US chemical companies on behalf of the myriad Vietnamese suffering from a continuing epidemic of deformed babies, miscarriages, and cancers.[1] The case was promptly thrown out by the US court in early March. By late March, the URL for every document about this agreement previously posted at the website of the National Institute of Environmental Health Sciences led to the following notice: 'LOST FILE (Error 404).' This is a relatively minor incident in the decades of economic, political, and cultural warfare waged by Washington against Vietnam *since* 1975. A recent book, Edwin Martini's *Invisible Enemies: The American War on Vietnam, 1975–2000*, may indeed force us to rethink our dating of the end of the war.[2]

The title of this chapter has two terms. First is 'Vietnam' – in quotation marks. Within the dominant American culture, 'Vietnam' is no longer a nation, a people, or even a war. 'Vietnam' is something terrible that happened to us, something that divided, wounded, and victimized America. As the grotesque title of one widely adopted history textbook puts it: *Vietnam: An American Ordeal.*[3] This 'Vietnam' that has come to substitute for the countries, the peoples, and the history of America's war in Southeast Asia is a byzantine construct of myths and fantasies. Three decades after the panicky US exodus from Saigon, this simulacrum of Vietnam operates as a powerful, sometimes decisive, force not only in American culture but also in American politics. It was used to help begin the Iraq War in 1991, led to the defeat of George H. W. Bush in the 1992 election, but permitted his son to win re-election in 2004 and thus to continue implementing the second term of my title, 'the New American Century.'

In case any readers are not familiar with the Project for the New American Century (although you all should be), let me briefly explain. This is the grouping that formulated and is now in charge of implementing a strategy for US total hegemony over planet Earth for at least the entire twenty-first century, what they explicitly call the 'global *Pax Americana*.'⁴ The plan was formulated in 1992 in the *Defense Planning Guidance* authored by Paul Wolfowitz under the direction of the then Defense Secretary Dick Cheney.⁵ In 2000, Wolfowitz and his cohort from The Project for the New American Century published an astonishing manifesto and master plan that envisions a world of endless imminent warfare where the land, sea, air, and heavens swarm with America's invincible weapons. They acknowledge that their program has 'elements of science fiction.' Writing in the year 2000, they see that 'the unresolved conflict with Iraq provides the immediate justification' for initiating their plan. They recognize with great regret that their vast military transformation is 'likely to be a long one,' unless it is fortuitously accelerated by 'some catastrophic and catalyzing event – like a new Pearl Harbor.'⁶

Before exploring how the fantasy Vietnam functions in the actual twenty-first century America, we need to peel away the layer after layer of distortions, myths, and outright lies that constitute the dominant narrative of the Vietnam War, to remind ourselves that the war did not begin when the United States came to the aid of some democratic nation known as South Vietnam which was threatened by subversion and invasion from some evil Communist nation known as North Vietnam.

It is easy to understand why most Americans cannot face the reality of our war in Vietnam. Because if we did, we would have to recognize that for decade after decade we waged unrelenting and sometimes genocidal war against a people and a nation that never did anything to us except ask for our friendship and support. The true history of this war begins in September 1945, the month after our Vietnamese allies had seized control of their country from the defeated Japanese occupiers and established the Democratic Republic of Vietnam. Ho Chi Minh, standing in front of half a million citizens in Hanoi, the capital of the new nation, began to read its Declaration of Independence: 'All men are created equal. They are endowed by their Creator with certain inalienable rights; among these are Life, Liberty, and the pursuit of Happiness.' This immortal statement was made in the Declaration of Independence of the United States of America in 1776.

In a broader sense, this means: all the peoples on the earth are equal from birth, all the peoples have a right to live, to be happy and free.

Suddenly two warplanes appeared overhead. The crowd looked up anxiously. When those hundreds of thousands recognized them as American P-38 fighter-bombers, they burst into a mighty cheer. To them, these planes were a token of support from the country they viewed as the world's great champion of the rights of self-determination and national independence. Little did they know that a few weeks earlier, the US government had promised France the military means to re-conquer and re-colonize Vietnam. Thus while the Vietnamese were cheering America and its support for the Democratic Republic of Vietnam, America was preparing to help wage war against this friendly people and nation.

In October, the first of eight, and possibly twelve, US troopships were diverted from their task of bringing GIs home from France and instead were loaded with an army to invade and conquer Vietnam.[7] This army was financed by the United States and armed by the United States. It contained units of the Nazi army, including SS units, that had been forced into the French Foreign Legion because General Dwight Eisenhower had declared that they were not prisoners of war but merely 'Disarmed Enemy Forces' with no legal rights whatsoever. Although this invasion army was under French command and its purpose was to restore French colonial rule, it was implementing part of Washington's global strategy. We need to remember that all this took place prior to the so-called Cold War, a chronological fact with immense historical significance.

If a large foreign power financed, armed, and helped organize an army, which it then transported to our shores to invade our nation, would any American doubt or question that this was a major act of war? If not, then we need to recognize that the US war against the DRV was not a sequel to the French war but an essential component of it. We also need to recognize that it took a very long time to get the American people to support hostilities against Vietnam. Indeed, the fall of 1945 was the beginning not only of the US war but also of the American movement against the war. When those US troopships arrived in Saigon, they were greeted and saluted on the docks by Japanese soldiers, uniformed and rearmed by British troops under the command of General Douglas Gracey. All the enlisted men on the crews of these troopships then drew up and signed letters and petitions to Congress and the President denouncing these 'imperialist policies' and the use of American ships 'to subjugate the native population' of Vietnam.

The American movement against the war, initiated by these hundreds of sailors, kept growing in the nine years leading to the French defeat in 1954. In April of that year, on the eve of the French surrender, Vice President Richard Nixon declared that because 'the Vietnamese lack the ability to conduct a war or govern themselves,' the United States may 'have to send troops there.'[8] This trial balloon launched by the White House sparked a firestorm of protest against what some called the 'Nixon War.'[9] Thousands of letters and telegrams opposing US intervention deluged the White House. An American Legion division with 78,000 members demanded that 'the United States should refrain from dispatching any of its Armed Forces to participate as combatants in the fighting in Indochina.'[10] There were public outcries against 'colonialism' and 'imperialism.' Senators from both parties rose to denounce any contemplation of sending US soldiers to Indochina. For example, Senator Ed Johnson of Colorado declared on the Senate floor: 'I am against sending American GIs into the mud and muck of Indochina on a blood-letting spree to perpetuate colonialism and white man's exploitation in Asia.'[11] By mid-May, a Gallup poll revealed that 68% of those surveyed were against sending US troops to Indochina.[12] So the Eisenhower Administration was forced into fighting a war hidden from the American people, a covert war. The first stage was creating in June the puppet regime of Ngo Dinh Diem, beginning to build a new proxy army, and launching terrorist and other secret operations masterminded by Colonel Edward Lansdale. All this began before the Geneva Conference concluded with its recognition that Vietnam was a single, independent nation and an agreement that French and DRV military forces would regroup on either side of the 17th parallel, a 'military demarcation line' that 'should not in any way be interpreted as constituting a political or territorial boundary.'[13] It would take Vietnam nineteen years to force Washington to accept these agreements.

Nine years after Geneva, the Kennedy Administration felt itself forced into another conspiracy, this one to remove Diem and replace him with generals on the Pentagon's payroll. As US Ambassador to Saigon, Henry Cabot Lodge, wrote in a top-secret cable in August 1963: 'We are embarked on a course from which there is no respectable turning back: the overthrow of the Diem government... there is no turning back because there is no possibility, in my view, that the war can be won under a Diem administration, still less that any member of the family can govern the country in a way to gain the support of the only people who count, i.e., the educated class in and out of government service – not to mention the American people.'[14]

The coup, including the assassination of Diem, took place in the first week of November. Three weeks later, President Kennedy was assassinated. Within seventy-two hours, newly installed President Lyndon Baines Johnson signed National Security Action Memorandum 273, the top-secret plan for a full-scale US war in Vietnam. A key section of NSAM 273, entitled 'Plausibility of Denial,' essentially asked for an assessment of whether the American people would be stupid or gullible enough to believe the government's lies when it denied the covert air, sea, and land attacks on northern Vietnam that would lead up to the open dispatch of combat forces. There are those who are old enough to remember that President Johnson's main foreign-policy campaign gambit in the summer and fall of 1964, repeated over and over again, was his promise that 'I shall never send American boys to Asia to do the job that Asian boys should do.' As soon as he was inaugurated as an elected president, after burying overtly hawkish Barry Goldwater in a record landslide, Johnson sent in the marines and began overt non-stop bombing of the north.

In that great 1974 documentary *Hearts and Minds*, Daniel Ellsberg outlines how 'the American people' were 'lied to month-by-month' about Vietnam by Presidents Truman, Eisenhower, Kennedy, Johnson, and Nixon, and says 'It's a tribute to the American public that their leaders perceived they had to be lied to.' But then he pauses and adds, 'It's no tribute to us that it was so easy.'

The lies did not stop when military combat ended in 1975, partly because they were necessary to legitimize that remorseless economic and political war Washington waged against Vietnam for the ensuing quarter of a century. Indeed, by 1978 a cultural juggernaut designed to re-image the war was beginning to overwhelm and replace everything we had remembered with its exact opposite. The key cultural text here is *The Deer Hunter*. Designated the best English-language film of 1978 by the New York Film Critics Circle, this lavishly financed celluloid fantasy was sanctified by four Academy Awards, capped by Best Picture – an award presented appropriately enough by John Wayne, that World War II draft dodger who received a Congressional Gold Medal for being a make-believe warrior hero. With wicked virtuosity, *The Deer Hunter* transformed the most powerful and influential images of the war, images deeply embedded in American culture, into their precise opposites. The first scene in Vietnam shows North Vietnamese helicopters napalming a South Vietnamese village, where the surviving women and children are then slaughtered by North Vietnamese Communists. This My Lai style massacre is halted by the first American to appear in this fantasy of Vietnam, Robert De Niro as a lone heroic guerilla. The tiger cages in which we tortured and crippled thousands of Vietnamese become tiger cages in which they try to cripple us. The bodies of Vietnamese prisoners being hurled from helicopters by American interrogators became American prisoners falling from helicopters. One of the most powerful and influential images of the real war was the photograph of Saigon secret-police chief General Loan killing an unarmed 'Viet Cong suspect,' his arms bound behind his back, with a revolver held to his right temple. *The Deer Hunter* artfully reverses this image, with American prisoners forced by sadistic Communist officers to play Russian roulette with a revolver held to their right temple below a portrait of Ho Chi Minh. The American POWs in *The Deer Hunter* are all working-class GIs, unlike the reality in which all but a handful of the POWs were flight officers. (And many of the enlisted POWs were in the Peace Committee, allied with their Vietnamese captors.)

The Deer Hunter succeeded not only in reversing key images of the war but in helping to transform US prisoners of war into the most potent symbols of American manhood for the 1980s and 1990s. It was the trailblazer for the POW/MIA cult movies, beginning with *Uncommon Valor* starring Gene Hackman (1983), the first of Chuck Norris's *Missing in Action* films (1984), and of course Sylvester Stallone's *Rambo* (1985). Wounded, tortured, imprisoned, victimized by bureaucracy and a feminized culture, American manhood now fought back as super-muscled heroes. By 1988, three years after he single-handedly won the last phase of the Vietnam War by freeing the POWs, Rambo was blasting the Russian hordes on another battlefield: Afghanistan.

The year after the Motion Picture Academy canonized *The Deer Hunter*, another Hollywood product – Ronald Reagan – brilliantly re-imaged the Vietnam War as part of his campaign to capture the White House. During the 1980 election campaign, Reagan coined the 'Vietnam syndrome' metaphor and, in the same speech to a Veterans of Foreign Wars conference, redefined the war as a 'noble cause.'[15] By 1982, then President Reagan was articulating a version of the history of the Vietnam War, every sentence of which was demonstrably false.[16] By the end of the 1980s, the matrix of illusions necessary for endless imperial warfare was in place and functioning with potency. The two great myths – the spat-upon veteran and postwar POWs – were deeply embedded in the national psyche. What was needed next was erasure of memory of the reality.

The cultural march from demonization of the Vietnamese in the late 1970s to eradication in the 1990s was vividly projected by Hollywood. Whereas the Academy Award for the Best Picture of 1978 went to *The Deer Hunter* with its meticulously reversed images of victims and victimizers, the winner of the Academy Award for the Best Picture of 1994 was *Forrest Gump*, which projects Vietnam as merely an uninhabited jungle that for inscrutable reasons shoots at nice American boys who happen to be marching through. And our iconic hero is now a man constitutionally incapable of understanding history.

How did we manage to gumpify 'Vietnam'?

Throughout the decades that the United States was waging war in Vietnam, no incoming president uttered the word 'Vietnam' in his inaugural address.[17] Ronald Reagan, in his 1981 inaugural speech, did include 'a place called Vietnam' in his list of battlefields where Americans had fought in the twentieth century. But it was not until 1989 that a newly elected president actually said anything about the Vietnam War. What he said was: forget it.

It was George H. W. Bush who broke the silence with these words explicitly calling for erasure: 'The final lesson of Vietnam is that no great nation can long afford to be sundered by a memory.' Note that by now 'Vietnam' was no longer a country or even 'a place called Vietnam,' as his predecessor had put it. It had become a war, an American war. Or not even a war. It was an American tragedy, an event that had divided and wounded America. Bush's speech went on to blame 'Vietnam' for the 'divisiveness,' the 'hard looks' in Congress, the challenging of 'each other's motives,' and the fact that 'our great parties have too often been far apart and untrusting of each other.' 'It has been this way since Vietnam,' he lamented.[18]

Two years later, Bush began the war against Iraq with the promise that 'this will not be another Vietnam.'[19] Inextricably intertwined with 'Vietnam,' 'Iraq' has also become a construct of simulations, an illusionary reality continually being spun – in all senses – by our culture. If the Vietnam War is the longest US war against a foreign nation or nations, the Iraq war is the second longest. After all, by now it has already been going on for fifteen years, through three American administrations.

Before US and allied ground troops withdrew from the parts of Iraq they had invaded in 1991, the United States, with assistance from Britain and France, began to set up a form of aerial occupation and control, the so-called no-fly zones. This was an application of a strategy for imperial rule from the air developed by Britain back in the 1920s, then named 'Control without Occupation.' Britain had tried this out first in 1922. Where? In Iraq. The first RAF report gleefully described the panic the air raids evoked among the 'natives' of Baghdad, especially the terrified women and children: 'Many of them jumped into a lake, making a good target for the machine guns.'[20] The northern no-fly zone was set up in April 1991, the southern no-fly zone in 1992. The no-fly zones in continual operation between the 1991 and the 2003 invasions had two interrelated purposes, both preconditions for eventual full occupation and control: first detaching the oil-rich regions of the north and south from central control, thus destroying the economic and political coherence of the nation; and second providing pretexts for ongoing aerial bombing campaigns designed to degrade and ultimately neutralize Iraq's military defense system.

The fantasy 'Vietnam' has proved crucial to launching and maintaining the war against Iraq. In 1991, the myth of the spat-upon Vietnam veteran was invoked to discredit the burgeoning antiwar movement and to create the emotional support necessary to start the war. How this was done is explored brilliantly in the 1998 book *The Spitting Image*, the landmark study of the spat-upon veteran myth by sociology professor Jerry Lembcke, himself a Vietnam veteran.

The elder Bush's administration had offered many different reasons for going to war: 'liberating' Kuwait; defending Saudi Arabia; freeing all those foreign hostages Iraq was holding (something I bet is mostly forgotten now); Saddam as Hitler; the threat to America's oil supplies; the 312 Kuwaiti babies dumped out of incubators by Iraqi soldiers (a story concocted out of thin air by the leading PR firm Hill and Knowlton); and so on. But the only one that succeeded in generating the required passion was 'Support our soldiers! Don't treat them like the spat-upon Vietnam vets!' From this flowed the ocean of yellow ribbons on cars and trucks and homes that deluged the American landscape. The yellow ribbon campaign, with its mantra of 'Support Our Troops,' 'dovetailed neatly,' as Lembcke wrote, with that other Vietnam issue 'about which the American people felt great emotion: the prisoner of war/missing in action (POW/MIA) issue.' So finally the war was not about political issues but about people. Which people? Again in Lembcke's words, 'Not Kuwaitis. Not Saudis... The war was about the American soldiers who had been sent to fight it.'[21]

In March 1991, gloating over what seemed America's glorious defeat of Iraq, President Bush jubilantly proclaimed to a nation festooned in its jingoist yellow ribbons, 'By God, we've kicked the Vietnam syndrome once and for all!'[22] Kicked? Syndrome? Had Vietnam become America's addiction? Its pathology? The President's diagnosis proved more accurate than his prognosis. Sixteen months after claiming to have cured us of our Vietnam disease, George Bush was on national TV shouting 'Shut up and sit down!' at MIA family members heckling him at the July 1992 annual convention of the National League of Families.

Inaugurated with a promise that he would heal America's Vietnam wounds, Bush tried to win the re-election by reopening them, turning Bill Clinton's anti-Vietnam War activities and draft avoidance into the Republicans' main campaign issue. But meanwhile Ross Perot, the original fabricator of the POW/MIA issue back in 1969,[23] now launched his own campaign as the wartime champion of the POWs and a Rambo-like hero who would rescue not only the dozens allegedly still alive in Indochina but also the nation itself. Perot masterfully played his role of the lone outsider from Texas ready to ride into Washington to save us from its sleazy bureaucrats and politicians who had betrayed the POWs and the American people.

Unlike the Republican and Democratic candidates, Perot had no national party apparatus. What he used as a remarkably effective substitute was a ready-made national infrastructure, a network of activists motivated by near religious fervor and coordinated by grassroots organizations: the POW/MIA movement. A master of symbolism, Perot chose ex-POW James Stockdale as his running mate and ex-POW Orson Swindle as his campaign manager. Homecoming II, an organization leading the Rambo faction of the POW/MIA movement, illegally turned the Vietnam Veterans Memorial into a perpetual campaign prop for Perot.[24] At his typical rally, Perot sat with former POWs and family members on a stage bedecked with POW flags. POW activists and their organizations were central to the petition campaigns that got Perot on the ballot in every state.[25] Without the Perot candidacy, Bush would undoubtedly have beaten Bill Clinton in a one-on-one race. Certainly in the televised debates, Perot's ferocious attacks on the Administration – spearheaded by his shrewd debunking of the glorious Gulf War – inflicted major damage while allowing Clinton to keep the blood off both his hands and his face. In the crucial third debate, when Bush attempted to focus on Clinton's draft records, Perot argued that the Bush Administration had given Saddam Hussein permission to 'take the northern part of Kuwait.'[26] Perot's 20 million votes, drawn disproportionally from Republican voters, amounted to almost four times Clinton's margin of victory over Bush, who got almost ten million fewer votes than he had received four years earlier. If Perot was responsible for Bush's defeat, then clearly the POW/MIA issue was central to the election's outcome, for without it Perot would surely not have been a national political figure much less a presidential candidate. In fact he would not have even made his first billion dollars, which largely came from favours accorded to him by the Nixon Administration for selling the POW/MIA issue to the American people in the first place.

But the first President Bush was right about one thing. The invasion of Iraq accelerated the continuing militarization of American culture, thus allowing us to 'kick' the 'Vietnam syndrome.' At the end of combat in Vietnam in 1975, a Harris poll indicated that a mere 20% of Americans between the ages of 18 and 29 trusted the leaders of the military. In December 2002, as the second Bush Administration was ramping up for a renewed invasion of Iraq, a Harris poll indicated that this number had more than tripled to 64%.[27]

What Lembcke wrote in 1998 about events that occurred in 1991 seems even more relevant today, when the ostensible reasons for the 2003 invasion of Iraq have all been thoroughly exposed as weapons of mass deception. Iraq of course had no arsenal of chemical or bacteriological, much less nuclear, weapons that was threatening the United States or anybody else, and this arsenal, we now know, was an Administration concoction based on cherry-picked and flagrantly bogus intelligence. Amnesiac America recognized no similarity to the bogus intelligence used to substantiate the White Paper of 1965, which provided the justification for overt US war in Vietnam.[28] Iraq of course had nothing to do with 9/11, but the war has been a bonanza for jihadists. Now we are supposed to believe that the war was designed to liberate the people of Iraq and bring them democracy. Well, maybe it was necessary to destroy the country in order to save it. But none of these rationalizations of the war today generate any pro-war fervour. No, those who fervently support the war today do so because they 'Support Our Troops,' rather than betraying them while they are fighting or spitting on them and calling them baby-killers when they come home.

In 2004 and 2005, the yellow-ribbon tsunami of 1991 swept over America once again, helped by a cute technological gimmick. Now, instead of those perishable actual yellow ribbons that festooned American homes and cars as a buildup to Operation *Desert Storm* in 1991, we have magnetic yellow ribbons, emblazoned with the slogans 'Support Our Troops' and 'God Bless America,' attached to millions of American cars and SUVs and vans and trucks, sometimes riding happily above the old-fashioned black-and-white POW/MIA bumper stickers.

George H. W. Bush failed to make the antiwar activities and draft evasion of Bill Clinton the central feature of the 1992 presidential race. But his son succeeded in making the combat experience and antiwar activities of John Kerry the central feature of the 2004 presidential race. 'Vietnam,' that construct of illusions, myths, fantasies, and lies that had replaced the realities of the Vietnam War, now became a defining test of character to determine who was fit to lead America during another construct of illusions and lies – the so-called 'war on terror.' In this psycho-cultural hall of mirrors, the President, who had used family connections to avoid serving in Vietnam or even fulfilling his minimal National Guard obligations, appeared as a towering figure of bravery and determination, while his challenger, who had received three purple hearts for combat wounds and five medals, including the Silver Star, for bravery and heroism, looked to millions of Americans like a cowardly wimp if not downright traitor. It turns out that it was none other than John Kerry, along with Jane

Fonda and all those pinko professors, who got Americans to betray our troops, spit on them, and call them baby killers.

The onslaught against Kerry was led by John O'Neill, who had first been recruited by Richard Nixon's dirty tricksters back in 1971 to discredit the combat veterans then leading the anti-war movement. The Nixon White House had been rattled by the Winter Soldier Investigation held by Vietnam Veterans Against the War, during which more than a hundred combat veterans testified about atrocities and war crimes they had witnessed or actually participated in; some showed pictures reminiscent of recent photos from Abu Ghraib, such as an interrogator yanking on a cord tied to the testicles of a Vietnamese prisoner. From April 19 through 24, Washington was besieged by antiwar demonstrators, eventually numbering half a million and led by thousands of Vietnam War veterans. The veterans' six-day demonstration, which they called Dewey Canyon III, climaxed when almost a thousand threw their medals over a hastily erected fence around the Capitol building and when their spokesman, Navy Lieutenant John Kerry, testified for two hours in nationally televised hearings of the Senate Foreign Relations Committee. Kerry included in his lengthy opening statement a very brief summary of the veterans' testimony at the Winter Soldier Investigation.[29] More than three decades later, those few words about the conduct of the war would be used as an explosive charge hurled with deadly effect at the Kerry campaign, thus demonstrating how thoroughly the realities of the Vietnam War have been replaced by jingoist fantasy. Never mind that Kerry's 1971 testimony, like that produced in the Winter Soldier Investigation, was contemporaneous with the trial of Lieutenant William Calley for the slaughter, rape, and sodomy in My Lai. Never mind that in April 2004, the *Toledo Blade* newspaper received a Pulitzer Prize for a series about systematic atrocities carried out by an elite US Army unit, as part of US policy, in the same province as My Lai a year earlier. Never mind that every one of Kerry's words about US atrocities and war crimes has been proved, over and over again, to be true. No, by 2004 the hideous record of US atrocities and genocide in Vietnam had been erased, and Kerry's 1971 testimony could be portrayed as a libelous if not downright treasonous attack on America and its soldiers.

Looking backward from the twenty-first century, the efforts of the Nixon administration to neutralize Kerry seem crude and primitive compared to what we saw in 2004. 'We found a vet named John O'Neill and formed a group called Vietnam Veterans for a Just Peace,' Nixon's Special Counsel Charles Colson boasted. 'We had O'Neill meet the President, and we did everything we could to boost his group.'[30] The White House engineered letters to newspapers demanding that they 'expose' Kerry as a 'fraud,' and Colson arranged an Op-Ed piece denouncing Kerry that was syndicated in 150 newspapers, with copies then mailed to 'all veterans organizations and military groups in plain envelopes with no cover letter.'[31] The Dick Cavett Show was chosen as the venue for a debate between Kerry and O'Neill.

Thirty-three years later, and months before Kerry became the Democratic candidate in July 2004, O'Neill, with massive financial support from Bush backers and unlimited media connections, launched the assault, twenty-first century PR style. An April interview on CNN and a May 4 Op-Ed in the *Wall Street Journal* headlined 'Unfit To Serve' set the stage for *Unfit For Command*, the book O'Neill co-authored with right-wing fanatic Jerome Corsi, and the made-for-TV film, 'Stolen Honor: Wounds that Never Heal,' both blaming Kerry for prolonging the war and causing the torture of American POWs. O'Neill and his Swift Boats organization got incessant media exposure on radio, TV, newspapers, magazines, and the Internet, including a free non-stop book-promotion blitz that turned *Unfit For Command* into the nation's top nonfiction bestseller for weeks during the crucial final months of the presidential race. Leading the circus was Rupert Murdoch's Fox network. Show after show on Fox featured such objective voices as former Iran Contra conspirator and now Fox News Channel host Oliver North, who claimed that the atrocities cited by Kerry in 1971 simply 'did not happen,' former Republican Speaker of the House and now regular Fox contributor Newt Gingrich, who invented a tale of secret 1970 meetings in Paris between Kerry and 'Communist leaders of a country that were [*sic*] killing young Americans while John Kerry is sitting in Paris talking to them,' and right-wing *Washington Post* commentator and regular Fox contributor Charles Krauthammer, who claimed that Kerry 'betrayed' his 'comrades' by 'telling the world that these soldiers left behind were committing atrocities, as Kerry has said on a daily basis.'[32] Over and over again, the wounded and decorated warrior was explicitly branded a 'traitor' responsible not only for the torture of POWs and the betrayal of his fellow soldiers, but even for the eventual defeat of the United States by the North Vietnamese Communists.

The main piece of evidence for all this was a picture of John Kerry in the War Remnants Museum of Ho Chi Minh City, a picture that John O'Neill and his cohort claimed to have discovered. *Unfit For Command* opens with a sensationalized account of this discovery by a touring Vietnam veteran: he realized that he had seen this face before – for the first time more than thirty years ago. It was John Kerry. The Vietnamese photo of a 1993 meeting of Kerry and Vietnamese leaders, including the General Secretary of the Vietnamese Communist Party Do Muoi, was to honour John Kerry's 'heroic' contributions to the North Vietnamese victory.[33] *Unfit For Command* later devotes an entire chapter to this terribly incriminating photograph, which is actually a picture of Kerry's reception in Vietnam as head of a congressional delegation seeking information from the Vietnamese about unaccounted for American servicemen.

Kerry and his campaign were criticized for not responding more aggressively to these scurrilous attacks. Some have argued that he should have reaffirmed the validity of his 1971 view of the war and his later efforts to resolve postwar issues and bring about normal relations with Vietnam. In fact, as co-chair of the Senate Select Committee on POW/MIA Affairs during its seventeen months of investigations in 1991 and 1992, Kerry had played a major role in the gradual beginnings of trade relations during the first Bush and Clinton Administrations and the eventual establishment of diplomatic relations in 1995.

Yet Kerry and his campaign dared not take this tack. Was this a mistake? To do so would have required confronting head-on the fantasy 'Vietnam.' Two-thirds of the American people still believe that Vietnam secretly held many US POWs after the war and therefore they are either still there or they were executed. The belief that Vietnam veterans were routinely spat upon and called baby killers is almost universal in America today, despite overwhelming evidence that this is pure myth. The depth of the irrationality on this issue is suggested by the accusation, made by a former San Diego mayor acting as guest host on the enormously popular Rush Limbaugh radio show that John Kerry 'was the one who coined the phrase "baby killers" ', 'the phrase returning veterans from Vietnam had to hear . . . when they were spit upon in airports.'[34] John Kerry was indeed a prominent activist against the Vietnam War, which explains some of the hatred and loathing evoked by his candidacy. But the fact that a prominent activist against the Vietnam War came very close to being elected President of the United States in 2004 suggests that the war in America over the Vietnam War has another side and has not yet been decided.

Although the fantasy 'Vietnam' is dominant in twenty-first century American culture and politics, the anti-war movement that arose from the realities of the war still exerts a profound and powerful counterforce. Demonstrations against the Iraq war have surpassed in size those against the Vietnam War, and the anti-imperial consciousness that emerged a little over three decades ago has deepened and gained a far wider constituency among the American people. The actual history of the Vietnam War has by no means been entirely forgotten, and whenever it bursts through the fantasy of Vietnam it threatens to obliterate the ignorance upon which current American politics and policy so precariously depend. So, no, I don't believe that the Vietnam War did end in 1975 or that its outcomes have yet been decided.

Notes

1. 'US Cancels Agent Orange Study in Vietnam,' *The New Scientist*, 19 March 2005, p. 7.
2. Edwin Martini, *Invisible Enemies: The American War on Vietnam, 1975–2000* (Amherst: University of Massachusetts Press, 2007).
3. This 1990 text written by George Donelson Moss and published by Prentice-Hall, a subsidiary of Viacom, had gone through three editions by 1998. Among the important studies that have explored how the war has been transformed into a trauma inflicted not by America on Vietnam but by Vietnam on America, see Susan Jeffords, *The Remasculinization of America: Gender and the Vietnam War* (Bloomington: Indiana University Press, 1989); Fred Turner, *Echoes of Combat: The Vietnam War in American Memory* (New York: Anchor Books, 1996); and Keith Beattie, *The Scar that Binds: American Culture and the Vietnam War* (New York: New York University Press, 2000).
4. *Rebuilding America's Defenses: Strategy, Forces and Resources For a New American Century. A Report of The Project for the New American Century* (New York: Project for the New American Century, September, 2000), pp. 2, 11, 13, 76.
5. 'A One-Superpower World' and 'Excerpts from the Defense Planning Guidance For the Fiscal Years 1994–1998,' *The New York Times*, March 8, 1992.

6. *Rebuilding America's Defenses: Strategy, Forces and Resources For a New American Century*, pp. 14, 51, 57.
7. Much of my account of the transport of this French invasion army by US troopships is based on Chapter 3 of Michael Gillen's extremely important 1991 NYU dissertation, *Roots of Opposition: The Critical Response to US Indochina Policy, 1945–1954.*
8. Reprinted in Marvin Gettleman, Jane Franklin, Marilyn Young, & H. Bruce Franklin, eds, *Vietnam and America: A Documented History, Revised and Enlarged Second Edition* (New York: Grove Press, 1995), p. 52.
9. Senator Ernest Gruening & Herbert Wilton Beaser, *Vietnam Folly* (Washington, DC: National Press, 1968), pp. 100–105.
10. Ibid., p. 105.
11. Gillen, *Roots of Opposition*, pp. 379–83, p. 402. As Gillen notes, some sources incorrectly attribute this speech to Lyndon Johnson.
12. Ibid., p. 402.
13. 'Final Declaration of the Geneva Conference,' July 21, 1954, in Gettleman *et al., Vietnam and America*, p. 75.
14. Cablegram from Ambassador Lodge to Secretary of State Rusk, August 29, 1963, reprinted ibid., p. 227.
15. Turner, *Echoes of Combat*, p. 63; Arnold R. Isaacs, *Vietnam Shadows: The War, Its Ghost, and Its Legacy* (Baltimore: Johns Hopkins University Press, 1997), p. 49.
16. Gettleman *et al., Vietnam and America*, p. xv.
17. Christian G. Appy, *Working-Class War: American Combat Soldiers and Vietnam* (Chapel Hill: University of North Carolina Press, 1993), p. 9.
18. George Bush, 'Inaugural Address,' January 20, 1989, *Public Papers of the Presidents of the United States: George Bush, 1989* (Washington, DC: Government Printing Office, 1990), Book 1, p. 3.
19. George Bush, 'Address to the Nation Announcing Allied Military Action in the Persian Gulf, January 16, 1991,' *Public Papers of the Presidents of the United States: George Bush, 1991* (Washington, DC: Government Printing Office, 1992), Book 1, p. 44.
20. Sven Lindqvist, *A History of Bombing* (New York: New Press, 2001), p. 43. C. G. Grey, *Bombers* (London: Faber & Faber, 1941), p. 71. See my discussion in *War Stars*, (New York: Oxford University Press, 1988), pp. 88–9.
21. Jerry Lembcke, *The Spitting Image* (New York: New York University Press, 1998), p. 20.
22. E. J. Dionne Jr, 'Kicking the "Vietnam Syndrome"', *Washington Post*, March 4, 1991.
23. H. Bruce Franklin, *M.I.A or Mythmaking in America* (New Brunswick, NJ: Rutgers University Press, 1993), pp. 50–6.
24. 'Veterans Raise Perot Banner,' *New York Daily News*, June 11, 1992.
25. David Jackson, 'MIAs' Kin Want Perot as President,' *Dallas Morning News*, May 19, 1992; interview with David Jackson, May 18, 1992; telephone interview with John LeBoutillier, June 12, 1992; 'It's Businessman Perot

and Not War Hero Bush Who Attracts a Following Among US Veterans,' *Wall Street Journal*, July 2, 1992.

26. The Third 1992 Presidential Debate, October 19, 1992, http://www.pbs.org/newshour/bebatingour destiny/92debates.
27. 'Trust in the Military Heightens Among Baby Boomers' Children,' *The New York Times*, May 27, 2003.
28. US Department of State, *Aggression from the North: The Record of North Vietnam's Campaign to Conquer South Vietnam*, Publication 7839, Far Eastern Series 130 (Washington, DC, 1965) in Gettleman *et al.*, *Vietnam and America*.
29. For the complete text of Kerry's statement, see *Vietnam and America*, pp. 456–62.
30. 'The Lies of John O'Neill,' *Media Matters for America*, http://mediamatters.org/items/printable/200408250002.
31. Tom Wells, *The War Within: America's Battle Over Vietnam* (New York: Henry Holt, 1994), p. 490.
32. Media Matters for America, http://mediamatters.org/items/printable/200408260004, 200409020010, 200409010004.
33. John E. O'Neill and Jerome Corsi, *Unfit for Command* (Washington, DC: Regnery Publishing, 2004), p. 7.
34. Roger Hedgecock, the former San Diego mayor, was acting as substitute host for Limbaugh when he made this claim on August 25, 2004. His claim that Kerry coined this term in his 1971 Senate testimony is demonstrably false as well as a bit illogical, since most Vietnam veterans returned prior to 1971. Media Matters for America, http://mediamatters.org/items/printable/200408270003.

4
Apocalypse Now Redux and the Curse of Vietnam

John Hellmann

In August 2001 Francis Ford Coppola released *Apocalypse Now Redux*, a re-edited and significantly expanded version of his 1979 surrealist epic of the Vietnam War *Apocalypse Now*. The occasion of the new version gave reviewers an opportunity to acknowledge that the film the press had once dubbed *Apocalypse When?* and *Apocalypse Too Late* had survived the controversy attending its release over two decades earlier. *Redux* was discussed as a revision of a masterpiece, even if a 'flawed' masterpiece, that now constituted perhaps the major single 'memory' of the Vietnam War. In this chapter I wish to discuss the expanded, re-released version of the film as a chance to consider the continued relevance of Coppola's film in the early twenty-first century. I will be discussing the meaning of *Apocalypse Now Redux* as above all a film about American culture staging its own values, albeit on a theatre set atop of the landscape of another country.

As much as the American war in Vietnam, memorable sequences in the film such as Colonel Kilgore's attack on a village to go surfing, the USO show with Playboy bunnies dancing to rock music, and the Do Lung Bridge sequence in which young black men are shown entrapped within what amounts to a burning slum night-marishly reflect major aspects of the United States in the 1960s. Likewise, the two figures at the center of the film, Captain Willard and Colonel Walter E. Kurtz, are recognizable character types of the culture back home. Significantly, however, they are icons not of the 1960s but rather of the time in which *Apocalypse Now* was filmed and originally released, the disillusioned and traumatized 1970s. The opening of the film establishes Captain Willard, who will be the identification-figure for the viewer throughout the film, as an embodiment of the loss of faith that was the prevailing mood of the 1970s. Colonel Walter E. Kurtz, who has 'set himself up like a god' and to whom the depressed and alienated Willard is attracted, mirrors the charismatic gurus offering certainty and fulfillment who during the 1970s drew such disaffected casualties of the 1960s as Willard to remote compounds.

Thus two time periods, the 1960s and the 1970s, are embedded within the film. As Karl French points out, the narrative action transpires sometime during the last two months of 1969 (this is indicated by the newspaper story about Charles Manson that reaches Willard's boat at the Do Lung Bridge).[1] The specific ethos of the film is retrospective. Willard's voice-over narration emanates from an undetermined point in the future, most logically at the end of the 1970s when *Apocalypse Now* was originally released ('Everyone gets everything he wants. I wanted a mission. And for my sins, they gave me one. Brought it up to me like room service. It was a real choice mission. And when it was over, I'd never want another).' Thus the film embeds within its narrative scheme its status as a searching look back from the disillusioned cultural moment of the 1970s to the tumultuous 1960s. *Apocalypse Now* is a 1979 film in which the narrative thread positions its original viewer with a protagonist and experiencing narrative filter who in his journey up the river in Vietnam is leading the viewer, through the retrospective vantage of reflective memory, in taking a look back at the previous decade in an attempt to find a way out of the despair and cynicism of the subsequent decade.

The 2001 version, *Apocalypse Now Redux*, retains these elements while bringing into view formerly discarded shots, scenes, and entire episodes. In one case, it also repositions an original episode. This new version, completely re-edited from the vantage of the twenty-first century, adds to the retrospective perspective of the original. *Redux* is not a so-called 'director's cut,' as Coppola had complete control over the original; rather, it is Coppola from the twenty-first century returning us to the Vietnam of *Apocalypse Now* from a later vantage. Encouraged to take a new look at Coppola's film from our more distant point of view, we can now see not only the representation of the 1960s in the scenes along the river, but also of the 1970s in the characters of Willard and Kurtz. The viewer comes back again, with the same narrator Willard, but this time with an implied author positioned more than thirty years after the events of the film. With this added frame, the structure of the film as a dialectic between the 1960s and the 1970s (the latter looking back at the former) emerges into sharper view, and we are positioned to see with the clarity of distance aspects of American culture that during the 1970s conveyed themselves with the vivid shock of first disillusion.

Captain Willard is a character who in late 1969 is already trapped within the disillusioned and depressed ethos that leads Philip Jenkins to entitle his study of the 1970s *Decade of Nightmares*.[2] The opening shot, in which helicopters drop fire upon lush jungle vegetation, is immediately revealed to be a nightmare taking place in the mind of the protagonist. The camera pans right as the imagery overlaps with one of a man's perspiring head, upside down on a bed. The collapsing of outer experience into inner experience, of hellish events into feverish consciousness, is further evoked on the soundtrack by the music of the Doors rock group. The singing voice of Jim Morrison expresses Willard's feelings and either articulates or comments upon his unconscious perceptions. Morrison sings lyrics from 'The End' stating that 'I'll never look into your eyes again,' and describing being 'lost in a Roman wilderness of pain.' Alone in a Saigon hotel room, Willard sets fire to a photograph of his ex-wife as the voice-over informs us that 'I hardly said a word to my wife until I said yes to a divorce' as we watch him hold her picture up to his cigarette and set it afire, a follow-up to his nightmare of helicopters setting the jungle aflame. Willard's personal crisis (divorce) is most immediately brought on by his society's imperial catastrophe (Vietnam), making him a representative of the Post-Traumatic Stress Disorder diagnosed in Vietnam veterans during the 1970s but also emblematic of the culture-wide crisis of faith. As Americans reeled from the disillusionment over Vietnam and the turmoil produced by the correlative personal and political upheaval at home, the 1970s witnessed the destabilizing of all its institutions, including a dramatic increase in the breakup of marriages.

Separating themselves, people turned inward toward quests for personal growth and liberation. Tom Wolfe labeled the 1970s the 'Me Decade' and Christopher Lasch saw a 'culture of narcissism.' As Jenkins notes, 'In a time of wide-ranging cultural crisis, it seemed natural to turn within to explore inner resources and needs.'[3] This withdrawal was marked by increased levels of escapist drug-taking, compensating adoption of Asian disciplines of self-control, and egoistic absorption in self. Willard's actions in the Saigon hotel room reflect a version of this isolating withdrawal. His voice-over tells us that each time he looked around 'the walls came in a little closer.' He descends into drunkenness while moving his body in the slow-motion martial arts exercises of Tai Chi in front of a mirror. At the end of the scene, having drunk himself into a self-destructive frenzy, he lashes out at his mirror-reflection, breaking the glass and sending himself over his empty bed naked and bloody, groaning in agony. The characterization of Willard in terms iconic of 1970s psychological withdrawal and disintegration amid the ruins of a fragmenting culture establishes him as an identification-figure for the culture-wide disillusionment and despair of a decade that at bottom was fueled by a failure in Vietnam confirming or catalyzing doubts about American society.

Cynicism concerning established authority was a pervasive aspect of the 1970s ethos, a time of intense skepticism toward all institutions and officials. The general at the headquarters in Nha Trang to whom Willard is taken is played by G. D. Spradlin, the same actor Coppola cast in *The Godfather II* (1974) in the role of a hypocritical senator who is ensnared by the Mafia in a bordello. The general cloaks his murderous intentions with fastidious manners and an elegant aristocratic Southern accent that sententiously moralizes with a quotation from Lincoln. He tells Willard that Colonel Walter E. Kurtz was 'one of the most outstanding officers this country's ever produced,' who fled when he was about to be arrested for murder, and that, 'very obviously, he has gone insane.' Willard outwardly accepts the general's categorization, but his voice-over narration confides to us his skepticism regarding established authority: 'Shit. Arresting a man for murder in this place was like handing out speeding tickets at the Indy 500. I took the mission. What the hell else was I gonna do? But I didn't really know what I'd do when I found him.'

While it is phrased in the hard-boiled language of a street-wise or battle-hardened tough guy, Willard is speaking the relativistic and skeptical sentiments of the radical liberalism that was ascendent in the 1970s. Jenkins points out that 'influential sociologists and criminologists who had been exposed to the currents of 1960s radicalism' supported a radical criminology in the 1970s that saw 'individuals who differed from the norm,' and who were therefore labeled 'criminal, lunatic, or heretical,' as perhaps having a 'moral legitimacy higher than that of the police or courts, especially in a society ruled by unchecked capitalism.'[4] And after he, and the viewer, in the next episode observes Colonel Kilgore's murderous rampage upon a Vietnamese village full of women and children in order to secure a beach for surfing, Willard comments, 'If that's how Kilgore fought the war...I began to wonder what they really had against Kurtz. It wasn't just insanity and murder. There was enough of that to go around for everybody.' As Willard proceeds up the river, his journey becomes an investigative expose of 'legitimate' American institutions as reflected in Vietnam and a growing identification with the man those in power have labeled criminally insane.

In an early analysis of *Apocalypse Now*, I focused on parallels between Willard and the hard-boiled detective of classic private-eye literature and film noir.[5] From the distant vantage of the *Redux* release, we can see that Willard more immediately resembles the major American culture hero of the 1970s, the investigative reporter who exposes the perfidy and hypocrisy of the Establishment. This heroic figure was created for the public by the success of the two young *Washington Post* reporters Bob Woodward and Carl Bernstein in exposing the Watergate cover-up. As Jenkins points out, 'Between 1973 and 1978, public corruption was never far from the headlines,' as reporters seeking to emulate Woodward and Bernstein 'began an era of furious efforts to root out the appearance of misconduct in public life.'[6] Their best-selling book recounting their experiences in pursuing the investigation, *All the President's Men* (1974), made into a highly successful 1976 motion picture starring Dustin Hoffman and Robert Redford, followed the narrative conventions of the hard-boiled detective genre. Willard thus fulfills the role of the private eye of film noir by enacting the reportorial exposé made iconic during the mid-1970s. As Willard proceeds up the river in search of Kurtz, he encounters three examples of 'misconduct in public life': the hypocritical brutality of Kilgore's enactment of war as a cult of celebrity, the degradation of the men and women of America into consumers and commodities epitomized by the Playboy bunnies USO sequence, and the racial and class exploitation evident at the Do Lung Bridge. Coppola structures each of these sequences on the model of the investigative reporter's experience exemplified in Woodward and Bernstein's account. In each case Willard comes upon a bewildering scene, vainly searches for a legitimate purpose and authority, and then categorizes the official perfidy. The effect of his discoveries echoes the obsession during the mid- to late 1970s with uncovering evidence of illicit force, corruption, and exploitation perpetrated by an authority no longer viewed as legitimate. The scenes of his investigation are surrealistic dramatizations, like the distorted metaphors in dream messages, of American culture in the 1960s.

In analyzing the exposé of the American society of the 1960s that Willard produces in his investigation of the American war in Vietnam, I will draw most importantly on perspectives concerning the society of the United States offered by historian Michael J. Sandel. His study *Democracy's Discontent: America in Search of a Public Philosophy* (1996) sees post-Vietnam discontent in the United States as rooted in economic and political developments during the first half of the twentieth century, with the cause being the gradual substitution of the ideal of the 'procedural republic' for the eighteenth- and nineteenth-century concern with republican political theory. Republican political theory guided economic and political arrangements calculated to form a citizenry with a character enabling them to be self-governing and to recognize their ties to community. The procedural republic, based in Keynesian economics, privileges the rights of citizens to pursue their own ends, in a society conceived as a field of desire populated by consumers, with the ideal character being an 'unencumbered self,' a citizen who is not burdened with obligations or situated by ties that she or he has not chosen. In his historical narrative of American political development, Sandel shows that the ideal of the procedural republic had taken precedence in the United States by the beginning of the Cold War in 1945 and completely dominated by the post-Vietnam 1970s.

Sandel suggests, however, that for two reasons the ideal of the citizen as unencumbered self cannot be fulfilled in American society as it has existed since 1945. First, the freedom for its enactment is not in fact available in a society dominated by the massive government and corporate structures that emerged from World War II. Second, it is in any case based on a fallacious concept of identity, since 'It fails to capture those loyalties and responsibilities whose moral force consists partly in the fact that living by them is inseparable from understanding ourselves as the particular persons we are – as members of this family or city or nation or people, as bearers of that history, as citizens of this republic.'[7] In Sandel's narrative, America's ascendancy to world domination and unprecedented affluence after World War II enabled Americans to at first enjoy an illusion of collective mastery enabling them to overlook their personal loss of identity and power. This illusion persisted during the 1950s, a spell broken only briefly by the shock of the Soviet launching of Sputnik in 1957 before reaching its apotheosis in the magical aura of President John F. Kennedy's Camelot. While Kennedy actually followed policies based on the technocratic premises of the procedural republic, his charismatic image and rhetorical call upon citizens for voluntary sacrifice offered an especially resonant and powerful identification figure in whom citizens could imagine their own mastery.

It was only after the Tet Offensive in Vietnam and the assassinations and other turmoil at home during 1968 that Americans experienced a general sense of loss of mastery. Sandel identifies the shocks of that year as only a crystallizing moment of a longer process: 'The mood of discontent that descended upon American politics in 1968 had been building for several years. The inner-city riots, campus protests, and antiwar demonstrations of the mid-1960s intimated the unraveling of faith in existing arrangements. . . . In 1968 the disillusion spread beyond the ghettos and the campuses to a broader American public.' One might add that the events to which Sandel refers were seen to begin with the assassination of John F. Kennedy in Dallas. The enduring result has been the loss of faith in America and of meaningful purpose for its citizens which has plagued the land ever since, and which the 1970s figure of Willard exemplifies. The 'twin curses' of JFK's assassination and Vietnam are deeply painful and resonant experiences of the helplessness created by the underlying perception of 'the loss of self-government and the erosion of community' that Sandel observes 'defined the anxiety of the age.'[8] From our relatively distant vantage from both the 1960s and the shocked perspective of Willard's 1970s narration, the realization of this loss is the legacy of Vietnam that the *Redux* of *Apocalypse Now* can help bring into our view. Sandel's perspective on the weaknesses of the public philosophy governing the life of the United States since World War II can help us to see the conditions of American life, governed by an inadequate public philosophy, beneath the appearances of phantasmagoric disaster and revelation associated with Vietnam.

The Kilgore episode and the Do Lung Bridge sequence, the first and last before Willard and the boat leave Vietnam to cross into Cambodia, may be examined as a pair. Both episodes are marked by a masculine ego which rises out of a field of chaotic violence in a display of radical individualism.

Significantly, on the threshold of his journey Willard finds himself under the orders of a news director (played by Coppola himself): 'Go on, keep going. It's for television. Don't look at the camera.' Willard is entering the looking-glass world of the media-driven American culture that in the 1960s began to confuse the realms of reality and entertainment. Willard asks where he can find the commander and is quickly led to the flamboyant and cocksure Colonel Kilgore, who with his contrived costume and self-conscious style presents himself as superstar. Kilgore turns everything about him into a stage, a devastation upon which he displays his own performing self. Ramrod straight, chest puffed out, shouting orders, he cuts a hyperbolic imitation of command that refers to the 1870s cavalry officer, the World War II commander, and the 1960s football coach. He wears the wide-brimmed black hat and yellow ascot, suggesting victors of the plains in Indian wars of the nineteenth century in John Ford films of the 1950s such as *She Wore a Yellow Ribbon, Rio Grande*, and *Fort Apache*. His sunglasses and celebration of battle respectively evoke the iconic World War II generals Douglas MacArthur and George Patton. His bullhorn-amplified shouts and crotch-grabbing gestures refer to the contemporary win-at-any-costs football coach. While he orders all about him, Kilgore has only the end of commanding attention. Kilgore's attack on a Viet Cong village to secure a beach for the enlisted man he embraces as a fellow star in a different sport ('You can cut out the "sir" crap, Lance. I'm Bill Kilgore. I'm a "goofy foot" ') is a parody of the 'pseudo-events' that Daniel Boorstin lamented at the outset of the 1960s, the public occurrences manufactured for an audience that he saw proliferating in response to the growth of the mass media. Kilgore himself is a walking instance of Andy Warhol's pop art, a self-made reproduction of his favorite icons, and just as emptied of meaningful historical reference or communal value.

This cult of celebrity is implicitly contrasted to the honor and integrity that Willard finds in Kurtz's dossier during scenes framing the Kilgore episode. Before meeting Kilgore, Willard reads of how Kurtz returned from his first tour in Vietnam demanding a personal meeting with President Johnson and the Joint Chiefs of Staff. When his report was rebuffed he gave up his superb career prospects ('He was being groomed for one of the top slots in the corporation') to join the Special Forces, which required going through arduous airborne training at twice the age of the other men and ensured never achieving a higher rank than colonel. After the Kilgore episode, Willard returns to dossiers on Kurtz to conclude that 'He could have gone for general, but he went for himself, instead.' In the dossiers, Willard as 1970s reader and storyteller begins on the boat to construct Kurtz as the antithesis of the society that exposes itself to him along the shore. After each such episode, Willard returns to the dossiers to find a virtue demonstrated by Kurtz that offers an alternative to the deficiencies of his contemporaries. In contrast to Kilgore's radical individualism and cult of celebrity, Kurtz gives up career won through empty display in favor of a virtuous pursuit of true victory. This is the fame that heroes of the early American republic sought as a meaningful identity embedded within service to a worthy community. As the authors of *Habits of the Heart*, a study of individualism and commitment in America life, put it, 'Madison and his contemporaries thought of the pursuit of virtue as the way to reconcile the desire to be esteemed by one's peers with publicly beneficial ends.'[9] The implicit contrast Willard finds between Kilgore and Kurtz establishes the motif in the film of Kurtz as Willard's nostalgic projection of an identity that might still be a viable alternative to the procedural republic.

Much later in the film, when Willard arrives at the Do Lung bridge, he can find no officer who claims to be in command. The darkness, fear, and chaos of the scene, in which black soldiers are under siege and fire machine guns in spasms of fear and rage, reveal no white commander dressed in the fetishes of the American Western. Instead, we are given a representation of young black Americans who are positioned at the bottom of the war just as they are of American society at home. The white courier exults of the release for himself acquired by delivery to Willard of the message he is carrying; leaving, he cries, 'You're in the asshole of the world, Captain!' The Do Lung Bridge is where those souls whom American society regards as waste products are trapped. As Willard and Lance move across the field in the darkness, the lights, smoke, and fire evoke the cycle of poverty and violence in the impoverished inner cities. When Willard asks two huddled black soldiers where the commanding officer is, he is told 'Right up the road there's a concrete bunker called Beverly Hills. Where the fuck else do you think it would be?' The soldier is pointing out to Willard that the familiar social, racial, and class geography of American society in California has been mapped upon that of Vietnam. As Willard and Lance proceed, they pass more black GIs, and trip over the body of one who angrily shouts that he is not dead, and finally come upon two black soldiers at a fifty-caliber machine gun. The gunner fires madly while pacing and swearing at the enemy, 'I told you to stop fucking with me! You think you're so bad, huh, nigga?' When Willard asks who is in command, the soldier looks into his white face and asks, 'Ain't you?'

In this hellish scene of the bottom of American society, in Vietnam or in California, a black hipster icon of the 1960s strides onto the stage as an underclass mirror to Kilgore's white celebrity. Upset by the cries of a Viet Cong trapped under bodies out by the perimeter wire, the gunner sends his spotter for a soldier named Roach. As music of the virtuoso black rock guitarist Jimi Hendrix plays in the background, a tall, preternaturally cool black man wearing beads and trinkets appears out of the night with an M-79 grenade launcher. Perfectly attuned to his instrument ('Do you need a flare?' 'No'), this Vietnam reflection of Hendrix with his Stratocaster points the weapon up in the air as he listens to his target's yelling; he fires, a sharp explosion is heard, silencing the screams of the waiting 'fan.' Willard looks up into his face and asks, 'Hey, soldier. Do you know who's in command here?' He looks back at him, says 'Yeah,' and turns and walks away.

Kilgore and Roach are at opposite poles of the racial, social, and economic landscape of the United States that has been placed over Vietnam; as mythic figures, they mirror the divide between the white California of the surfer boy Lance and the south Bronx 'shithole' of Clean. Yet they actually have much in common. Both are supreme expressions of masculine confidence and skill. Kilgore commands men, machines, all the power of American technological resources with precision and results; his name suggests an exhilaration in the ability to devastate. Roach, at the bottom of the hierarchy, commands only the M-79 grenade launcher, but he does so with dazzling effectiveness; his name suggests both the lowly insect that nevertheless has no peer in survival in a slum environment and the marijuana cigarette enhancing a jazz or rock musician's outsider perspective. Both the white colonel and the black grunt have style, apparent in their costumes and bearing. Kilgore and Roach are both stars.

The significance of the parallels between Kilgore and Roach is that they are both manifestations of the kind of success most celebrated in the American society that Sandel labels the 'procedural republic.' They are both stars, a triumph of individual ego that separates them from the mass. As such, their awe-inspiring performances and style captivate those around them, turning them into mere audiences for their self-display. The careful evocation of their Americanized Vietnam worlds as those of blond surfing beaches and black ghettos suggests more than that the Vietnam War was a massive imposition of American society upon the Vietnamese landscape and culture, though that is certainly true; it also enables these episodes to comment upon the economic and political arrangements of American society at home. Within those arrangements the stardom of Kilgore and Roach looms as a self-isolating reign of a radical individualism: as isolating to the self as it is devastating to others. Kilgore and Roach are figures of hollowness, the first unaware and contemptible, the second lonely and forlorn, that stand in contrast to the austere sacrifice Willard finds in the Kurtz who abandoned the lure of career.

The other episodes that portray American society in *Apocalypse Now Redux* center around the Playboy bunnies, and represent a sustained critique of the consumer society. As the boat pulls up to the stage and audience awaiting the USO performance, Willard has come upon the spectacle of consumer hedonism of the 1960s, emphasized by the row of motorcycles and other consumer goods as well as the *Playboy* centerfolds behind the supply sergeant's desk. When we watch the brilliant headlight of the helicopter with a white *Playboy* bunny logo descending from the night sky toward us, we are being shown the true god of the American empire, signifying its ultimate value of commodity worship. From the inaugural issue *Playboy* in late 1953, editor and publisher Hugh Hefner propagated a 'playboy philosophy' in which the girl-next-door was advertised as a potential playmate who could take her place in a playboy's pad among the other shiny consumer items. Hefner's magazine enjoyed instant and dramatic success, attaining its peak of influence in the 1960s because it was in fact moving so exactly with the logic of the consumer society. Indeed, back in the 1950s a motivational researcher had declared that 'One of the basic problems of prosperity, then, is to demonstrate that the hedonistic approach to life is a moral, not an immoral one.'[10]

By 1965 advertisers had inferred from the success of *Playboy* that they could sexualize formerly sacrosanct objects. Stephanie Coontz cites the example of an advertisement in which the 'Statue of Liberty suggestively modeled a new zipper.' The irreverence elicited no condemnation, apparently because it was perceived as one with the patriotic value of free enterprise.[11] When the three Playboy bunnies emerge from the helicopter scantily clad in costumes designating them as Indian, cavalryman, and cowboy, the spectacle sexualizes the frontier myth along the same lines as the zipper advertisement does the idea of liberty. The Indian and cavalry bunnies, both Play-mates of the Month, emerge from opposite sides of the helicopter, hanging out at opposite angles from the same level, suggesting their status as opposed elements of savagery and civilization in a histor-ical dialectic. The climactic appearance on top of the helicopter of the cowboy – the lead part played by the bunny who has won the highest designation, Playmate of the Year – represents the cowboy's emergence in the American frontier myth as triumphant, uniquely American synthesis. Significantly, the bunnies playing the Indian and cavalryman hump M-16 rifles as part of their dance, suggesting the satisfaction they acquire from their roles in the violent legend, while the cowboy repeatedly rubs her twin six-guns against her inner thighs before firing them at the audience. The cowboy receives the phallic sexual power of the violent myth and then 'shoots' that potency to the contemporary male audience.

This symbolic dance is accompanied by the rock song 'Suzie Q.' Like *Playboy*, the song appropriates the girl-next-door ideal of American innocence to a fantasy of guileless, obtainable sexual satisfaction. Behind the shouting, wildly stimulated male audience stand erect the phallic symbols formed by giant rocket-like lipsticks. The fetishes of female sexual allure contain the destructive potency of rockets to form 'pillars' of a society in which female sexuality is used to sell consumer items of all types. In the climax of the USO episode the aroused men break through barriers to reach the advertised 'Suzie Q' and frontier myth, only to find the promise of satisfaction withdrawn in a cloud of smoke laid down by the bunnies' agent.

Barbara Ehrenreich has argued that the complaint of the counter-culture about the consumer culture was simply that it 'had always promised much more than it advertised: Not just a car, but sexual adventure; not just a pack of cigarettes, but heroic vistas and a soaring sense of freedom.'[12] In her analysis, the counterculture did not critique the logic of hedonism but rather the false promises that the commodities it displayed would bring satisfaction. In *Apocalypse Now Redux* the scene in which Clean turns on the armed forces radio station and dances to the Rolling Stones' song, '(I Can't Get No) Satisfaction,' follows shortly after the USO sequence. The three stanzas of the lyrics of the famous Stones' song successively denounce news on the radio, a commercial on television, and a girl on her period for arousing desire ending only in frustration. While the song plays, we witness the 'boys on the boat' in thrill-seeking obliviousness to the disruption of traditional society, here Vietnamese but by extension the family values of American society; as Clean dances and Lance water-skis behind, the waves produced by the boat swamp the washing being done by women along the shore and capsize a sampan from which men are at work fishing.

The subsequent Medevac scene comically emphasizes the futility of a society that has assimilated women and sexuality to the field of commodities. While he stands apart himself, Willard barters petrol to the bunnies' agent in return for their sexual favors to the boat crew. The encounters that ensue show the young men obsessed with remaking the flesh-and-blood women into the images they have obsessed over in the magazine, opening their blouses, placing a wig on one, make-up on another; as they do so, they are deaf to the women's tales of insecurity about their self-worth, experience of being pressured to pose in a manner against their wishes, and desire to be truly seen and heard. This fetishistic comedy of errors climaxes in the bunny with Lance screaming in fright at seeing Clean at the window. When she asks who he is he answers, 'I'm next.' His inadvertent identification of his status as someone hopefully waiting, defined in his society by race, ironically repeats Clean's delight in the previous scene at telling about a Vietnamese 'gook' whom a GI shot full of holes for putting pinholes in a Playmate centerfold. The satire is complete when the frightened bunny bumps against a coffin, knocking aside a lid that reveals a dead GI full of holes. The overall import of the bunny sequences is to portray a society in which eros has been diverted into a degrading fetishism that enforces a separation between self and object rather than a coming together of two beings.

In Ehrenreich's analysis, the counterculture decided that drugs were the 'ultimate commodity and the negation of all other commodities' that could bring true satisfaction: 'Drugs could dissolve the boundary between self and object and thereby render the mere possession of things redundant' in a 'fairyland where all desires can be instantly gratified.'[13] Back on the boat, Chief later asks Lance why he is putting green paint on his face as he studies himself in a compact paint that we saw him placing on his bunny to make her up once again like an Indian brave in preparation for possessing her fetishized identity as savage. He answers, 'Camouflage. So they can't see you. They're everywhere, Chief.' Lance has transferred the sexual fetish to a primitive fetish, in either case a magical object aimed at warding off direct encounter with the other, and in taking on the power of the feminine and the savage with face paint enacts the countercultural move of using drugs and costume to turn the mainstream culture's use of fantasy to manipulate consumers into a self-determined dissolution of reality and subjectivity. Somewhat later Lance reads aloud a letter from a friend who tells about a recent visit while on drugs to Disneyland and poses the question: 'There could never be a place like Disneyland, or could there? Let me know.' Lance, who has turned to LSD to transform his tour of Vietnam into a psychedelic trip, answers as he gazes wondrously around at his Vietnam, 'Jim, it's here. It really is here.' A moment later he opens a flare to let loose colored smoke, declaring 'Purple Haze! Look!' and then, 'Rainbow reality, man. Get a good whiff.' The sum effect of these episodes is to suggest that the American culture of the 1960s, as manifested in the mainstream consumer culture as well as the 'opposing' counterculture, is in its totality an expression of the organizing of society after 1945 as a field of desire in which utopia is conceived as a place in which to play, to pursue a fantasy, to fulfill desire.

In the report that Kurtz wrote, Willard reads his complaint that failure to demand true commitment results in a military of 'dilettantes in war, and tourists in Vietnam.' He scathingly denounces a culture in which 'cold beer, hot food, rock'n'roll, and all the other amenities remain expected norm,' resulting in 'conduct of the war' that achieves 'only impotence.' Asserting that the 'tragedy' of the war is that the 'world's greatest technocracy' is being duped by its own 'strategic rhetoric,' Kurtz concludes that 'We need fewer men, and better.' While this critique is specifically aimed at American policies in the Vietnam War, it is implicitly a broader critique of the American society at home and the character of citizens who have become 'impotent' voyeurs and 'tourists' – consumers of spectacle; in effect, Kurtz wants an American force in Vietnam made up of a virtuous minority that is distinctly superior in its values to the culture at home.

Willard has returned to Vietnam because he is convinced that he cannot find out who he is 'working in a factory in Ohio.' Realizing that his society is not providing him a place at home in which he can achieve a viable identity, he has sought definition in the 'mission' in Vietnam. Thus his outrage, mirrored in enlarged terms by the story of Kurtz, at the values he finds American society is staging in Vietnam. Willard hopes to find in Kurtz's outlaw approach the 'home' that is no longer either in the United States or in the war.

After the boat leaves Vietnam and enters the forbidden territory of Cambodia, however, *Redux* first provides Willard a tempting diversion. The French plantation sequence is the major addition to the text of *Apocalypse Now Redux*. Milius says that he conceived of the boat's journey upriver as a trip back in time, with the visit with the French family that has refused to leave Indochina representing a return to the 1950s. Willard and the crew come upon the plantation through clouds of fog, with the French soldiers emerging like the ghosts from another time that in fact they are. In a sense, it is also a journey into the pre-Vietnam War American past, the America of simple verities. The sense of the uncanny is reinforced in the funeral with full military honors that the French give the recently slain Clean. A bugler plays taps as the fallen soldier's body is solemnly carried to its grave on a funeral bier, with Chief handing a carefully folded American flag to Willard and telling him, 'Captain, accept the flag of Tyrone Miller, on behalf of a grateful nation.' This scene is shot with wooden camera work, tinny soundtrack, and muted artificial color that suggest a television melodrama of the era, reinforcing the effect that we are viewing a part of Willard's journey that has departed from the psychedelic and accelerated atmosphere of the late 1960s in Vietnam to enter his nostalgic fantasy of what he expected it, still wishes it, to be. Willard has re-entered the 1950s French plantation to experience a world strangely like the lost 'home' he has earlier confided to us no longer exists 'back there.'

In the dinner table scene, when Willard asks the patriarch Hubert DeMarais why they don't return to France, the Frenchman answers that France is no longer their home, and insists on their right to the land because it was 'nothing' when they found it and they 'built' something on it. He contrasts their own fight to keep what is theirs with the American war in Vietnam, which he scathingly characterizes as fighting 'for the biggest nothing in history.' Willard is subsequently taken to bed by a beautiful French widow, Madame Roxanne Sarrault, who tells him of how she would sooth the pain of her husband when 'He would rage and he would cry, my lost soldier. And I said to him, "There are two of you, don't you see? One that kills and one that loves." ' When she asks Willard if he will return home after the war, and he replies in the negative, she says, 'Then you are like us. You will stay here.' Along with the opium she gives him to smoke, Roxanne offers Willard a tempting rest from the journey he is making, a temptation to join her in the spell in which she and her family have enveloped themselves. Rather than displays of celebrity and consumerism, the French colonials present the possibility of an identity made meaningful through encumbrances of family and tradition. Thus Roxanne represents for Willard, and for the viewer, the temptation to give up the vacuous idealism of the American fight for global freedom and replace it with the unabashed pleasures and clear interests of an imperial identity. The scene is shot with an emphasis on Willard's passivity. He is shot from above lying very still and very tired on the bed, a position that rhymes with our first view of him in the film alone with the relics of his former marriage as he awoke from his nightmare in the Saigon hotel room. Roxanne slips her robe off to reveal her nude body. At the same time she mystifies the view by untying the strings of the filmy bed canopy. The viewer looks up from Willard's point of view as he reaches up to her. Roxanne offers him the relief from pain that his unknowing wife back home could not, addressing to her new lover the words she spoke to her husband: 'There are two of you, don't you see? One that kills ... and one that loves.' The film cuts from this scene to Willard back on the boat, continuing his journey toward Kurtz. He is released from the spell of the renegades who have abandoned France in their determination to preserve what France lost; Willard must confront the same possibility in his American double Kurtz.

If Willard is a personification of the disaffected alienation of the 1970s looking for a restored sense of order and meaning, placed back into the Vietnam setting of the 1960s that catalyzed that disillusionment, Colonel Walter E. Kurtz is a version of the 1970s guru who promises an alternative. One of the symptoms of the post-1960s disillusion was the proliferation of cults and charismatic gurus that offered guidance to the disaffected on a 'quest for self-exploration and personal growth.' As Jenkins points out, these movements 'adopted the communitarian ethos' of the late 1960s 'and gathered their followers together in communal settlements, often in isolated areas,' but 'the new movements claimed to offer absolute certainty and authority, usually symbolized by a charismatic leader, a guru or messianic figure.'[14] Back in Nha Trang Willard was told that Kurtz's followers 'worship the man like a god, and follow every order, however ridiculous.' Willard admits to himself midway on his journey that for him personally Kurtz is 'turning from a target into a goal.'

In the dossiers Willard finds a Kurtz who has the major traits that enable a guru to attract and hold followers. Kurtz possesses a charismatic aura, in his case conferred by his outstanding degrees, class standing, and performance reports ('Like they said, he had an impressive career. Maybe too impressive. I mean, perfect.'). He has acquired secret knowledge that if accepted by the society would achieve great ends; after his first tour in Vietnam he demanded a confidential meeting with Lyndon Johnson and the Joint Chiefs of Staff to give them his Top Secret report but they rejected his recommendations ('Seems they didn't dig what he had to tell them.'). He has rejected the rewards of conformity and instead dropped out and entered the wilderness to do things his way; Kurtz committed career suicide over the thrice-made objections of his superiors and joined the Special Forces, requiring him at the advanced age of thirty-eight to undergo arduous training with full knowledge ('I did it when I was nineteen, it damn near wasted me. A tough motherfucker') that he will never be able to advance beyond colonel ('He could have gone for general, but he went for himself, instead'). He has displayed the power of his ideas in near-miraculous feats that defied authority and attracted positive attention, conceiving and executing an operation that had unprecedented success ('They were going to nail his ass to the floorboards for that one. But after the press got a hold of it, they promoted him to full colonel instead.') Finally, he has set himself up according to his own authority and disappeared into the wilderness; after ordering the assassination of four double-agents he has identified among South Vietnamese government officials, he is about to be arrested for murder when he disappears into the jungle ('They lost him).' As he reads Kurtz's dossier Willard finds a philosophy and evidence of success that offer him, from a remote place in nature, an alternative vision seemingly answering his inner sense of emptiness.

Kurtz's function as 1970s-style guru of a cult is signaled explicitly as Willard nears his goal. Approaching Kurtz's compound, Willard opens a new message from the army command back at Nha Trang. It constitutes a warning. Willard's predecessor on the identical mission is reported to have joined Kurtz. The warning is accompanied by evidence, a scrawled note from Captain Richard Colby to his wife telling her to 'SELL THE HOUSE SELL THE CAR SELL THE KIDS FIND SOMEONE ELSE FORGET IT! I'M *NEVER* COMING BACK FORGET!!!' The convert's message exactly fits the total rejection of one's past life in conventional society typical of cult members; it is expressed in the ecstatic terms of someone who is convinced he has found the truth and the way, its frenzied tone suggesting the 'brainwashing' that a cult member's abandoned family often presumed in the 1970s to be the case, but which, as Andreas Killen has pointed out in discussing the conversion in 1974 of Patty Hearst to the Symbionese Liberation Army (SLA), was 'a disturbing object lesson in the new fragility of the American psyche brought on by a decade of social turmoil and oedipal conflict.'[15]

This connection of Kurtz to an ominous cult leader is further signaled when Chef reads aloud from a newspaper that 'Charles Miller Manson ordered the slaughter of all in the home anyway, as a symbol of protest.' Manson's arrest in the last months of 1969 marks for many the end of the utopian dreams of the 1960s, and his notoriety marked the coming into public consciousness of the gurus and cult compounds that in the 1970s replaced egalitarian communes. It is also in this scene that Lance reads the letter reporting his friend's trip to Disneyland, eliciting Lance's claim that he is somewhere even better. Kurtz's compound comes into view as an elaborately planned addition to the several 'worlds' of Disney's park, a murderously *kitsch* display of longtime Hollywood visions of Oriental horror and decadence, with nearly naked painted savages, mutilated bodies hanging from trees, and decapitated heads staring out from their ornamental placement on the temple steps. The words 'Apocalypse Now!' are scrawled in red blood on one of the steps, echoing the 'Helter Skelter' that Manson's followers painted on the wall in the victims' blood as a proclamation of the race war that would clear the earth of all but Manson and his cult. Willard finds his predecessor Colby a mute automaton, the mindless fanatic that Americans in the 1970s worried would be the fate of one of their own if lured into a cult. The photographer played by Dennis Hopper greets Willard in a freaked-out gibberish exaggerating his iconic performance in *Easy Rider* (1968), in which he played a hippie version of Wild Bill Hickok heading toward the dream of an absolute Wild West. Personifying the 1960s counterculture dream of freedom and adventure turned into a mindless search in the 1970s for some new god to bow down to, he exalts Kurtz as the great man who has expanded his mind.

In seeking to live out the republican ideal of virtue, Kurtz has succeeded only in becoming a cult leader who has lost the moral bearings exercised by the restraint and judgment offered by one's fellow citizens. His radical individualism has led him, like Captain Ahab, to break with society on a paradoxical quest to achieve its aims elsewhere. Thus his quest for moral excellence has brought him somewhere beyond the American frontier trek west, to absolute nihilism. Willard tells Kurtz that he doesn't 'see any method at all.' Kurtz is in the ironic situation of having cut himself off from family and society by his willful determination to serve it as a self-reliant individual. As his letters to his son poignantly show, his insistence on following his duty and honor without the sanction and against the orders of his society has cut himself off from the collective story of American history that he is attempting to live out. As a result, his radical individualism has left him only, to quote Willard as he prepares to execute him, a 'rag-assed renegade.'

Cut off from the American story, the story by which Americans can connect their present to their past and imagine a future, Kurtz's story has become exactly the genre that began to command Americans' fascination during the 1970s and has to the present day. As Willard warned us before beginning his story of Walter E. Kurtz, it is really a 'confession.' Indeed, as Willard has read the newspaper clippings about Kurtz in the dossiers, and finally decides to execute him, the story has also deteriorated into those staples of our time, a celebrity scandal and a sensational trial. Such stories of the 'scandalous, the sensational, and the confessional' are precisely the forms of narrative that Sandel observes have come to preoccupy political discourse in the post-Vietnam United States. Sandel points out that without a restoration of a collective story, and social and economic arrangements that can support it, in which Americans can see their identities as selves encumbered with ties and obligations to each other in a republic that is more than an abstract 'democracy' manipulated by powerful and mysterious forces, the only alternative to such fragmented and narcissistic storytelling is 'narrow, intolerant moralisms.'[16] It is such a fundamentalism of course that Willard had hoped to find in Kurtz. Viewed from a vantage more than thirty years after the failure of the American mission in Vietnam, *Apocalypse Now Redux* offers a vision of the futility of attempting to spread a democracy abroad that is so far from achievement at home.

Willard accomplishes his mission, slaying his ideal self turned 'horror' even as he smashed his mirror image in the opening sequence. He also declares, 'They were gonna make me a major for this, and I wasn't even in their fucking army anymore.' He then leads Lance, dancing among Kurtz's Montagnard worshippers in paint and loincloth, back to the boat to begin their long journey back. Lance has enacted the journey of the 1960s youth culture, from surfer boy to playboy to acid head to mindless cult follower. Willard has completed the journey of the 1970s culture of narcissistic self-reflection. Some thirty years after, they and their fellow Americans have yet to find home.

Notes

1. K. French, *Karl French on Apocalypse Now* (New York: Bloomsbury, 1998), pp. 154–5.
2. P. Jenkins, *Decade of Nightmares: The End of the Sixties and the Making of Eighties America* (Oxford: Oxford University Press, 2006).
3. Ibid., p. 38.
4. Ibid., pp. 42–3.
5. J. Hellmann, *American Myth and the Legacy of Vietnam* (New York: Columbia University Press, 1986), pp. 188–202.
6. Jenkins, *Decade of Nightmares*, pp. 48–9.
7. M. J. Sandel, *Democracy's Discontent: America in Search of a Public Philosophy* (Cambridge: Harvard University Press, 1996), p. 14.
8. Ibid., pp. 294–6.

9. R. Bellah, R. Madsen, W. M. Sullivan, A. Swidler, and S. Tipton, *Habits of the Heart: Individualism and Commitment in American Life* (New York: Perennial, 1986), p. 254.
10. S. Coontz, *The Way We Never Were: American Families and the Nostalgia Trap* (New York: Basic Books, 1992), p. 171.
11. Ibid., pp. 172–3.
12. B. Ehrenreich, *The Hearts of Men: American Dreams and the Flight from Commitment* (New York: Anchor, 1983), p. 113.
13. Ibid., p. 113.
14. Jenkins, *Decade of Nightmares*, p. 38.
15. A. Killen, *1973 Nervous Breakdown: Watergate, Warhol, and the Birth of Post-Sixties America* (New York: Bloomsbury, 2006), pp. 268–9.
16. Sandel, *Democracy's Discontent*, pp. 322–3.

5
Imagining Vietnam: Tim O'Brien's *The Things They Carried*

Subarno Chattarji

The critic and activist H. Bruce Franklin relates an encounter with a woman during the campaign against napalm in the suburban town of Redwood City, California, in early 1966. 'Asked to sign a petition against the local production of napalm, she responded: "Napalm? No thank you. I'm not interested. I always use Tide." '[1] The story is indicative of a general level of indifference toward and ignorance of a war that continues to haunt the American imagination. The ways in which John Kerry's Vietnam service record surfaced as an issue during the 2004 presidential election is just one example of the presence of that conflict in the American landscape.

The cultural, political, psychological, and sociological aspects of Vietnam have been analyzed in depth and I will not enter into those debates here, except where they touch upon Tim O'Brien's *The Things They Carried* (1990). That O'Brien is a writer of distinction is undeniable. Accolades such as 'the best American writer of his generation' (*San Francisco Examiner*) and the seven-and-a-half pages of tribute that preface the Broadway Books 1998 edition of *The Things They Carried* are indicative of the centrality of the Vietnam stories he tells. More than one reviewer has noticed the connections between truth, memory and fiction that O'Brien weaves so well. The *St. Louis Post-Dispatch* said *The Things They Carried* is 'One hell of a book... You'll rarely read anything as real as this.' The *Tampa Tribune & Times* claimed that 'In *The Things They Carried*, Tim O'Brien expertly fires off tracer rounds, illuminating the art of war in all its horrible and fascinating complexity, detailing the mad and the mundane... *The*

Things They Carried joins the work of Crane and Hemingway and Mailer as great war literature.'

This chapter examines the ways in which O'Brien writes the Vietnam War as reality and fiction, focusing on the implications of the constant blurring between the two, and indicating that the elements of 'story-truth' and fantasy are a mode of recuperating the war for contemporary times. The chapter also attempts to place O'Brien within a larger context of American literature, with particular reference not to the fictions of Crane, Hemingway, or Mailer but to the figure of Huckleberry Finn.

As the newspaper reviews suggest, O'Brien is undoubtedly a war writer, with all his works emerging from and based on the war in which he fought. In an interview in March 1990 he acknowledged the inescapable heritage of Vietnam as it impacted upon his subsequent vocation: 'The war made me a writer.'[2] However, he does not wish to be read purely as a war writer. Interviewed in 1987 he declared: 'I don't think of myself as a "war writer." I don't think my writing is very political.'[3] Given the nature of the Vietnam War and the centrality of that war to all of O'Brien's writings, the disavowal of politics is either naïve or disingenuous. In an interview with Tobey Herzog in 1997 he repeated his rejection of the label of war writer: 'It's like calling Toni Morrison a black writer or Shakespeare a king writer.'[4] While such labels are indeed reductive, O'Brien's response reflects a desire to move beyond the political and cultural ambit of the Vietnam War while writing about the war and its aftermath. He wishes to place his war experience and the writings of those experiences within a larger fictional and cultural framework that is not defined solely as 'war literature.' This stated desire leads to the constant negotiation between reality and fiction, and the impression that the Vietnam War can be perceived in meta-fictional terms.

The immediate impact of *The Things They Carried* is based on O'Brien's fidelity to detail:

The things they carried were largely determined by necessity. Among the necessities or near necessities were P-38 can openers, pocket knives, heat tabs, wristwatches, dog tags, mosquito repellent, chewing gum, candy, cigarettes, salt tablets, packets of Kool-Aid, lighters, matches, sewing kits, Military Payment Certificates, C rations, and two or three canteens of water. Together these items weighed between 15 and 20 pounds, depending upon a man's habits or rate of metabolism.[5]

This is the Jamesian 'solidity of specification' that helps create the 'reality' of Vietnam for readers.

The catalogue not only creates a welter of detail but simulates the weight of the things carried by the grunts. These facts are combined with the intangible and the psychological: 'They all carried ghosts'; 'They shared the weight of memory'; 'They carried all the emotional baggage of men who might die.'[6] The fighting machine of the US is described in microcosmic terms and is symptomatic of a culture of production, consumption, and waste, as O'Brien indicates a little later:

> Purely for comfort, they would throw away rations, blow their Claymores and grenades, no matter, because by nightfall the resupply choppers would arrive with more of the same, then a day or two later still more, fresh watermelons and crates of ammunition and sunglasses and woolen sweaters – the resources were stunning – sparklers for the Fourth of July, colored eggs for Easter – it was the great American war chest – the fruits of science, the smokestacks, the canneries, the arsenals at Hartford, the Minnesota forests, the machine shops, the vast fields of corn and wheat – they carried like freight trains; [...] for all the ambiguities of Vietnam, all the mysteries and unknowns, there was at least the single abiding certainty that they would never be at a loss for things to carry.[7]

In the manner of classic satirists such as Jonathan Swift, O'Brien relentlessly builds the structure of a catalogue to highlight the sheer absurdity of things, the belief that things could win the war, and draws attention to the yawning chasm between the US and its opponent, a point that is specifically driven home when the belongings of a dead VC boy of about 15 or 16 are described: 'At the time of his death he had been carrying a pouch of rice, a rifle, and three magazines of ammunition.'[8]

There is an element of romanticizing of the enemy as peasant fighters with little more than revolutionary zeal in their armoury (and more so in the chapter, 'The Man I Killed'), a romantic image ably fostered by anti-war activists such as Mary McCarthy and Susan Sontag. This portrait of saintly peasant warriors ignores not only the military hardware and capability that the NVA possessed, but also overlooks the atrocities of which they and the NLF were capable. What is undeniable, however, is the technological gap between the US and the Vietnamese, and the sheer volume of firepower that the US brought to bear on a tiny country. O'Brien also hints most accurately at a cultural difference between the two nations, one in which objects can be endlessly produced and reproduced and thrown away, and one in which things are scarce and therefore more precious.

O'Brien's primary focus is on war stories, their telling, and their truth-value. The chapter 'How to Tell a True War Story' begins with the simple statement: 'This is true.'[9] The work overall is labeled 'a work of fiction' and throughout we have a complex interplay between 'fact' and 'fiction.' O'Brien's authority to tell the tale arises from the fact that he was there, he lived to tell the tale, an authority that is evoked by narrators ranging from Ishmael in *Moby Dick* (1851) to Huck Finn. In the context of the Vietnam War it is almost imperative that the narrator be a Vietnam veteran since no one else can actually tell the truth. This is a myth that has been fostered by veterans' writings and testimonies and it perpetuates the idea of a closed circle of understanding and truth. As Lorrie Smith observes, 'O'Brien often depicts war as inaccessible to non veterans, creating a storytelling loop between characters within stories that excludes the uninitiated reader and privileges the authority of the soldier's experience.'[10] Smith's critique is primarily concerned with representations of masculinity in *The Things They Carried*, and her point about exclusivity is important in our understanding of an underlying assumption that drives and controls the narrative.

Assuming authority, O'Brien proceeds to define the parameters of a 'true' war story:

> A true war story is never moral. It does not instruct, nor encourage virtue, nor suggest models of proper human behavior, nor restrain men from doing the things men have always done. If a story seems moral, do not believe it. [...] There is no rectitude whatsoever. There is no virtue.[11]

O'Brien rejects the idea of war stories as vehicles for change and restitution, although this is later challenged in 'The Lives of the Dead' where stories are indeed seen as redemptive. In this chapter the focus is on representations of war:

> War is hell, but that's not the half of it, because war is also mystery and terror and adventure and courage and discovery and holiness and pity and despair and longing and love. War is nasty; war is fun. War is thrilling; war is drudgery. War makes you a man; war makes you dead.[12]

The irreconcilable opposites must be held together because it is in their oxymoronic togetherness that the opposing terms articulate the 'reality' of war.

O'Brien writes that the recollection of Curt Lemon's death is possible by capturing the 'surreal seemingness, which makes the story seem untrue, but which in fact represents the hard and exact truth as it *seemed*.'[13] Here he grapples with the problem of representation, the (in)adequacy of language as a mode of conveying the meaning, the feelings, the flavor, the terror, and the boredom of war. It is only through inscription and re-inscription that he can hope to communicate the 'truth' of war, and that is one reason the narrative is both repetitive and circular. Every assertion of 'truth' needs to be qualified and re-presented if it is to be perceived as 'authentic.' O'Brien creates an aesthetic of anti-sentimentalism whereby there is no morality or heroism that can be extracted from the experience of combat. This is unexceptionable and ties in with his sense of the injustice of the Vietnam War.

The yoking of contraries mentioned earlier is not as value neutral as the narrative might imply. In a long passage, O'Brien indicates some of the problems:

> It can be argued, for instance, that war is grotesque. But in truth war is also beauty. For all its horror, you can't help but gape at the awful majesty of combat. You stare out at tracer rounds unwinding through the dark like brilliant red ribbons. You crouch in ambush as a cool, impassive moon rises over the nighttime paddies. You admire the fluid symmetries of troops on the move, the harmonies

of sound and shape and proportion, the great sheets of metal-fire streaming down from a gunship, the illumination rounds, the white phosphorus, the purply orange glow of napalm, the rocket's red glare. It's not pretty, exactly. It's astonishing. It fills the eye. It commands you. You hate it, yes, but your eyes do not. Like a killer forest fire, like cancer under a microscope, any battle or bombing raid or artillery barrage has the aesthetic purpose of absolute moral indifference – a powerful, implacable beauty – and a true war story will tell the truth about this, though the truth is ugly.[14]

The irresistible beauty of combat is something that soldier-writers have testified to across wars. In Vietnam, Robert Stone, W. D. Ehrhart, and William J. Broyles, among others, write of this 'awful,' 'astonishing' spectacle. Broyles who served in Vietnam in 1969 and 1970, explained the allure of war in terms not too dissimilar from O'Brien, in an article, 'Why Men Love War':

Part of the love of war stems from its being an experience of great intensity; its lure is the fundamental human passion to witness, to see things, what the Bible calls the lust of the eye and the Marines in Vietnam called eye fucking.[15]

The idea of war as fascinating spectacle has been bolstered in the post-Vietnam era by television coverage, particularly CNN's of the first Gulf War in 1991: 'The skies are illuminated over Baghdad.'

As in descriptions by other writers, O'Brien projects war as a disembodied presence with a life of its own, where instruments of death such as white phosphorus and napalm are magically transformed into morally indifferent objects of beauty. He is astute enough to acknowledge that the recognition of such destruction as 'beautiful' is in itself an ugly truth, but the telling of that truth is justified on the basis of its truth function. Ugly 'truths' such as the fascination that war begets must be expressed, yet in their expression such 'truths' tend to aestheticize and domesticate war. The 'absolute moral indifference' that he attributes to artillery barrages or bombing raids is only tenable if there was no human agency behind those barrages or raids. Since, alas, there is always human agency behind war, and since, as O'Brien portrays so eloquently, war maims and kills, it is difficult to maintain a stance of aesthetic or moral distance when these monstrosities are unleashed. In articulating an alternative moral paradigm he seems to perpetuate a mythic fascination with the horrors of war, of combat as a crucible for growth toward manhood and maturity.

Underlying this valorization of participating and witnessing war is O'Brien's larger concern with truth-telling and stories. The intertwining of 'fact' and 'fiction' is a narrative strategy that all critics of his work have noted. Tobey C. Herzog writes:

> O'Brien's assertion of a purportedly factual story or piece of information later contradicted by his confession of its fictive nature is his method for effectively introducing listeners to the complex intermingling of facts, history, fiction, truth, lies, memory, and imagination underlying all of his writings.[16]

The interplay of fact, fiction, memory, and imagination is crucial in literary representations of the Vietnam War. In contexts where language itself was debased and inadequate as a mode of representing the horrors of combat, a purely 'factual' representation might seem incomplete. Hence there is the need for the commingling of fact, fiction, and meta-fiction.

This need explains O'Brien's insistence on the importance of story telling in his writings and interviews. In the chapter 'Spin' he writes: 'Stories are for joining the past to the future. [...] Stories are for eternity, when memory is erased, when there is nothing to remember except the story.' In 'Good Form': 'What stories can do, I guess, is make things present.' In 'The Lives of the Dead': 'The thing about a story is that you dream it as you tell it, hoping that others might then dream along with you, and in this way memory and imagination and language combine to make spirits in the head.'[17] In an interview O'Brien stated: 'I'm a believer in the power of stories, whether they're true, or embellished, and exaggerated, or utterly made up. A good story has a power... that transcends the question of factuality or actuality.'[18]

Stories are a mode of recuperating the past and they are seen as redemptive in the way in which the boy Timmy resuscitates Linda and through that resurrection salvages the life of the narrator, O'Brien himself. There is a touching faith in the power of the word, the story well told that adds value to the narration. Steven Kaplan says that *The Things They Carried* 'is O'Brien's expression of his love of storytelling as an act that can wrestle tolerable and meaningful truths from even the most horrible events.'[19]

Whether it is the actuality of combat and death in Vietnam or the death of Linda, narrative seems to be a mode of retelling and thereby healing. Much of the writing by Vietnam veterans originates from and perhaps performs a therapeutic function and while one may debate the value of writing as psychological catharsis, one is willing to accept the premise of stories as regenerative. A problem arises, however, when narrative is seen as a purely performative act, a game with endless possibilities. The stress on ambiguity and uncertainty in Vietnam War stories reflects part of the actuality of combat. In 'Ghost Soldiers' O'Brien indicates the sense of a haunted landscape in which the Americans were aliens:

It was ghost country, and Charlie Cong was the main ghost. The way he came out at night. How you never really saw him, just thought you did. Almost magical – appearing, disappearing. He could blend with the land, changing form, becoming trees and grass. He could levitate. He could fly. He could pass through barbed wire and melt away like ice and creep up on you without sound or footsteps.[20]

One has only to read accounts and stories by 'Charlie Cong' to realize that there was nothing 'magical' in his existence, but the stereotypical representation of the enemy creates a mimesis of the Vietnam War as a phantasmagoric game, with no definite 'facts.' The stress on ambiguity and uncertainty in Vietnam overlooks unambiguous facts such as the deaths of American soldiers and Vietnamese soldiers and civilians, of the depredations wrought by napalm or cluster bombs, of the NLF assassinating village chiefs in South Vietnam, and the list can go on. O'Brien indicates some of this reality in the graphic, multiple descriptions of the deaths of Curt Lemon and Kiowa.

Yet in asserting the value of storytelling as a means of ameliorating the horrors of Vietnam, he creates an overall mythic structure of love, comradeship and forgetfulness in the very process of recovering that horror: 'You become part of a tribe and you share the same blood – you give it together, you take it together.' Any outsider who is not a part of this 'tribe' is just a 'dumb cooze' who cannot really comprehend the story[21]. Nevertheless stories are vital and O'Brien reiterates the overwhelming power of the story in an interview:

> I think two hundred years, seven hundred years, a thousand years from now, when Vietnam is filled with condominiums...the experience of Vietnam – all the facts – will be gone. Who knows, a thousand years from now the facts will disappear – bit by bit – and all that we'll be left with are stories.[22]

One need not wait as long as O'Brien predicts for the facts to disappear, or be rewritten, or distorted. As Bruce Franklin and others have pointed out, the Vietnam War has been effectively rewritten in American politics, popular culture, and imagination so that, in a sense, all that we are left with are stories. O'Brien's stories have greater integrity and truth than the ones told by Hollywood or Washington, but there is every danger that the privileging of story *qua* story will contribute to the further dehistoricizing of the Vietnam conflict. To perceive the Vietnam War purely or largely in terms of ambiguity, mystery, and endlessly multiplying narratives is to fall into a typically postmodernist trap. The problem of 'facticity' in representations of the Vietnam War gives rise to a postmodern illusion of the free play of meaning whereby any set of 'facts' can be wheeled out to prove or disprove any ideological or political view of the war. The way in which 'facts' are wielded can alter perceptions of the conflict. For example, reading Al Santoli's oral history of the Vietnam War, *To Bear Any Burden* (1985), one might be convinced that every Vietnamese hated communists and communism, and that the US involvement was a glorious and noble, if slightly muddled, intervention. Santoli's strategy is to include in his book the voices of North Vietnamese defectors and anti-war protestors, thereby creating an illusion of pluralism.

This kind of all-encompassing pluralism, as Fredric Jameson points out, is dubious:

> Pluralism is one thing when it stands for the coexistence of methods and interpretations in the intellectual and academic marketplace, but quite another when it is taken as a proposition about the infinity of possible meanings and methods and their ultimate equivalence with and substitutability with one another.[23]

This is arguably a ubiquitous condition, but it is exacerbated in the context of the Vietnam War where disembodied facts are bandied about without any moral discrimination, and any set of facts can be counterbalanced by another. One person's fact is another's fiction, and the war and its aftermath can be mired in post-modern ambiguity and free-play of meaning. Bruce Franklin cites 'Jim Neilson [who] has cogently argued in *Warring Fictions: Cultural Politics and the Vietnam War Narrative*, [that] the widespread *intellectual* perception of the Vietnam experience as too alien to be comprehended has helped to establish a canon of Vietnam War literature that enshrines indeterminacy, incoherence, ambiguities, strangeness, and unknowability, with critics exalting Michael Herr's *Dispatches* as the quintessential truth about the war.'[24] Several critics have placed O'Brien within this mould because, as Franklin also suggests, he 'spins a complex dialectic between what he calls "story-truth" and "happening-truth"' and they 'have interpreted his fiction as validating their own view of the Vietnam War as unknowable or crazy or "unreal."'[25]

From the combat soldier's point of view Vietnam was a mystery or unknowable simply because he was not equipped with any knowledge of the country and its people. Stunning ignorance coalesced with the fear that combat engendered to create the sense of an inscrutable enemy. In purely epistemic terms the problem seems to be not whether Vietnam was/is unknowable, but the extent to which fear, ignorance, and prejudice made it so. O'Brien's fiction-memoir-autobiography interface does not steer clear of ugly, ignoble truths, but there is the discomfiting possibility that endless interpretations are not only possible but desirable, because stories are all that we have to comprehend the war.

To conclude here would be to place O'Brien among the legion of dubious writers on the Vietnam War and that would create an incomplete picture of a complex writer. As in his stories, there are contraries that need to be taken into account. Despite the enthusiastic embrace of postmodern and conservative critics, O'Brien himself has attacked the interpretations that see the Vietnam War as unknowable and crazy. 'For me, Vietnam wasn't an unreal experience, it wasn't absurd. It was a cold-blooded, calculated war,' he said in an interview in 1984.[26] In a later interview with Tobey Herzog O'Brien expressed his sense of personal moral responsibility:

In my case I committed an act of unpardonable cowardice and evil. I went to a war that I believed was wrong and participated in it actively. I pulled the trigger. I was there. And by being there I am guilty.[27]

This awareness distinguishes O'Brien from veteran writers such as Philip Caputo or W. D. Ehrhart who went to Vietnam believing they were fighting for God and country and who were disillusioned only when they experienced the war.

This pre-war knowledge and the choices it involved are expressed in the chapter 'On the Rainy River.' O'Brien's discomfort with the war is expressed clearly:

In the June of 1968, a month after graduating from Macalester College, I was drafted to fight a war I hated. I was twenty-one years old. Young, yes, and politically naïve, but even so the American war in Vietnam seemed to me wrong. Certain blood was being shed for uncertain reasons.[28]

The story of this chapter has been narrated earlier by O'Brien in his memoir, *If I Die in a Combat Zone* (1973), and its repetition is testimony to the intensity of his conviction. The basis of opposition is his belief that the war was unjust:

It was my view then, and still is, that you don't make war without knowing why. Knowledge, of course, is always imperfect, but it seemed to me that when a nation goes to war it must have reasonable confidence in the justice and imperative of its cause. You can't fix your mistake. Once people are dead, you can't make them undead.[29]

One can hardly disagree with these statements, but O'Brien seems to overlook or forget that US Presidents and policy-makers were confident of the justice and imperatives of their cause, that they believed the domino theory, and that only the US could save the world for democracy. Of course, as *The Pentagon Papers* and other documents subsequently proved, there were clear elements of mendacity, but those lies arose out of a core belief in the justice of the US cause.

Even retrospective statements testify to the conviction of the people who made and prosecuted the war. Just two examples, the first from Richard Nixon's *No More Vietnams* (1986) and the second from Robert McNamara, writing almost a decade later, encapsulate this element of retrospective justification. Nixon wrote:

> Today, after Communist governments have killed over a half million Vietnamese and over 2 million Cambodians, the conclusive moral judgment has been rendered on our effort to save Cambodia and South Vietnam: We have never fought in a more moral cause.[30]

McNamara acknowledges errors and his sense of unease at the way the war was conducted, but he concludes *In Retrospect* (1995) with a reiteration of basic goals:

> Let me be simple and direct – I want to be clearly understood: the United States of America fought in Vietnam for eight years for what it believed to be good and honest reasons. By such actions, administrations of both parties sought to protect our security, prevent the spread of totalitarian Communism, and promote individual freedom and political democracy.[31]

The convictions expressed during and after the war by the Nixons and the McNamaras are open to question but they were deeply held: a point that O'Brien seems to ignore.

In *The Things They Carried*, 'On the Rainy River' is a crucial chapter, however, because it encapsulates the dilemmas of choice and conscience so central to the American imagination. In an interview with Steven Kaplan in 1991 O'Brien expressed his belief that all great fiction explores moral quandaries and portrays characters who are confronted with making a difficult choice: 'The reason choice seems to me important as a word and as a way for me to think about stories is that it involves values. It's most interesting when the choices involve things of equally compelling value.'[32] Thus the narrator O'Brien grapples with two kinds of fear when contemplating escape to Canada: 'I feared the war but I also feared exile.' Finally it is the fear of exile and shame that triumph: 'What it came down to, stupidly, was a sense of shame. [...] I did not want people to think badly of me. [. . .] I was ashamed of my conscience, ashamed to be doing the right thing.' This searing confession concludes with a summation of the self that continues to haunt the narrator: 'I was a coward. I went to war.'[33] At an obvious level this statement overturns heroic models of manhood and courage nurtured in the crucible of war.

William Broyles's essay 'Why Men Love War' is just one example of the generic glorification of war that O'Brien questions. In O'Brien's narrative, cowardice is related to a state of being where conscience and morality fail to influence and shape action. In his interview with Herzog, he declared that all individuals have 'the possibility of action, virtuous action, coming out of a desire for pure virtue, the world notwithstanding.'[34] In referring to his conscience and fear of social obloquy O'Brien indicates that it is precisely this possibility of 'virtuous action' 'the world notwithstanding' that has been rejected. In articulating that rejection and failure, he ceases to be only a war writer, reflecting also on quintessentially American themes of choice, morality, and the endless possibility of fashioning oneself anew. The last possibility is one which animates the American imagination from the Pilgrim Fathers to Walt Whitman, from Huck Finn to *The Great Gatsby* (1925).

O'Brien thus taps into a cultural, imaginary reservoir to express his moral quandaries in a time of war. In Mark Twain's *The Adventures of Huckleberry Finn* (1884), there are two episodes when Huck faces the 'most interesting' of 'choices [which] involve things of equally compelling value.' The first is in Chapter 16 when he lies to the slave hunters to save Jim's freedom. The second more extended and significant conflict occurs in Chapter 31, when he reflects on the consequences of helping a runaway slave:

> It would get all around, that Huck Finn helped a nigger to get his freedom; and if I was to ever see anybody from that town again, I'd be ready to get down and lick his boots for shame. [. . .] The more I studied about this, the more my conscience went to grinding me, and the more wicked and low-down and ornery I got to feeling. And at last, when it hit me all of a sudden that here was the plain hand of Providence slapping me in the face and letting me know my wickedness was being watched all the time from up there in heaven, whilst I was stealing a poor old woman's nigger that hadn't ever done me no harm, [. . .].[35]

While Huck had set himself in opposition to the 'sivilizing' mission of the Widow Douglas he believed that helping Jim escape was a humane thing to do. However, the extent to which Huck has internalized the dominant ideology of his society is perceptible in his sense of remorse and sin at 'stealing a poor old woman's nigger.' This is his socialized conscience that grinds him and leads him to write a note to the widow letting her know the whereabouts of Jim.

After writing the note Huck says he 'felt good and all washed clean of sin for the first time I had ever felt so in my life, and I knowed I could pray now.' Then he recollects the journey that he and Jim have shared: 'I see Jim before me, all the time, in the day, and in the night-time, sometimes moonlight, sometimes storms, and we a floating along, talking, and singing, and laughing.' His recollections lead him back to the message he has written and this is the moment of reckoning:

> I was a trembling, because I'd got to decide, forever, betwixt two things, and I knowed it. I studied a minute, sort of holding my breath, and then says to myself: 'All right, then, I'll go to hell' – and tore it up. It was awful thoughts, and awful words, but they was said. And I let them stay said; and never thought no more about reforming.[36]

Huck Finn rejects the morality of his times that justifies the dehumanizing institution of slavery and overturns moral paradigms; it is better to go to hell to save a fellow human being.

As John Seelye puts it:

> In declaring himself against the laws of man Huck becomes an outlaw, but he is in truth an avatar of the higher laws of humanity, beyond the reach of society's often unfair rules, his raft a dwelling reminiscent of Natty Bumpo's cabin in *The Pioneers* or the hut at Walden Pond, being a sanctuary of both sanity and sanctity.[37]

The sanctuaries that Seelye describes may be temporary ones but they represent crucial alternatives, territories of conscience in times of injustice and strife.

In his hallucinatory vision list in *The Things They Carried*, O'Brien mentions Huck Finn.[38] The reference is a deliberate one in the context of Huck's struggle with his conscience. Huck's decision to protect Jim – ' "All right, then, I'll go to hell" ' – is a decision of conscience and courage, as opposed to O'Brien's one to go to war: 'I was ashamed of my conscience, ashamed to be doing the right thing'; 'I was a coward. I went to war.'[39] While overturning the heroic paradigm of war, O'Brien distinctly highlights his inability to do 'the right thing.' Despite the realistic improbability of a 12-year-old white boy helping a slave escape in the 1840s, Huck is an iconic figure of anti-authoritarianism, the drive for freedom that animates a part of the American imagination. Huck always has the option of 'light[ing] out for the Territory.'[40]

That imaginative space in O'Brien's narrative has now shrunk to a choice between a shaming exile in Canada and a morally dubious war in a distant land, fought in the name of ideals that were betrayed from the outset. The Vietnam War led to a constriction of choices and moral possibilities in much the same way as slavery desensitized and corrupted an entire society.

John Balaban, a conscientious objector and poet of the Vietnam era, concludes his poem 'After Our War' with the following lines:

> After the war, with such Cheshire cats grinning in our trees,
> Will the ancient tales still tell us new truths?
> Will the myriad world surrender new metaphor?
> After our war, how will love speak?[41]

Perhaps stories are a mode of restoring the worlds of metaphor, truth, and love shattered by the Vietnam War. As O'Brien writes: 'The thing about a story is that you dream it as you tell it, hoping that others might then dream along with you, and in this way memory and imagination and language combine to make spirits in the head.'[42]

Notes

A version of this chapter was presented as a public lecture for the 'One Book, One Philadelphia' project in February 2005. I am grateful to John S. Baky, Curator and Director of Libraries, for his generous help during my tenure as Fulbright Senior Research Fellow at the Imaginative Representations of the Vietnam War Archive, Connelly Library, La Salle University, Philadelphia.

1. H. Bruce Franklin, *Vietnam & Other American Fantasies* (Amherst: University of Massachusetts Press, 2000), p. 71.
2. Gail Caldwell, 'Staying True to Vietnam,' *Boston Globe* (29 March 1990), p. 75.
3. Judith Slater, 'An Interview with Tim O'Brien,' *The Short Story Review*, Spring 1987, Vol. 4, No. 2: 1, 4–5.
4. Tobey C. Herzog, *Tim O'Brien* (New York: Twayne Publishers, 1997), p. 23.
5. Tim O'Brien, *The Things They Carried* (New York: Broadway Books edition, 1998), p. 2.
6. Ibid., pp. 10, 14, 21.
7. Ibid., pp. 15–16.
8. Ibid., p. 13.
9. Ibid., p. 67.
10. Lorrie Smith, ' "The Things Men Do": The Gendered Subtext in Tim O'Brien's *Esquire* Stories,' *Critique*, Fall 1994, Vol. XXXVI, No. 1: 16–40.
11. O'Brien, *The Things They Carried*, pp. 68–9.
12. Ibid., p. 80.
13. Ibid., p. 78.
14. Ibid., pp. 80–1.
15. William J. Broyles Jr, 'Why Men Love War,' in Walter Capps (ed.), *The Vietnam Reader* (New York and London: Routledge, 1990), p. 71.
16. Herzog, *Tim O'Brien*, p. 2.
17. O'Brien, *The Things They Carried*, pp. 38, 180, 230.
18. Cited in Maria S. Bonn, 'Can Stories Save Us? Tim O'Brien and the Efficacy of the Text,' *Critique*, Fall 1994, Vol. XXXVI, No. 1, pp. 2–15.
19. Steven Kaplan, *Understanding Tim O'Brien* (Columbia, SC: University of South Carolina Press, 1995), pp. 186–7.
20. O'Brien, *The Things They Carried*, p. 202.
21. Ibid., pp. 68, 192.
22. Cited in Kaplan, *Understanding Tim O'Brien*, from Timothy Lomperis, *'Reading the Wind': The Literature of the Vietnam War* (Durham, NC: Duke University Press, 1987), p. 10.
23. Fredric Jameson, *The Political Unconscious* (London: Methuen & Co. Ltd., 1987), p. 31.
24. Franklin, *Vietnam & Other American Fantasies*, p. 32.
25. Ibid., p. 35.
26. Eric James Schroeder, 'Two Interviews: Talks with Tim O'Brien and Robert Stone,' *Modern Fiction Studies*, Spring 1984, Vol. 30, No. 1, p. 146.
27. Herzog, *Tim O'Brien*, 14.
28. O'Brien, *The Things They Carried*, p. 40.
29. Ibid., pp. 40–1.
30. Richard M. Nixon, *No More Vietnams* (London: W.H. Allen edition, 1986), p. 209.
31. Robert S. McNamara, *In Retrospect: The Tragedy and Lessons of Vietnam*, with Brian Van De Mark (New York: Times Books, 1995), p. 333.

32. Steven Kaplan, 'An Interview with Tim O'Brien,' *Missouri Review* 14.3 (1991), p. 108.
33. O'Brien, *The Things They Carried*, pp. 42, 54, 61.
34. Herzog, *Tim O'Brien*, p. 32.
35. Mark Twain, *The Adventures of Huckleberry Finn*, edited with an introduction by John Seelye (New York: Penguin Books edition, 1986), p. 233.
36. Ibid., pp. 234, 235.
37. John Seelye, 'Introduction,' Ibid., p. xxv.
38. O'Brien, *The Things They Carried*, pp. 58–9.
39. Ibid., pp. 52, 61.
40. Twain, *The Adventures of Huckleberry Finn*, p. 321.
41. John Balaban, 'After Our War,' *Locusts at the Edge of Summer: New and Selected Poems* (Washington: Copper Canyon Press, 1997), p. 41.
42. O'Brien, *The Things They Carried*, p. 230.

6
The Vietnam War: (Post-)Colonial Fictional Discourses and (Hi-)Stories

Walter W. Hölbling

Never was so much false arithmetic employed on any subject as that which has been employed to persuade nations that it is in their interest to go to war. Were the money which it has cost to gain at the close of a long war a little town, or a little territory, the right to cut wood here or catch a fish there, expended in improving what they already possess, in making roads, opening rivers, building ports, improving the arts, and finding employment for their idle poor, it would render them much stronger, wealthier, and happier. This I hope will be our wisdom.

(Thomas Jefferson, *Notes on the State of Virginia*)

There are still governments that sponsor and harbor terrorists – but their number has declined. There are still regimes seeking weapons of mass destruction – but no longer without attention and without consequence. Our country is still the target of terrorists who want to kill many, and intimidate us all, and we will stay on the offensive against them, until the fight is won.

(George W. Bush, 'State of the Union Address,'
January 20, 2005)

Happy is he who can say 'when,' 'before,' and 'after.' He may have been struck by hard luck, or he may have been writhing with pain: the moment he is able to narrate the events in the order of their temporal sequence he feels as comfortable as if the sun were shining upon his belly.

(Robert Musil, *Man Without Qualities*)

Close to the end of Herman Meville's intriguing tale about racist and nationalist stereotypes, 'Benito Cereno' (1855), the American captain Delano asks Benito Cereno what causes his gloom, now with all African slave rebels punished and their leader's head stuck on a pole for public display. Delano cannot really fathom the Spanish captain's answer:

'You are saved, Don Benito,' cried Captain Delano, more and more astonished and pained; 'you are saved; what has cast such a shadow upon you?'
'The Negro.'
There was silence, while the moody man sat, slowly and unconsciously gathering his mantle about him, as if it were a pall.

Reading this passage over 150 years later, with our knowledge of what has happened since, Melville's sparse dialogue succinctly articulates what many Europeans (as well as good number of Americans, from Henry James and Mark Twain to Ernest Hemingway, Norman Mailer, J. William Fulbright, Ward Just, *et al.*) consider a peculiar American attitude towards foreigners in general and ethnics of darker skin colour in particular that seems to have undergone only minimal changes until this day. One might call it a combination of innocence, ignorance, and arrogance. Delano is unable – or unwilling – to understand Cereno's gloom that results from the Spaniard's recognition, based on his experience during the slave revolt, that Africans are at least as intelligent and able as Europeans, and that it is therefore wrong by all religious and moral standards to treat them like chattels or commodities. While the Spanish captain suffers from growing depression under the weight of his insight, Delano considers the case closed: for him, the mutiny of the slaves is just an incident which, thanks to American arms, has been resolved; law and order have been reestablished, justice has been done.

The American war story – literary and historical conventions

The following argument rests on the premise that stories of war display essential cultural concepts, expectations, and self-images more prominently than most other kinds of fiction. In the extreme situation of war, the community demands from its (usually young) citizens that they risk their lives for the common good; traditionally, situations like these have been occasions for questioning the validity of those individual and collective values and self-concepts in whose name one might die prematurely. Thus, fictions of war can be considered as fictional models of a nation's (or a people's) 'storifying of experience,' as acts of 'literary sense-making'[1] (or the lack of it) in response to historical problems of national importance. In an essay on British literature about World War I, Paul Fussell talks of 'cultural paradigms,' defining them as 'the systems of convention and anticipation that determine which of the objective phenomena of experience will be registered by the individual – what we "make of things," and how we fit them into the conceptual frames our culture has taught us to consider important.'[2] Together with the personal experience and individual vision of the author, as well as the powerful influence of literary conventions, these 'cultural paradigms' establish specific symbol systems that provide the conceptual frame for what N. Luhmann calls 'fictional responses' to an historical situation.[3] If they have sufficient explanatory power, these models of literary sense-making persist as established conventions even in the face of political and historical changes.

American war stories have perpetuated, up to the present day, a number of myths and self-images that originated in 17th- and 18th-century colonial narratives of Indian war and captivity. As studies by Richard Slotkin, R. Van der Beets, R. H. Pearce and others have shown, 'the Indian wars proved to be the most acceptable metaphor for the American experience.'[4] Pervasive elements of these early narratives are a *strong sense of mission*, the firm belief to lead a *just war* in a *unique historical situation* (and, by definition, win it, if only after considerable efforts and trials), as well as a distinct component of *racial warfare*.

James Aho, in his *Religious Mythology and the Art of War* (1981), distinguishes between 'immanentist-cosmological' (Buddhism, Hinduism, early Christianity) and 'transcendent-historical' religious

symbol systems (Hebrew, Muslim, later Christianity, and Prot-
estantism), each of which maintains specific concepts about the
functions, methods, and goals of war. Whereas for immanentist-
cosmological creeds war is a ceremonial ritual conducted to restore
disturbed cosmic harmony, the following quotation sums up the
characteristics of transcendent-historical religions: they put justice
as the supreme norm and its defence in a holy war as a sanctified
mission in the name of God:

> As a rule, in Judaism, Islam, and Protestantism, responsibility for
> the world's sin is projected onto minority populations, strangers,
> and foreigners; those with tongues, customs, and pantheons alien
> to God's faithful. In collectively objectifying evil and positing it
> upon this external enemy, a sense of cleanliness of His 'remnant'
> is created symbolically. Analogous to the Levitical rite of the
> scapegoat (Lev. 16: 20–12), the projectors can 'escape' from
> acknowledging the possibility of their own blemish. [. . .] Thus,
> mythologically, the holy war will be fought between the absolutely
> righteous and the equally absolute incarnation of Evil. Insofar as
> it exorcises the objectified evil, the ferocity of the violence in
> the war must reflect the enormity of the crime against God and
> man. [. . .] The Hebraic, the Muslim and Christian holy wars, both
> in myth and enactment, are among the most ruthless in human
> experience.[5]

Aho's examples, taken from periods of Hebrew and Muslim history
as well as from the confessional wars in early 17th-century Europe
(especially the 30-Years' War), very well apply to the situation in colonial America. By the end of the 17th century, the discourse of war in
American narratives exhibits the characteristics of 'holy war' as stated
by Aho; they provide the dominant model for future writings on the
subject, are seriously questioned only by the experience of Vietnam,
and seem to have returned in force in the official US rhetoric around
the Iraq War of 2003. A representative example of such prevailing
early attitudes is provided by John Underhill in *Newes from America*,
published in 1639:

> Many were burnt in the fort, both men, women, and chil-
> dren. Others forced out, [. . .] which our soldiers received and

entertained with the sword. Down fell man, women, and children. [...] Great and doleful was the bloudy sight to the view of young soldiers that never had been in war, to see so many souls lie gasping on the ground, so thick, in some places, that you could hardly pass along. [...] Sometimes the Scripture declareth women and children must perish with their parents. Sometime the case alters; but we will not dispute it now. We had sufficient light from the word of God for our proceedings.[6]

By the end of the 18th century the struggle for souls has largely given way to struggles for soil, and the religious and spiritual understanding of 'God's special providences' is gradually replaced by more pragmatic ideas that anticipate the concept of 'manifest destiny' of the 19th century. Or, as Slotkin puts it somewhat differently:

After 1700 apocalyptic jargon is increasingly overlaid by the vocabulary of secular concerns, which identify the perfection of American life not with that of a Bible commonwealth, but with our possession of republican virtue, democratic idealism, or a perfect economic system.[7]

Yet the basic elements in the discourse about the new nation's 'errand into the wilderness' remain unchanged. They continue to justify the use of collective and individual force in the process of appropriating the promised land and create a cluster of concepts that subsume the destruction of the indigenous culture under the comprehensive symbol system of 'cultivating the wilderness.' The symbolic opposition 'civilization/wilderness' perpetuates the traditional image of white European man as superior cultivator, reinforced by Lockean ideas of 'nurture' and by the new key image of the 'national family' that has gained popularity in the second half of the 18th century.[8]

General Benjamin Lincoln, on his way to sign an Indian treaty at Detroit in 1793, sees civilized agrarian power divinely ordained and rhapsodizes in his journal, when surveying the landscape at the shore of Lake Erie:

When I take a view of this extensive country, and contemplate the clemency of its season, the richness of its soil [...] consider the many natural advantages [...] possessed by this country [...]

that is capable of giving support to a hundred times as many inhabitants as now occupy it [...] I cannot persuade myself that it will remain long in so uncultivated a state; especially, when I consider that to people fully this earth was in the original plan of the benevolent Deity. [...] So that if the savages cannot be civilized and quit their present pursuits, they will, in consequence of their stubbornness, dwindle and moulder away, from causes perhaps imperceptible to us, until the whole race shall become extinct.[9]

Today, this reads like a cynical understatement of the rather percept-ible causes of the American Indians' extinction, and one might recall the passage from John Underhill quoted before. Not unexpectedly, there is no indication that the newly proclaimed democratic rights of the young republic should or could be extended to the inhabitants of the wilderness.

Historically, after the War of 1812, neither the British, let alone the Indians, any longer constitute a serious threat to the powerful young nation; yet literary convention perpetuates a rhetoric that subsumes natural obstacles, Indians, and foreign powers alike as malevolent forces endangering America's historical mission. Not until after the Civil War does the symbolic opposition of 'civilization/wilderness' begin to lose its mythic explanatory power. In the works of perceptive writers like Stephen Crane (*The Red Badge of Courage*, 1895) and Ambrose Bierce (*Tales of Soldiers and Civilians*, 1891), the opposition 'civilization/wilderness' begins to be replaced by that of 'peace/war,' thus questioning what Russell Weigley calls the American 'strategy of annihilation'[10] as an accepted means sanctioned by ennobling ends. In the writings of these two authors, the actual experience of battle and its effects on the fighting individuals become the central themes, unadorned by patriotic, religious, or nationalist rhetoric. The 'face of battle,' rendered closely for the first time without recourse to idealizing imagery, shows few glorious traits. By its rather incidental character, the 'red badge of courage' in Crane's novel suggests that the myth of war as a proving ground for manly qualities and cultural superiority has become obsolete; and Bierce's bitter tales of soldiers and civilians, as in 'Chickamauga,' present impressive vignettes of senseless and grotesque dying. Crane's novel is also the first since the

Revolutionary era to depart from the family romance as the preferred literary convention in writing about war.

Texts like these, to which one may add Mark Twain's gruesome vision of the final showdown between 19th-century technology and medieval knighthood in *A Connecticut Yankee in King Arthur's Court* (1889), or Melville's *Israel Potter* (1855) and *Billy Budd* (1924), prepare the ground for the disillusioned war fictions of Hemingway, Dos Passos, and e. e. cummings in the wake of World War I. They also testify to a more general change of attitudes towards war, as Stanford historian David Kennedy suggests:

> Nineteenth-century America saw war as a great danger to democratic institutions and to economic prosperity, but as a promising arena for personal fulfillment. In the 20th century we have lost all illusions about the heroic possibilities of war; but now, ironically, we regard military preparedness as the essential guarantor of our way of life – and as an apparently indispensable stimulus to the economy.[11]

Already in Mark Twain's novel, several basic 'articles of faith' of the progress-oriented industrial age become central images for his critique of American civilization: the obsession of his countrymen with technical innovation and their (mis)understanding of it as progress; the (still unbroken) belief – in good faith and often with the best of intentions – that it is every American's duty to share the blessings of an industrialized democratic civilization with any other culture on the globe, regardless of the specific characteristics of this culture's society; the leading US role in the invention of new and more destructive weapons; and the effects of these technological devices on those who employ them.

Twain's concluding vision of thousands of corpses between barbed wires reads like an eerie prophecy of the mass slaughter in the trenches of World War I; like no other work of its time it voices the author's deep skepticism towards a simple belief in a kind of technical progress that opens up unprecedented ways for mass destruction.[12] Of interest in our context is the fact that the novel clearly shows structural characteristics of the 'captivity narratives,' though with the traditional situation of the captive turned upside down. It takes Hank Morgan, the representative of the 'civilized' world, only a few years to destabilize King Arthur's medieval society and threaten it with extinction. Equipped with advanced technology and a strong sense of mission that puts social, economical, and military 'improvement' as the highest goals, he goes about his reform project. Whenever he meets with serious resistance he employs the traditional strategy of annihilation to decide the conflict in his favor. Twain's projection of 19th-century American symbol systems onto the European Middle Ages can thus be read as a reflective and corrective fiction about dominant American myths. For the traditional figure of the Puritan in the wilderness, left with his faith in God as the only recourse from the evil that surrounds him, Twain's satirical re-vision substitutes the foreman of an arms factory who defends himself against the onslaught of God's knights by means of superior technology and firepower.[13] That he cannot, in the end, succeed is due to the logic of the story but does not invalidate the critical discourse.

In spite of these critical attitudes towards war in the works of Hawthorne, Melville, Twain, Bierce, and Crane, the majority of American novels about World War I continue to employ the conventional pattern of the 'historical romance' and updated versions of the 'civilization/wilderness' opposition. Stanley Cooperman's *World War I and the American Novel* (1967) and David Kennedy's *Over Here* (1980) both emphasize the enormous impact of war propaganda and its 'atrocity stories' about the enemy.[14] The first sophisticated public relations campaign in US history was highly effective and largely responsible for the fact that the official battle cry 'to make the world safe for democracy' and to join the 'Great Crusade' translated well into the fictional rendering of events.[15]

Without underestimating the influence of public propaganda, it appears appropriate to also point to other likely explanations of this sudden enthusiasm for war in a nation which, one year before it entered the conflict, elected Woodrow Wilson president exactly for his promise to stay out of it. As early as 1915, two years before the US entered the war, Mary Raymond Shipman Andrew wrote in her novel *The Three Things*: 'Civilization against barbarism; Gentlemen against Huns; Englishmen and Frenchmen whom we know to be straight and clean against – the unspeakable Germans. From the Kaiser down – seventy million of canaille.'[16] The national stereotype of the righteous American hero defending Faith and Civilization against the onslaught of barbarian hordes lends itself (too) easily for use in the somewhat abstract American view of the situation in Europe, conditioned as it was by distance in space as well as culture. Americans as 'Knights of Democracy' in the 'Great Crusade' against 'the Hun,' in order to save 'La Belle France,' 'Innocent Belgium,' and 'Classical Italy' (symbolizing European culture) from destruction – this conceptual framework projects the symbol system of the 'captivity narratives' onto the international arena, complete with all the major components of missionary zeal, racial warfare, gender-specific roles of victim and saviour, and their not so implicit sexual connotations.[17]

The disillusionment, after all has been slain and done and President Wilson's peace plan has shattered on European power politics, is painful and deep, a direct reversal of the initial idealizing euphoria. It produces not only the 'classics' by Hemingway, Dos Passos, Faulkner, and e. e. cummings, but, with some delay, also fierce novels of 'rhetorical protest,' like William March's *Company K* or Dalton Trumbo's *Johnny Got His Gun*, which bear remarkable resemblance to some of the bitter novels written by Vietnam war veterans – one might think of Larry Heinemann's *Paco's Story*, James Webb's *Fields of Fire*, or Ron Kovich's personal narrative *Born on the 4th of July*.

The literary legacy of the World War I authors is rich and proves to be adaptable to the experience of the next generation of authors who, sooner than they have expected after the 'war to end all wars,' are living through one of their own. As Malcolm Cowley remarks, somewhat tongue-in-cheek:

> One might say that a great many novels of the Second World War are based on Dos Passos for structure, since they have collective heroes in the Dos Passos fashion, and since he invented a series of structural devices for dealing with such heroes in unified works of fiction. At the same time, they are based on Scott Fitzgerald for mood, on Steinbeck for humor, and on Hemingway for action and dialogue.[18]

Given the broad consensus, in World War II, that war against the Nazis and fascists in Europe and their allied Japanese imperialists in the Pacific was justified on political and moral grounds, it must be considered a sign of intellectual sincerity that US fiction about the war brings forth any critical works at all; not even to mention the general climate of the Cold War years that was not very congenial for critical voices or texts. Yet authors like Norman Mailer, J. H. Burns, and in a different vein also Irwin Shaw, Stefan Heym, Alfred Hayes, and John Hersey are among those who, while supporting the war goals, point to its potentially dangerous effects for the victors. Not unexpectedly these voices remain, like their literary predecessors after World War I, an influential minority. Most novels about World War II tell the kind of 'war stories' that follow the conventional popular mythology, as Ward Just sums them up in his *Military Men*:

> Since American wars are never undertaken for imperialist gain (myth one), American soldiers always fight in a virtuous cause (myth two) for a just and goalless peace (myth three). [...] American wars are always defensive wars, undertaken slowly and reluctantly, the country a righteous giant finally goaded beyond endurance by foreign adventurers.[19]

It was these kind of war stories and their trivialized versions, as well as the host of glorifying Hollywood and TV productions in the same vein, that were popular in the years before and during the Vietnam War.[20] They shaped the ideas about war of those young Americans who were sent to Vietnam. Not surprisingly, the gap between their expectations and the reality in Vietnam turned out to be as profound and disillusioning as that of their military forefathers who grew up with Sir Walter Scott's ideas of gallant individual heroism and were then sent to experience anonymous mass slaughter on the battlefields of World War I.

The discourses of American war fiction

After World War II, the dominant literary discourse available to tell a war story is that of the mimetic mode: it tells a chronological story and introduces pyschologically more or less realistic characters acting in a traditional plot structure. War is seen as an exceptional historical event limited in time and space; with its end, society returns to normal, as do the characters of the story, if they survive. The majority of war fiction is written in this mode, following the goal to 'tell how it really was,' according to an understanding that the task of literature is to represent reality/historical events as faithfully as possible. To this purpose, authors mostly employ three well-established conventions:

the combat novel, the ideological melodrama, and novels that portray the military as a microcosm of (American) society.[21]

Combat novels present a limited number of characters, focus on the intensity of their personal experiences as individuals and in smaller military units, and usually pay scant attention to wider strategic, social, or political contexts. The characters' attitudes towards war range from considering it an unpleasant and dangerous job that has to be finished to a vocation that offers great personal satisfaction in serving a good and/or patriotic cause. Frequently, inexperienced or power-hungry officers and (military) bureaucracy in these novels constitute more of a threat than the actual enemy. For World War II, Harry Brown's *A Walk in the Sun* (1941) established itself as a classic in this category; for Vietnam, one may think of Robin Moore's *The Green Berets* (1965) or, quite differently, Larry Heinemann's *Close Quarters* (1977).

In melodrama, as Robert B. Heilman defines it, 'one attacks or is attacked; it is always a kind of war.'[22] Daniel C. Gerould argues that melodrama, originally imported from Europe, during the 19th century became 'a direct expression of American society and national character' and 'by the mid-twentieth century, American melodrama – particularly film – would be exported throughout the world, viewed on a global scale and widely imitated.'[23] Accordingly, Frederick J. Hoffman uses the term 'ideological melodrama' in his discussion of American novels of World War II and names as its standard ingredients 'the intellectual who must mature, the external menace or bogey, the signs of inner corruption that resembles the enemy.'[24] The ideological component usually appears as an historical mission to defend democracy against the menace of Nazi Fascism, Japanese Imperialism, or World Communism and always carries strong moral and ethical connotations. Most of the American novels about World War II show a 'pattern of triumph' in which, after initial individual differences, the official national consensus about the war prevails and the struggle is won by the good side. The much more numerous critical voices about the Vietnam War tend, especially with the progression of the conflict, towards a 'pattern of defeat' and illustrate the division among Americans about 'their nation's highly disconcerting historical experience.'[25] Examples for World War II are Irwin Shaw's *The Young Lions* (1948) or John Hersey's *The War Lover* (1959) and for Vietnam, Graham Greene's *The Quiet American* (1955), Morris L. West's *The Ambassador* (1965), or John Briley's *The Traitors* (1969).

The American literary tradition that presents the army as a microcosm of society dates back to John Dos Passos' novels about World War I, *One Man's Initiation, 1917* (1920) and *Three Soldiers* (1921). Both shocked their contemporary American audience, but with their innovative literary technique ('camera eye,' 'newsreel,' 'lives') they became models for authors writing about wars to come, like Norman Mailer (*The Naked and the Dead*, 1948) or John Del Vecchio (*The 13th Valley*, 1982). In these novels, authors present a panoramic view of how war affects society and its representative members, also reflecting on the role of the military in a democratic society and, often critically, on contemporary value systems and the official rationale for the war. Readers are introduced to characters from a representative cross-section of the whole military hierarchy, even though the focus of sympathy mostly remains with the simple soldiers and low-rank officers who are responsible for maintaining morale and who do the actual fighting.

The Vietnam War also brought into existence a new thematic subgenre of the mimetic mode. Since the mid-1980s war narratives have been complemented by a growing number of stories which no longer focus on the traumatic experience of soldiers fighting 'in country,' but examine instead the effects of the war upon the home front and depict, sometimes from a female perspective, both the severe adjustment problems of returned veterans, who suffer from Post-Traumatic Stress Disorder (PTSD), and the complex fates of war widows and children who cope with the death of their loved ones. Bobbie Anne Mason's *In Country* (1985), Susan Fromberg-Schaeffer's *Buffalo Afternoon* (1989), and Larry Heinemann's *Paco's Story* (1986) will suffice here as examples. Also new, if mostly in quantity, are the hundreds of published personal narratives trying to exorcize the horrors of jungle warfare, captivity, traumatic service in field hospitals, as well as many veterans' inability to re-adapt to the civil world after their return to the US.[26]

Radically different from these novels in the mimetic mode that write about war as a concrete historical event are – both in *what* they say and especially *how* they say it – those fictions that deviate from traditional ways of storytelling because their authors believe that one can no longer make sense of war within the framework of chronological plots and 19th century – derived teleological concepts of history as continuous progress towards some final goal. In these texts, war is no longer seen as an exceptional moral or historical state of limited duration with a specific beginning and end. Separated from its concrete historical contexts, war becomes one of many possible patterns of collective behaviour on a scale that ranges from local military action to global nuclear destruction. In the vision of these authors, war also turns into a complex metaphor for – as well as a critique of – a world in which individual as well as collective aggressive behaviour seems to have become a generally accepted model of social and political interaction. At the beginning of the 21st century, in the age of 'real time' newsbreaks, we have become quite accustomed to the fact that war is no longer an exceptional state limited by its temporal duration, but that there is always some war going on somewhere on the globe, and the media tell us about it. In short, since World War II war has become a *spatial* event that affects us even if we happen to live in a peaceful space.

Several intrinsic characteristics of the Vietnam War further contribute to a de-centered writing about events: it follows a strategy of containment in which no traditional concept of 'victory' or 'progress' applies and the same hills, villages, towns, access routes, bridges, and so on are fought over again and again. The one-year rotation scheme of soldiers as well as the long duration of the war leaves most of them with only a rather fragmented perspective and no sense of closure; swift transportation by jet from and to the world of war creates the impression of war as an event in a limited geographical space, and the high-tech speed of relocation between 'Nam' and 'The World' gives many soldiers a sensation of being caught in a surreal sequence of events. Media coverage is as diverse as it is abundant; and the growing anti-war movement in the US reflects a nation strongly divided about the war. As an American reviewer of fiction about Vietnam put it in 1978: 'The novelist's disadvantage is that this was a war with no center, no decisive battles; it was all circumference and it is therefore difficult to filter the thing through unified plot and point of view.'[27]

My argument here is also that the authors writing about war in a non-mimetic mode respond to very real changes in the American as well as the global sociocultural and political environment since the end of World War II. These include the mostly repressed but always residual fear of the possibility of a nuclear apocalypse in humankind's final military confrontation during the Cold War; numerous smaller-scale military actions across the world, mostly with US involvement; increasing domestic violence in Europe, the Near East, and the United States during the 1960s and 1970s (political assassinations, riots, radical political groups); the knowledge – thanks to our rapidly developing information society – of (civil) wars or terrorist attacks anywhere on the globe; as well as the recognition that, as Marshall McLuhan once put it so aptly in 1965, 'the medium is the message,' that is, language and images used in the media create their own realities rather than 'objectively' inform a fact that becomes particularly relevant for the Vietnam War.

Early examples for texts that focus on the power of literary language and discourse to create – rather than represent – (hi)story are John Hawkes' *The Cannibal* (1949) and Joseph Heller's *Catch-22* (1961), followed by Norman Mailer's *Why Are We in Vietnam?* (1967), Kurt Vonnegut's *Slaughterhouse-Five* (1969), as well as Tim O'Brien's *Going After Cacciato* (1978) and *The Things They Carried* (1990). To some extent, also, William Eastlake's *The Bamboo Bed* (1969) and Robert Mason's *Chickenhawk* (1983) show elements of this mode. Even though they use a specific war as referential context, these authors' intentions are no longer 'to tell how it really was;' their aim is to go beyond the surface and to reflect on as well as question the very concepts and language patterns with which we make sense of our world, including slogans like 'patriotic duty,' 'just war,' 'crusade for democracy,' and so on. The following discussion of several exemplary Vietnam novels illustrates dominant characteristics of the different categories outlined above.

The war that did not fit the mould

Though the American historical experience in Vietnam – America's 'longest war,' as George C. Herring calls it – even on the level of individual combat experience, runs counter to most established conventions in American war fiction, this does not mean that they are not frequently applied.[28] Robin Moore's *The Green Berets* (1964), one of the earliest fictions and most likely the commercially most successful book about the US engagement in Vietnam, employs all of them, and more. It is an example of the glorification of the 'professional warrior' who loves his job and does it well. Its animated cartoon figures share their characteristics with the heroes of James Jones gritty combat novels and James Bond's explosive professional self-sufficiency, as well as with a number of various American popular culture heroes. A well-blended concoction of macho American stereotypes serves us patriotism, adventure, secret-mission suspense, and heroic individualism, with more than enough brutalizing rhetoric to drive home how tough and professional these guys are who successfully complete one dangerous mission after another on the new frontier of democracy. Moving expertly in the limbo along the borderlines of civilized society, Moore's supermen are *gestalts* of the heroic frontier man, the 'good gunman' as State Marshal, the stubborn 'good detective,' and so on. They fight for law and order in spite of their corrupt or weak superiors and the bungling military bureaucracy; the good cause justifies their practice of deceit and brutality, and they usually surpass the enemy in their efficiency. Yet they are basically good chums, with a soft spot for comrades in arms, gentle women, and helpless children. Moore dutifully differentiates between 'good good guys' and 'bad good guys'; the latter's names usually suggest non-WASP ethnic groups and their stereotypical attributes: German = Nazi (Korn, Schmelzer); Armenian = cruel and sly (Ossidian); Mexican = passionate and crafty, and so on.

Their enemies are 'Communists,' 'black hordes,' 'monkeys,' or simply the Vietnamese in general, 'gooks,' 'dinks' (female 'slanteyes') – inferior, subhuman creatures who are invested with anthropomorphous qualities only when dying in 'brilliant white pools of napalm.' Then, 'human torches cry their last.'[29] Moore's presentation leaves no doubt that they will share the fate of their predecessors in American popular literature, the devilish 'injuns'. Conceiving of the Vietnam conflict in symbol systems derived from trivialized versions of historical racial warfare, Moore demonstrates his fundamental inability (or unwillingness) to understand the real issues in Vietnam and reduces the representatives of a foreign culture to the abstracts of Evil, Exotic, and Inferior. By necessity, his American heroes become equally abstract and stereotyped agents of the Good Cause. The bestseller status of Moore's book (by 1975: 3.2 million copies sold; 1983, a new Ballantine paperback edition of unknown quantity, a 5th printing in 1985; and most recently a paperback edition by St Martin's Press, Dec. 2002) makes it a notorious fictional equivalent to and forerunner of the Rambo movies. In the early phase of the war – and, it seems, again more recently – Moore's adventure stories seem to have sufficient explanatory power for a statistically significant number of Americans to let them conceive of their country's involvement in Vietnam as another just mission in the fight for democracy and freedom.[30]

Yet there is a dimension to Moore's discourse that runs counter to his traditional 'war stories' about successful military action: strangely enough, the enemy in Moore's book never ceases to be a threat, even though an infinite number of black-pajama wearing fanatics are blown to kingdom come on the Berets' perfectly executed missions. Intentional or not, the repetition of identical success stories also foregrounds the continuing existence of a dangerous opponent, thus questioning the significance of all the victorious actions. Moore's fictional strategy turns out to be that of commercial popular series and cartoons: removed from any specific historical context, the war in Vietnam becomes ideological pulp fiction in which the 'good guys,' week after week, forever not quite defeat their opponents in their struggle for world power. Rather than telling 'how it really was,' *The Green Berets* serves as an example for a rather colonizing mindset that perpetuates (white) American supremacy in Asia and Cold War clichés in general; the historical outcome of the Vietnam War apparently has not diminished the readers' attraction for this type of American 'guts and glory' writing.

Right from the beginning, though, there are a number of authors who refuse to tread the worn path of patriotic 'gung-ho' war stories; works like Brian Garfield's *The Last Bridge* (1966), Smith Hempstone's *A Tract of Time* (1966), Daniel Ford's *Incident at Muc Wa* (1967), Victor Kolpacoff's *The Prisoners of Quai Dong* (1967), David Halberstam's *One Very Hot Day* (1967), or John Briley's *The Traitors* (1969) are early examples for a growing awareness that this war may not fit the traditional pattern. Of them, Briley is the only one to attempt a comprehensive and coherent political-ideological presentation of the US engagement in Vietnam, following in the critical footsteps of two British predecessors, Graham Greene (*The Quiet American*, 1955) and Morris L. West (*The Ambassador*, 1965). Briley's book, like those of Green and West, is given a rather cool reception by American reviewers and is barely mentioned even in recent studies of American Vietnam fiction.[31] This is somewhat surprising, as Briley basically uses the same fictional model of ideological melodrama that, Irwin Shaw, for example, employed in his bestselling World War II novel, *The Young Lions* (1948), and his critique is scarcely more radical than that in James Jones' *From Here To Eternity* (1951), Joseph Heller's *Catch-22* (1961), Kurt Vonnegut's *Mother Night* (1967) and *Slaughterhouse-Five* (1969), or Thomas Pynchon's *Gravity's Rainbow* (1973).

Apart from certain habits of canon formation in literature, one reason for the neglect of Briley's novels by American critics may be that he writes a rather conventional naturalist discourse which, as Beidler suggests, is not adequate to the experience in Vietnam.[32] Yet so do most of the American writers about Vietnam without being ignored by critics, so there is reason to assume it is the story rather than the discourse that has condemned this novel to oblivion. What is it about? The 'action story' consists of the adventures of a group of US soldiers captured by a special Viet Cong unit in order to help them free an important politician imprisoned in South Vietnam who would be able to end the war by establishing a government of the 'third force,' with the support of the Buddhists and independent-minded Vietnamese nationalists. With the Viet Cong is an American collabor- ator, Evans, whose main task is to win the support of his fellow Amer- icans for this mission. As in many novels of ideas, the plot is at times a little bizarre and constructed; but parallel to this action story Briley is telling a much more interesting one. As in practically all American novels about Vietnam, the Vietnamese characters, especially – if they appear at all – those of the 'other side,' remain abstract and function as a supporting cast for American protagonists. Briley's novel is no exception, and the real battle fought on 450 pages is an ideological one among the American prisoners of war – and for the mind of the critical reader. Briley's Americans represent the divided social, polit- ical, and ethnic groups on the US homefront, and their respective atti- tudes: Evans, the collaborator (leftist-liberal drop-out from a wealthy Southern, Roman Catholic family); Lt Janowitz (Jewish liberal intel- lectual); Sgt Pershing (black Roman Catholic professional soldier); the GIs, Russell (Southern poor white redneck), Miller (Midwest farmer), and Hill (black Philadelphia slum survival artist). In their often heated discussions about whether or not to co-operate in their captors' plans they give voice, quite convincingly, to major issues of the 1960s in the US – the peace movement, President Johnson's 'Great Society,' civil rights movements, liberal-leftist reform movements, 'Law and

Order' mentality, military career as a chance for the underprivileged, and so on. As is to be expected, Janowitz and Hill finally consent and, together with Evans, successfully carry out the plan; but when they return to their base camp with the rescued politician, the loyalists lead by Sgt Pershing have overwhelmed their guards and are in command. Pershing provokes a bombing run by the US Air Force that wipes out the camp, and the only survivor of the carnage is Hill. He lets himself be picked up by a US helicopter as an escaped prisoner of war and coolly listens to the reports of the crew about their successful attack of the camp: ' "We zapped them babies to kingdom come. [. . .] We blew the piss out of them, man. Bodies lying all over the place". Hill managed to nod.'[33] Returning to 'his' army, Hill has a few days of transfer leave and uses the time to re-establish his authority in the Saigon black market business. With sufficient gains in his pocket, he contently strolls the bustling streets of Saigon when, unexpectedly, he catches a glimpse of one of his former Viet Cong guards in the crowd. Suddenly, all the displaced memories of the past weeks and months come flooding back and, in the end, effect a drastic change of his perspective:

> The Saigon he knew – the GIs, the pretty dollies, the shined shoes, the flashing cars, the shining neon, the big, solid buildings – all sort of blurred [. . .] It was the same city, the same streets, but he saw the poor kids hanging around the doorways, the old women with rubber tires for shoes hawking beads to the dollies in their patentleather high heels; he saw the smug, fat-gutted Vietnamese being pulled by men thinner than Thai's old man, pumping their pedicabs and sucking ass for their tips. He saw the rows and rows of crowded ramshackle streets, with hundreds of people huddled together off the treelined avenues where American cars floated by with their stereo radios and air conditioning. [. . .] He walked toward the river where there were no buildings of concrete and glass, no cars, no roads for cars. Where there were flies and stench and heat. Where people stared at him with fear and suspicion and dabbed their bony fingers into wooden bowls of rice, while overhead the rumble of the million-dollar jets shook their litter of tin and clapboard 'homes.' [. . .] Hill walked and walked. He was five miles along the road to Long Binh when he finally turned off the road . . . and into the underbrush.[34]

Hill's sudden change from an exploiter of the system to a morally enraged social reformer on the last page of Briley's novel quite suggestively serves up the moral of the story. It is reminiscent of the change of vision Yossarian, in J. Heller's *Catch-22*, experiences in his 'night journey' through Rome and which, in the end, motivates his final decision to (literally) jump out of the system.

While Yossarian's moral conversion is built up slowly throughout the novel, Hill's change happens a little unexpectedly; yet he is basically motivated by the same vision of a 'just society' which, in various shapes, appears or is implied in other US war novels that, by criticizing the war, also castigate the sociocultural and political structures that support it. To make clear that these contradictory views are all rooted within US thinking and in no way 'anti-American,' Briley has Evans, the collaborator, point to the American tradition: 'My country is the country of Jefferson and Lincoln, of John Quincy Adams and Robert E. Lee – men who would despise what is being done here in the name of the country they love.'[35] Maybe what makes Briley's novel much more controversial than other highly critical novels like *Catch-22*, *Slaughterhouse-Five*, or *Going After Cacciato* is not only the time of its publication, 1969, when the US public as well as the military were having a hard time recovering from the psychological effect of the Tet Offensive. His use of a conventional literary discourse in presenting the sensitive theme of desertion and collaboration with the enemy puts the central issues much more squarely, and by translating into a realist fictional scenario the possible consequences of dissent, he strikes uncomfortably close to life.

Not many American novels about Vietnam take on the task of clearly spelling out the basic contradictions of their country's involvement in Southeast Asia within a comprehensive cultural and political context. Most prefer to stay within the range of individualized doubts and problems; for example, Halberstam's *One Very Hot Day*, Webb's *Fields of Fire*, Heinemann's *Close Quarters*, or Groom's *Better Times Than These*. An interesting example of an attempt to eat the cake and have it, too, is John Del Vecchio's novel *The 13th Valley* (1982), written with the declared intention to tell 'what it was really like.'[36] One of the most voluminous American novels to come out of the Vietnam war, the book is an ambitious 'naturalist epic' in the literary tradition of Dos Passos, Shaw, and Mailer. Del Vecchio supports his claim to historical truth with military maps, after-action reports, a list of military terms, and GI jargon, as well as a host of details about the soldiers' everyday life. He presents us a company as microcosm of American society, with several main characters that are representative of the social configuration of US troops in Vietnam: company commander Lt Rufus Brooks, educated black intellectual with a BA in English and an excellent military leader, whose tolerance and understanding, together with that of the company's black medic Doc Johnson, keep racial tension within the company to a minimum; Daniel Egan, a more intellectual version of Sgt Croft in *The Naked and the Dead*, is cast in the role of the white 'ultra-soldier' on their side; under his guidance, the 'new guy,' V. 'Cherry' Chelini, trained psychologist and now serving as a radioman, is introduced to the business of war. The story relates the mission of the company in the hills between Hue and Khe San and, finally, into the Khe Ta Laou valley, where the goal of destroying a major, well-fortified NVA command centre is achieved at the price of heavy US losses. Brooks, Johnson, and Egan are killed in the final battle while attempting to save each other. Chelini, who has matured from innocent intellectual civilian to battle-worn soldier, survives 'to tell the tale,' suggesting a parallel to Ishmael in *Moby-Dick*.

The merits of this novel are obvious, yet so are its contradictions and Del Vecchio's final inability or unwillingness to integrate the special qualities of the US experience in Vietnam into his tale. Intentionally or not, the author uses two kinds of discourses that are hermetically sealed from each other. One is that of the traditional story of a patrol in enemy country, with all its ups and downs, sensitively rendered details of soldiering life, shocks and little pleasures, up to the somewhat melodramatic ending. However, none of the problems that are considered typical of this war seem to exist on this level of the book: here, the US soldiers fight NVA regulars in an uninhabited mountain valley with no civilians in sight, so it is soldiers against soldiers – a war like it should have been, and as it often was in World War II.

The specific problems of the US experience in Vietnam make up the second discourse – that of meditation and discussion, campfire talks, and so on. Here we learn about all the social, cultural, ethnic, political, moral, and military issues – racial tensions, anti-war protesters, personal problems, and so on; but they leave the level of action curiously unaffected. In keeping these two discourses isolated on parallel and never-intersecting planes, Del Vecchio practices a narrative immunization strategy which allows him to avoid tackling the real issues of the conflict without leaving them out of the picture altogether.

The overall effect is that, historical geographical setting and contemporary weapons systems apart, Brooks and his men might as well be fighting on one of the Pacific islands in World War II, or in any other war: their timeless tale of battle and death would not be significantly different. To say this is not to classify Del Vecchio's novel as just a slightly anachronistic attempt to write an epic of the World War II kind – with sometimes jarring naturalist symbolic imagery – about Vietnam. As in most wars, GIs have little time to think about what they are doing and why, as they are kept busy with staying alive. And yet – the high awareness of the war's problematic issues, which Del Vecchio's philosophizing 'boonierats' reveal in their campfire discussions, might have encouraged the author to incorporate the real contradictions of Vietnam into the overall structure of his novel rather than bury them under a surplus of personal and military facts and details.[37]

Staying alive certainly is a major issue for every soldier, in history as well as in fiction, and in American fiction about Vietnam, for many protagonists it seems to have become the only purpose during war time. Few authors have better managed to incorporate the American soldiers' experience in Vietnam into their work than Tim O'Brien in his *Going After Cacciato* (1978).[38] In his first book about his Vietnam experience, *If I Die in a Combat Zone, Box Me Up and Ship Me Home* (1969), O'Brien, like many other veterans, wrote a personal narrative that accepted the day-by-day sequence of events, with occasional attempts to establish suggestive connotative relations by means of recurring phrases and images. In *Going After Cacciato*, he uses a much more sophisticated approach that involves a third-person (self-conscious) narrator and three interacting levels of narrative discourse that roughly correspond to different activities (remembering, imagining, perceiving) in the mind of the sensitive narrator-protagonist, Paul Berlin. He is dropped into a world which he thinks he knows from various secondary sources: his father's tales of World War II, movies and TV-series, daily media coverage, and supposedly true-to-life training in boot camp. Once in-country, his attempts to comprehend Vietnam reality by applying the rules of this media-engendered 'reality' fail abysmally and provide for a rock-bottom experience of fundamental ignorance.[39] A fellow soldier's 'death of fright,' which Paul witnesses on his first patrol, becomes for him 'the ultimate war story' Like the key motifs in earlier American war novels – Dresden in *Slaughterhouse-Five*, Snowden's death in *Catch-22*, Hennessy's death on the beach in *The Naked and the Death*, or the retreat from Caporetto in Hemingway's *A Farewell to Arms* – Billy Boy's 'death of fright' makes the protagonist shockingly aware of his own precarious situation.

The figure of the sensitive and critical intellectual has been with American war fiction ever since Dos Passos' *Three Soldiers* (Andrews), but O'Brien introduces a number of innovative elements. In order to involve the reader in his protagonist's struggles for sense-making, or his 'storifying of experience,' he uses two clearly distinguishable modes of literary discourse. One renders Berlin's memories of past events ('what happened'), the other his imaginative pursuit of Cacciato across Eurasia to Paris ('what might have happened').[40] Differently from Del Vecchio's strategy, though, these two levels interact and interfere with each other: while imaginatively leaving the dangerous world of war in his pseudo-legitimate pursuit of the deserter Cacciato, Paul Berlin, mostly involuntarily, remembers – and finally comes to terms with – the horrors of war in an alien environment.

What I consider original is that O'Brien uses his sophisticated 'dialogue of contradictory discourses' for a juxtaposition of the 'factual' (modern) and the 'fictional' (postmodern) modes of literary sense-making. The discourse of Berlin's memories recalls the phenomenological style of the Hemingway tradition and consciously places itself in the context of American war literature. In one passage, for example, Paul remembers a fire-break during a patrol in a mountain area that has been devastated by air bombardment and been dubbed 'World's Greatest Lake Country' by the caustic Doc Peret. Cacciato, the archetypal young innocent/ignorant GI, casts an improvised fishing line into one of the bomb-craters filled with rain water:

> He tied a paperclip to a length of string, baited it up with bits of ham, then attached a bobber fashioned out of an empty aerosol can labeled Secret. Cacciato moved down to the lip of the crater.

He paused as if searching for proper waters, then flipped out the line. The bobber made a splashing sound.[41]

The obvious allusion here is to Hemingway's famous short story 'Big Two-Hearted River,' where Nick Adams, back from the war, attempts to regain his bearings in the world by the familiar ritual of trout fishing. For both youths, the ritual of fishing is meant to (re-)constitute a sense of personal identity, but its form and its significance are notably different. Hemingway's Nick, symbolically placed between the burnt land around Seyney behind him and the swamp before him, is able to determine his position in the world – the river and his campsite – by doing the right things, or rather by 'doing things right,' and thus establishes a working relationship with his natural environment.

Compared to this, the very materials Cacciato uses for fishing – some string, paperclip, a piece of canned ham, an empty aerosol can – signify more than just a low grotesque version of Yankee ingenuity. In the world of the 17-year-old Cacciato, no piece of untouched nature is left between the burnt land and the swamp: both (symbolic) landscapes have been fused in the lifeless wasteland of 'World's Greatest Lake Country.' Interaction with such an environment to constitute one's identity must take different forms, and Cacciato's fishing becomes an ambiguous symbolic gesture: an expression of boyish helplessness and withdrawal into oneself, it also signals individual self-assertion by clinging to a familiar ritual whose situational inadequacy makes it a striking poetic image for the youth's despair.

Opposed, and sometimes complementary to the disturbing memories of despair and death, Paul Berlin's imaginative discourse creates an alternative reality, one very much in contradiction to the reality of his memories. Berlin makes it clear that his imaginings are more than mere escapist daydreaming or pretending: 'Not a dream, but an idea. An idea to develop, to tinker with and build and sustain, to draw out as an artist draws out his visions. [. . .] It was a working out of the possibilities. It wasn't daydreaming and it wasn't pretending. [. . .] It was a way of asking questions.'[42] While Berlin's memories contain all the horrors of war, his imaginings are full of the popular myths and stereotypes an American 20-year-old may come up with in his attempts to build 'a smooth arc from war to peace.' As the quoted passage indicates, Paul Berlin's imaginings serve three major purposes: they are artistic visions of an alternative reality as well as intellectual hypotheses, and they also are cognitive models for questioning traditional patterns of perception and understanding – all of this, quite realistically, within the limits of the imagination of a 20-year-old college drop-out with an inherent gift for 'pretending,' especially in the face of unpleasant and shocking demands of the world of war. As readers, we see the 'story within stories' unfold before us, flounder along and, finally, shatter on the senselessness of war. The dialogue of discourses, towards the end of the novel, has turned into a battle, and the apparent winner is the discourse of the factual when, in the last chapter, we are definitely thrown back in the world of 'what happened.'[43]

Yet the contradictions inherent throughout the novel are far from resolved. With a sharp eye for the incongruity of popular myths and historical realities, O'Brien inverts the motif of the American Westward Movement: 'Going West' does not take Cacciato and his pursuers to untouched new continents but to Paris – the city where American independence was officially ratified in 1783; the city that served as the symbol of European culture in World War I and was celebrated by Americans in World War II. But here, in 1968, Paris is the city where negotiations for peace in Vietnam are dragging their feet around the notorious oval conference table. Paris as the literal 'vanishing point' of Cacciato's and Paul Berlin's imaginative journey – 'Imagination, like reality, has its limits'[44] – suggests that the American Westward Movement has come full circle, and also alludes to the ironic fact that the US, themselves a former colony, have taken up the colonial heritage from France in Indochina.

At the end of the novel, Cacciato, the enigmatic symbol of American innocence and ignorance, is MIA (missing in action). Thus O'Brien, while not entirely foreclosing Cacciato's eventual resurfacing, makes it understood that traditional concepts of 'just war,' 'unique historical mission,' or 'crusade for democracy' have lost their power as explanatory symbol systems for the US involvement in Vietnam. Now they are stories, overtaken and contradicted by historical realities. Paul Berlin, while still unable to make sense of the war, has at least taken a significant step towards self-definition: his imaginative questioning of war's realities has yielded no smooth solutions, but a heightened awareness that helps him to distinguish clearly between 'what happened and what might have happened.' In other words, his attempts at a literary 'storifying of experience,' even if unsuccessful on their own, have taught him to accept the contradictory qualities of his situation.

Acceptance of basic contradictions as a painful yet unavoidable component of existence is also characteristic of the large number of personal narratives written about Vietnam. Most of their authors have little or no experience as writers, and only few have written more than one account of the events that drastically changed them and often enough came (too) close to destroying their lives. For many of them, writing about this is not only a desperate attempt at sharing their experience with an audience of fellow citizens who, in their majority, are (and often would prefer to remain) unaware of the indelible scars this war has left on those who actually fought it. For Vietnam veterans, writing is also a way of spelling out – quite literally – their rage and disillusionment and to make use, by articulating themselves, of the therapeutic power of writing. I am aware that one might argue about whether these personal narratives should be properly included under the heading of 'fiction,' and there is no question that 'literariness' of the traditional academic kind is not their forte. Yet we should, I believe, acknowledge the fact that autobiography is also a kind of fiction – the one we tell (about) ourselves in the attempt to make sense of our lives beyond the mere chronological sequence of days and events.

Michael Herr, in *Dispatches*, points out that 'war stories, after all, are stories about people'; personal narratives about Vietnam in particular are war stories by and about the people who have lived through extreme situations and still suffer from it, because this experience more often than not has shattered, or at least seriously shaken, their fundamental beliefs, value systems, and their understanding of the world. So it is no surprise that events in their works are stated starkly, and often with outrage. In particular, this becomes apparent in personal narratives as well as novels about Vietnam veterans trying to re-accommodate to civil life back home: they discover that they have to lead a many-sided battle – against their haunting war memories, against discriminatory public rhetoric as well as hostile personal attitudes among their local communities or even their own families. Some never escape from the war, like Hicks in Robert Stone's chilling

Dog Soldiers (1973); some keep running forever, like the protagonists in John Balaban's *Coming Down Again* (1985), or the rootless hero of Larry Heinemann's *Paco's Story*. Others live through painful struggles and, with the help of understanding 'Others,' manage to accept their past, as do Griffin in Stephen Wright's *Meditations in Green* (1983), and Christian Starkman in Philip Caputo's *Indian Country* (1987); or they are able to gather enough strength out of their bitterness to speak out about an experience that has almost destroyed them, physically and/or mentally, as do Ron Kovic in *Born on the Fourth of July* (1976), Robert C. Mason in *Chickenhawk* (1984), or William D. Ehrhart in *Vietnam-Perkasie: A Combat Marine's Memoir* (1985). These works are very personal, pragmatic, and fundamental: they show men who did, in good faith, believe they would become heroes serving their country in a(nother) just war. Instead, they have to discover that they endured hardships and risked their lives just to find themselves ostracized by their fellow citizens upon their return home; suffering from physical injuries and Post-Traumatic Stress Disorder, they find themselves pushed onto the fringe of their communities and, more often than not, are conscious of the possibility that they may be on an irreversible slide down the social ladder. The laconic final sentence in Mason's *Chickenhawk* tersely sums up the overall effect: 'No one is more shocked than I.'

The return of the repressed

As this survey has tried to indicate, American discourses and stories of Vietnam exist in dazzling variety and multitude, to which one still has to add other genres like poetry, drama, cartoons, graphic novels, diaries, film, and television.[45] What all of them share is the attempt to understand – or at least come to terms with – a war that went terribly wrong by all traditional American standards. Even the 'gung-ho' tales in print and screen testify to this endeavour, clinging, as they desperately do, to old patterns of military success and individual heroism that have become obsolete in the face of a new reality. Yet these familiar beliefs of fighting a just war with a strong sense of mission in a unique historical situation are radically shaken by the Vietnam experience, which gives rise to a serious questioning of basic American values on the personal as well as the collective level. The prolonged and painful soul-searching has yielded a rich, if diversified, harvest. One might argue that Meville's Captain Delano would find himself among a minority in today's United States (admittedly, though, at times a governing one), as his stereotype of colonial Americans is mostly apparent only in early fictions about the Vietnam War. The majority of later works display a much more self-critical, almost post-colonial perspective. This relates, in the wake of the Watergate and Iran-Contra affairs, to US domestic as well as international politics; many more Americans can now understand the depression of Melville's Benito Cereno. What one might find a bit disconcerting is how little of this awareness is reflected in recent US politics; the collective trauma of the terrorist attacks of 9/11 not only offered apparently irresistible incentives for 'backsliding' into old concepts but even for condoning a new doctrine of 'pre-emptive strike' that carries all the dangers of opening a Pandora's Box of unbridled military aggression on a global scale.

The concluding words of Mason's *Chickenhawk* – 'No one is more shocked than I' – may express succinctly the experience of many American soldiers in the current US military engagement in Iraq. Once more they are thousands of miles from home, in a country whose language, customs, and cultural codes mostly remain alien to them; once more they find it difficult to distinguish between friends and enemies (and therefore tend to shoot first and ask questions later); and once more they discover that the people whom they were sent to protect more often than not consider them invaders rather than liberators. Even for an observer not directly afflicted by this war, it is heartbreaking to read the personal narratives and blogs of yet another generation of young Americans suffering through the process of disillusionment, despair, trauma, and anger when they discover that the 'just war' their government started rests on rather weak premises, to put it politely.[46] In spite of the different political and historical contexts of the Iraq engagement, the experience of American soldiers is painfully reminiscent of that of their parents' generation in Vietnam; so is the media coverage, whose daily reports of soldiers and civilians wounded or killed in Iraq resemble the notorious 'body counts' of the Vietnam years. Also domestically, events and practices show almost eerie similarities to those of over 30 years ago. In 1971, Senator J. William Fulbright warned of the detrimental effects of long wars on a democratic society:

> When a war is of long duration, when its objectives are unascertainable, when the people are bitterly divided and their leaders lacking in both vision and candor, then the process of democratic erosion is greatly accelerated. [...] Beset by critics and doubt, the nation's leaders resort increasingly to secrecy and deception.[47]

After more or less continuous involvement in military actions around the globe since the end of World War II, and in view of the stunning quality and volume of writing about the American experience in Vietnam, one wishes that American politicians were listening more closely to the voices of their best and brightest; they could recognize that real (hi)stories are made not by Jefferson's 'false arithmetic' of missiles and bombs but by images and words that make sense – and the world safe for democracy – domestically as well as internationally.

Notes

1. P. Beidler, *American Literature and the Experience of Vietnam* (Athens, Georgia: University of Georgia Press, 1982), considers 'sense-making' (in life as well as in fiction) as the key problem of the US Vietnam experience.
2. P. Fussell, 'Der Einfluss kultureller Paradigmen auf die literarische Wiedergabe traumatischer Erfahrung,' in K. Vondung, ed., *Kriegserlebnis: Der Erste Weltkrieg in der literarischen Gestaltung und symbolischen Deutung der Nationen* (Goettingen: Vandenhoek, 1980), pp. 175–87, p. 175 passim (my translation).
3. For a detailed discussion of discourses in US war fiction until 1986, see W. Hölbling, *Fiktionen vom Krieg* (Tübingen: Narr, 1987) and P. K. Jason & M. A. Graves, eds, *Encyclopedia of American War Literature* (Westport, CT: Greenwood, 2001). See also N. Luhmann, *Soziologische Aufklärung. Aufsätze zur Theorie sozialer Systeme* (Cologne: Westdeutscher Verlag, 1970).
4. R. Slotkin, *Regeneration Through Violence* (Middleton, CT: Wesleyan University Press, 1973), p. 68. See also R. Slotkin, *The Fatal Environment: The Myth of the Frontier in the Age of Industrialization, 1800–1890* (Middleton, CT: Wesleyan University Press, 1985); R. H. Pearce, *Savagism and Civilization* (Baltimore: Johns Hopkins Press, 1965); R. E. Berkhofer, *The White Man's Indian* (New York: Vintage, 1979); and Philip H. Melling, *Vietnam in American Literature: The Puritan Heritage* (Boston: Twayne,

1990). For reprints of popular Indian captivity narratives, see R. Van der Beets, ed., *Held Captive by Indians: Selected Narratives 1642–1836* (Knoxville: University of Tennessee Press, 1973), and J. Leverner and H. Cohen, eds, *The Indians and Their Captives* (Westport, CT: Greenwood, 1977).

5. J. Aho, *Religious Mythology and the Art of War* (London: Aldwych, 1981), p. 151.
6. Quoted in Slotkin, *Regeneration Through Violence*, p. 76.
7. Slotkin, *The Fatal Environment*, p. 62.
8. See for example J. Fliegelman. *Prodigals and Pilgrims: The American Revolution against Patriarchal Authority 1750–1800* (New York: Cambridge University Press, 1982).
9. Quoted in Pearce, *Savagism and Civilization*, p. 69.
10. R. Weigley, *The American Way of War* (Indiana: Indiana University Press, 1978).
11. David Kennedy, 'War and the American Character,' *The Stanford Magazine* 3:1 (Spring/Summer 1975), pp. 14–18, 70–2.
12. U. Brumm, 'Amerikanische Dichter und Europäische Geschichte: Nathaniel Hawthorne und Mark Twain,' in A. Weber, ed., *Geschichte und Fiktion* (Göttingen, 1972), pp. 85–108, argues that Twain did not intend generally to criticize technical progress. Likewise, T. Tanner, 'The Lost America – The Despair of Henry Adams and Mark Twain,' in Henry Nash Smith, *Mark Twain: A Collection of Essays* (Englewood Cliffs, NY: Prentice Hall, 1963), pp. 159–74, sees Morgan's failure as grounded in the inadequate historical conditions of the European Middle Ages. On the other hand, W. Fluck, 'The Restructuring of History and the Intrusion of Fantasy in Mark Twain's *A Connecticut Yankee in King Arthur's Court*,' in W. Fluck *et al.*, eds, *Forms and Functions of History in American Literature* (Berlin: Schmidt, 1981), p. 147, emphasizes Twain's social critique: 'What makes the *Yankee* such a remarkable and disconcerting book, however, is the fictional revelation that the Yankee himself, Twain's embodiment of his moral idealism, emerges as a prisoner of certain popular aspirations and fantasies of the "Gilded Age" '.
13. D. Aaron, *The Unwritten War, American Writers and the Civil War* (New York: Alfred A. Knopf, 1973), pp. 140–5, sees the novel primarily as Twain's belated contribution to the Civil War, in which he did not serve personally. Yet a more contextual socio-cultural interpretation seems appropriate: two years before the novel was published, the Dawes Act, an attempt to integrate American Indians into society, yielded results that were about as fatal for the Indians as Hank Morgan's reforms are for the medieval feudal system. In 1890, the year after the publication of Twain's book, the *Indian Barrier* was abolished and the American 'frontier' officially closed.
14. Stanley Cooperman, *World War I and the American Novel* (Baltimore: John's Hopkins University Press, 1967), and David Kennedy, *Over Here* (New York: Oxford University Press, 1980).

15. G. Creel, *How We Advertised America* (New York: Harper & Brothers, 1920). Creel chaired the Committee on Public Information instituted by President Wilson, and the book describes in detail the work of his agency. See also J. R. Mock & C. Larson, *Words That Won the War: The Story of the Committee on Public Information, 1917–1919* (Princeton: Princeton University Press, 1939); H. Lasswell, *Propaganda Technique in the World War* (New York: Peter Smith, 1938); G. T. Blakey, *Historians on the Home-front: American Propagandists for the Great War* (Lexington, KY: University Press of Kentucky, 1970); E. M. Coffman, *The War To End All Wars: The American Military Experience in World War I* (New York: Oxford University Press, 1968); and S. I. Rochester, *American War Narratives, 1917–1978: A Study and Bibliography* (New York: David Lewis, 1969). Other relevant works are cited in the bibliographies of S. Cooperman & D. Kennedy.

16. Mary Raymond Shipman Andrew, *The Three Things* (New York, 1915), p. 1.

17. S. Brownmiller, *Against Our Will: Men, Women and Rape* (New York: Simon & Schuster, 1975), p. 44, points to the far-reaching sexual aspects of the feminine allegorization of France in American propaganda of World War I: ' "The Rape of the Hun" became an instant byword in this country. It came to symbolize the criminal violation of innocent Belgium. It dramatized the plight of La Belle France. It charged up national patriotism and spurred the drive for Liberty Loans by adding needed authenticity to the manufactured *persona* of an unprincipled barbarian with pointed helmet and syphilitic lust who gleefully destroyed cathedrals, set fire to libraries, and hacked and maimed and spitted babies on the tip of his bayonet. As propaganda, rape was remarkably effective, more effective than the original German terror. It helped to lay the emotional groundwork that led us into the war.'

18. M. Cowley, *The Literary Situation* (New York: Vintage, 1958; 1969), p. 41.

19. W. Just, *Military Men* (New York: Knopf, 1970), p. 7.

20. See J. Smith, *Looking Away: Hollywood and Vietnam* (New York: Scribner's, 1975) and T. Doherty, *Projections of War: Hollywood, American Culture and World War II*, revised edition (New York: Columbia University Press, 1999).

21. Excluded from more detailed analysis here are texts like the ubiquitous and timeless formulaic adventure stories with exchangeable war settings.

22. Robert B. Heilman, *The Iceman, the Arsonist and the Troubled Agent: Tragedy and Melodrama on the Stage* (Seattle: University of Washington Press, 1973), p. 46.

23. Daniel C. Gerould, *American Melodrama* (New York: Performing Arts Journal Publication, 1983), p. 7.

24. Frederick J. Hoffman, *The Mortal No: Death and the Modern Imagination* (Princeton: Princeton University Press, 1964), p. 237.

25. G. Raeithel *et al.*, eds, *Vietnamkrieg und Literatur* (Munich: Fink, 1972), p. 96 (my translation).

26. See the REMF Bibliography, part of the Sixties Project sponsored by Viet Nam Generation Inc. and the Institute of Advanced Technology in the Humanities at the University of Virginia, Charlottesville: http://lists.village.virginia.edu/sixties/HTML_docs/Resources/Bibliographies/REMF_bib_entry.html.

27. E. Pochoda, 'Vietnam, we've All Been There,' *The Nation*, March 25 (1978), p. 344. (Book review of Tim O'Brien's *Going After Cacciato*.)

28. G. C. Herring, *America's Longest War: The United States and Vietnam, 1950–1975*, 2nd edn (New York: Knopf, 1986). For examples, see R. Newhafer, *No More Bugles in the Sky* (New York: New American Library, 1966); T. Taylor, *A-18* (New York: Crown, 1967), *A Piece of this Country* (New York: Norton, 1970); G. D. Moore, *The Killing at Ngo Tho* (New York; Norton, 1967).

29. Robert Moore, *The Green Berets* (1964). The reference is from the 1983 Ballantine paperback edition, p. 64.

30. In addition to the new edition of Moore's book, titles like Nicholas Proffit's *Gardens of Stone* (1983) and Brian Freemantle's *The Vietnam Legacy* (1984) show a tendency to combine patriotic glorification of comradeship with a sense of duty reminiscent of Oliver North and a fairly open pro-war attitude. Crossing the borderline to a 'pornography of violence' is Barry Sadler's *Phü Nam* (1984), which – like Rambo II – employs well-worn melodramatic simplification and reduces the essence of the war to a gruesome showdown between two superkillers. Recent heroic tales in this vein are Larry Chambers, *Death in the a Shau Valley* (1998), Ray Hildrer, *Hill 488* (2003), and John J. Culbertson, *13 Cent Killers: The 5th Marine Snipers in Vietnam* (2003).

31. After the end of the Vietnam War, Greene's novel repeatedly was recognized by US critics as a prophetic vision of things to come, although at the time of its publication in 1955 it was considered to be outrageously anti-American. See, for example, Gloria Emerson, *Winners and Losers* (New York: Random House, 1977), James C. Wilson, *Vietnam in Prose and Film* (Jefferson, NC: McFarland & Co., 1982) and Thomas Myers, *Walking Point* (New York: Oxford University Press, 1988). Briley's novel received a rather ambivalent review from R. Rhodes in the *New York Times Book Review* (September 7, 1970, p. 50 passim) and continues to go unmentioned in all major American studies on the subject, except for a short comment in Beidler's *American Fiction and the Experience of Vietnam*, pp. 46, 65. K. M. Puhr, 'Novelistic Responses to the Vietnam War' (unpubl. PhD Dissertation, St. Louis University, 1982, pp. 189–93), briefly mentions *The Traitors* as 'the strongest political propaganda novel to emerge from the Vietnam War,' and attests to its political and ethical seriousness.

32. Beidler, *American Literature and the Experience of Vietnam*, p. 47.

33. John Briley, *The Traitors* (New York: Putnam's House, 1969), p. 438 passim.

34. Ibid., p. 441.

35. Ibid., p. 198.
36. John Del Vecchio, *The 13th Valley* 1982.
37. Myers, in *Walking Point*, p. 57, calls Del Vecchio's novel the Vietnam War's 'first true leviathan' and interprets it with regard to the fair number of quite explicit references to Melville and the author's use of nature symbolism, and points to the ambiguous conclusion.
38. Tim O'Brien, *Going After Cacciato* (1978). References are from the Dell paperback edition, 1979.
39. On the impact of movies and TV, see M. Mandelbaum, 'Vietnam: The Television War,' *Daedalus* (Fall 1982), pp. 157–69; J. Smith, *Looking Away: Hollywood and Vietnam* (New York: Scribner's, 1975); L. Suid, *Guts and Glory: Great American War Movies* (Reading, MA: Addison-Wesley, 1978); and the interviews with Vietnam Veterans published in R. J. Lifton, *Home From the War* (New York: Simon & Schuster, 1973), especially, pp. 161–88.
40. The third discourse, discernible in the 'Observation Post' chapters which serve as the (relative) present in this novel, may be called that of perception, as it mostly renders Paul Berlin's sensory perceptions and meditations/speculations stimulated by them.
41. O'Brien, *Going After Cacciato*, p. 283.
42. Ibid., pp. 43–6.
43. See T. C. Herzog, 'Going After Cacciato: The Soldier-Author-Character Seeking Control,' *Critique*, 24:2 (Winter 1983), pp. 88–96.
44. O'Brien, *Going After Cacciato*, p. 378.
45. See A. Louvre and J. Walsh, eds, *Tell Me Lies About Vietnam* (Milton Keynes & Philadelphia: Open University Press, 1988).
46. For example, Jason Hartley, *Just Another Soldier: A Year on the Ground in Iraq* (New York: HarperCollins, 2005), Colby Buzzell. *My War: Killing Time in Iraq* (New York: Berkley Trade, 2006); John R. Crawford, *The Last True Story I'll Ever Tell: An Accidental Soldier's Account of the War in Iraq* (New York: Riverhead Trade, 2006). Also see http://iraqblogcount.blogspot.com/, http://iraqthemodel.blogspot.com.
47. *Congressional Record*, Senate, March 12, 1971, p. 6395.

7
King Philip's Shadow: Vietnam, Iraq and the Indian Wars

Philip H. Melling

The 'war on terror' in the United States is often accompanied by fears and anxieties that come to us from previous disputes. The rhetoric delights in rituals of commemoration – Elaine Showalter calls them 'infectious stories', 'rituals of testimony'[1] – the meaning of which reveals the character of a Puritan regime. In the aftermath of September 11, for example, George Bush's diary entries and policy speeches referred to an historical moment that had placed his country at the epicenter of new world history and made it, what he called, 'freedoms defender' in an age-old war against 'barbarism'. Bush's tendency to see new war in terms of old, linguistic separations and divisions – righteous purity on the one hand; 'men without conscience' on the other – received its initial inspiration from World War II. In a speech he gave on the 50th anniversary of Pearl Harbor on the deck of the US Enterprise, Bush harped back to the fight against 'tyranny' in World War II; in particular, the brave pilots in their P-40 fighter planes who, although vastly outnumbered, gave chase and shot down four enemy aircraft. In the modern war against terrorism and the leaders of those who live 'in caves' in the United States, he said, would need to deploy 'new capabilities and technologies'. It would also need to enlist the support of the nation's 'military' (in memory of the pilots of Pearl Harbor and their planes) to achieve 'decisive and total victory'.[2]

The importance of military interdiction as a way of counteracting primitive 'barbarism' was first alluded to by the Secretary of Defense, Donald Rumsfeld. On 20 September 2001, Rumsfeld claimed that the campaign against Bin Laden and his supporters would 'combine military, political, intelligence and diplomatic initiatives' to '*drain the swamp they live in*'. The Undersecretary of Defense, Paul Wolfowitz, repeated this idea and extended the metaphor in a meeting with NATO ministers in Brussels when he said that 'while we'll try to find every snake in the swamp, the essence of the strategy is *draining the swamp*'. For Wolfowitz, the snake in question was Saddam Hussein and the swamp of swamps was Saddam's Iraq.[3]

Iraq and Vietnam

It is clear from these references that the lessons of the Vietnam War – in 1985, for example, Paul Kennedy referred his readers to a 'military establishment that nervously questions itself about when and in what circumstances it can intervene abroad without getting bogged down in an unpopular, divisive war'[4] – had been long forgotten. In the 1990s, says Richard Drayton, faith in technology became the new mantra in America's military universities. 'Born up by the high tide of techno euphoria' military theorists preached a philosophy of 'full-spectrum dominance', by which the United States through its technological pre-eminence could 'fight and win multiple, simultaneous major-theatre wars'. Among these theorists was Lieutenant Colonel Ralph Peters at the Army War College who announced, in 1997, an 'age of constant conflict'; Thomas Barnett at the Naval War College, a vigorous advocate of 'network-centric warfare'; and General John Jumper who 'predicted a planet easily mastered' by US force 'from air and space'. Behind these boasts, says Drayton, lurked a virulent and 'violent hysteria' which came to the surface when third-world factions refused to adopt a subservient role when faced with overwhelming American force.[5]

At the time of the invasion of Fallujah, Peters told Fox News that 'the best outcome, frankly, (for the people of the city) is if they're all killed'.[6] Third-world nations and militia regimes could not be allowed to repeat their triumph in the Vietnam War. Attrition technologies could not be denied. Overwhelming force would always defeat those who relied for their inspiration on a guerilla landscape as well as a terminology of swamps and quicksands. Vietnam was of no military relevance. Historians and journalists who had spoken out against intervention in Vietnam and used the swamp as a metaphor of entrapment were neither useful nor reliable. Writers like David

Halberstam (*The Making of a Quagmire*, 1969), Arthur Schlesinger, Jr (*The Bitter Heritage*, 1968), Townsend Hoopes (*The Limits of Intervention*, 1969), Chester L. Cooper, (*The Last Crusade*, 1970) – all of whom had pointed out the folly of wading 'waist deep' in an Indian war were regarded as dinosaurs in a world governed by 'shock and awe'.[7]

In the later years of the 1990s the author of this particular phrase, Harlan Ullman of the National Defense University, was already well established as an intellectual guru for neoconservative, imperial strategists. Donald Rumsfeld, Richard Perle and Paul Wolfowitz eagerly embraced the principle that the Vietnam War had wrongly undermined the principle of technological power as a precondition for social and economic reconstruction. Ullman's strategic documents eschewed compromise and persuasion, says Drayton. Instead, they preached the virtue of adversarial 'impotence': namely, that 'one must always inflict brutal reprisals against those who resist' and that 'fear' always leads to 'submission'. As such, they provided the intellectual rationale for the destruction of Iraq's infrastructure in the March bombardment of 2003.[8]

The United States invaded Iraq in 2003 on the basis of a theory rather than a plan. The formulation of that theory proved conclusively, says Charles Krauthammer, that Vietnam was still 'in our heads' and that the Vietnam Syndrome, for good or ill, had not been 'kicked'. The 'war on terror' was a clear indication that after thirty years the memory of failure in Southeast Asia had 'no cure'.[9] Yet failure was the one thing that could not be overcome by military tactics which tried to disinvent it. The lessons of Vietnam were non-negotiable. Martin Jacques puts it succinctly:

> The Vietnamese proved, with extraordinary courage and intelligence that people's war could triumph against the most formidable and frightening odds. The Americans may have possessed awesome weapons, but the Vietnamese commanded the hearts and minds – and eventually even managed to convince the American public that the war could not be won. Their victory was to transform the conduct of American foreign policy for a quarter-century – until the arrival of the Bush regime, which declined to accept the verities of the Vietnamese conflict and preferred to believe that defeat was a consequence of a lack of US military resolve.[10]

Rumsfeld's decision in 2001 to dredge up his country's fears of Vietnam has all the characteristics of his predecessor Robert McNamara who, in rejecting pacification as an operational strategy in Vietnam, elected to fight with massed firepower whenever and wherever he could. McNamara had used the success of conventional military operations in the Ia Drang Valley in November 1965 to justify a huge increase in American ground troops, while General William C. Westmoreland, as Kenneth J. Hagan points out, 'adopted the macabre practice of using "body counts" of dead Vietnamese as the standard of victory'. To the army's campaigns of massed firepower we must add 'the bombing raids of the US Air Force and Navy that began under Lyndon B. Johnson ("Rolling Thunder", 1965–68) and reached a crescendo of barbaric ferociousness with Richard M. Nixon's "Line-backer" raids of 1972'. Hagan concludes his analysis with a prescient anecdote: 'Nixon said at the time of the Easter Offensive: the bastards have never been bombed like they're going to be bombed this time. For once in his life, he was true to his word.'[11]

The bleakness of Rumsfeld's military philosophy of 'slogging our way through Iraq' shows the extent to which the Vietnam war implanted itself 'on the collective brain' of the Bush administration. Even though previous administrations had spent over three decades trying to eliminate its legacy 'from the American memory', war managers like Rumsfeld and Wolfowitz did little to discourage the Iraqi people from believing that the policies and practices of Vietnam, both in the use of firepower and in the treatment of suspect communities, would once again govern the conduct of the American military. Indeed, the removal of Vietnamese peasants from rebel-controlled areas and their forced resettlement in government-controlled strategic hamlets during the 1960s soon found their equi-valent in detention centers like Guantanamo Bay, Cuba. The creation of interrogation centers to house and interview suspected terrorists, a practice known as 'extraordinary rendition', was yet another of those links to the Vietnam War in which local people, innocent as well as guilty, were taken away from their families and homes. America's refusal to understand its failure to pacify insurgent theatres remained a source of inspiration for guerilla movements throughout the Middle East. The source of that inspiration was always Vietnam. Before the invasion of Iraq in 2003 rebellious Shiites in the Baghdad slum of Sadr City were writing 'Vietnam Street' on walls and streets (as in: 'This is called Vietnam Street because this is where we kill Americans').[12]

In Vietnam, the destruction of rural and urban village society and the use of massed firepower proved wholly inadequate as a counterinsurgent strategy. Iraq continued to reinforce this message. In the early stages of the war in Iraq and as the devastating effectiveness of the self-proclaimed strategy of 'shock and awe' was beginning to unfold, Rumsfeld declared: 'The United States doesn't do nation-building.' 'Whatever the precise motivation', says Kenneth J. Hagan, the statement reflected 'the pre-war refusal of the Dept. of Defense to plan for the occupation and governance of Iraq once the Americans destroyed Saddam Hussein's army and political infrastructure'. It also reflected the overwhelming influence which the flawed philosophy of Carl Von Clausewitz had come to exert on the Joint Chiefs of Staff and the higher echelons of the American military during the 1980s (a philosophy which says nothing about what wars mean for postwar policy).[13] As a result, the generic reason for the failure of errand in South Vietnam was repeated almost immediately in Iraq. According to Max Hastings:

> it is impossible to study any informed critique . . . of operations in Iraq without recalling the Vietnam debacle. There, too, most Americans treated ordinary Vietnamese with contempt, whatever their political allegiance. American convoys forced Vietnamese vehicles off the road, killed peasant livestock with impunity, brought down fire on suspected enemy positions heedless of civilians in the target zone, and treated even educated, professional Vietnamese with condescension. All this is being repeated in Iraq, with predictable and identical consequences.[14]

The Puritan heritage

Vietnam is an important point of reference for the war in Iraq.[15] Both wars reveal, what might be called, a failure of civilian understanding as well as a disdain for 'barbarism' and those who live beyond the teachings of His church.[16] We see an early sign of this particular antipathy in Puritan New England. In the journals and sermons of New England theologians, says Linda Colley, fear of the Indians was often synonymous with the threat of kidnap by the Barbary

Corsairs. The terror inspired by the Indian captivity narratives, she argues, was deeply rooted in the stories of capture and abduction 'by the powers of Barbary', particularly for 'the 400,000 or so men and women from Scotland, Ireland, Wales and above all England who crossed the Atlantic in the course of the seventeenth century' and took these stories 'with them'. For early modern Britains, the personality of Indians and Corsairs was interchangeable. Each was a servant of the antichrist and had powers which were derived from the black arts of 'magic and conjuring and trickery'. In this new 'transatlantic' affiliation, Indians and Corsairs were characterized by elusiveness and surprise attack and the ability to materialize at will – personality traits that long outlasted the capacity of either 'to do serious harm'.[17]

The trace or tail of an elusive other can still be detected in contemporary theaters. For the Barbary pirate read the Viet Cong guerilla and for the Viet Cong guerilla read Mohammad Atta leading the attack on the Twin Towers. In Iraq, the radical Islamist, al Zakarwi, is often depicted as a 'wild beast'[18] – the words are those of William Hubbard in describing the fears of English soldiers during The Great Swamp Fight of 1676 – whose followers come without warning to the souks and wreak havoc with their suicide bombs. Indeed, when Donald Rumsfeld refers his audience to the menace of the swamps he impersonates the imperialist hatreds of Puritan theologians like Nathaniel Saltonstall who, in 1676, described New England as 'a Moorish Place, overgrown with Woods and bushes but soft like a Quagmire or Irish Bog'. In his sermon, Saltonstall made explicit the challenge posed by the forces of the antichrist – Islam or Barbary activity – and 'the dismal thickets of America' in which the Narragansetts of King Philip were 'entirely invisible'. The draining of the swamps was the logical fulfillment of the Indian Wars of the seventeenth century and a way of confronting the fear of being 'in swamped'.[19] Wilderness errand (from sea faring to garrison life) created multiple insecurities and the particular anxiety that one was always 'vulnerable to capture'[20]. In subsequent campaigns where the nation went abroad (despite John Quincy Adams' admonition from a later century) 'in search of monsters to destroy', the errand to civilize a degenerate landscape and a dangerous other remained a powerful and seductive force.

In Steven Wright's Vietnam novel, *Meditations in Green*, the ecology that lies beyond the perimeter of the fire support base is a constant threat to the 1069th. As Winehaven says: 'it's not as if the bushes were innocent'. For soldiers like Winehaven who 'stare at the tree line for a while' the movement of nature is progressively forward, 'slow but inexorable, irresistible, maybe finally unstoppable'. Others like Griffin who appear puzzled – 'what movement, what are you talking about!' – are quickly put in their place: 'The trees of course, the fucking shrubs. And one day we'll look up and there they'll be, branches reaching in, jamming our M-60s, curling around our waists.' Sexual paralysis comes to those who stray too near the tree line. This is a sickness the Vietnamese swamp is able to transmit. When Kraft goes missing in the forest, he too becomes paralysed, full of 'helpless amazement', 'obviously useless'.[21] As Philip Caputo puts it in *A Rumor of War*:

> When the helicopters flew off, a feeling of abandonment came over us. Charley Company was now cut off from the outside world. We had crossed a line of departure all right, a line of departure between the known and the unknown. The helicopters had made it seem familiar. Being Americans, we were comfortable with machines, but with the aircraft gone we were struck by the utter strangeness of this rank and rotted wilderness.[22]

This fear of an enemy who becomes invisible in the forest translates, in the work of William Eastlake, into an enduring and essentially American fear. In his novel *The Bamboo Bed* (1969), Eastlake describes an infantry captain who has led his men into a restaging of Custer's last stand:

> Clancy blundered. Clancy blundered by being in Vietnam.... Clancy had blundered by not holding the ridge. Clancy had blundered by being forced into a valley, a declivity in the hills. It was the classic American blunder in Vietnam of giving the Indians cover. The enemy was fighting from the protection of the jungle. You couldn't see them. Americans love the open. Americans do not trust the jungle. The first thing Americans did in America was clear a forest and plant the cities.[23]

In Vietnam, policies of cleansing and eradication denied the need for social contact with the Vietnamese, as well as a knowledge of religious belief, philosophy and religion. When Mary McCarthy visited the country she was given, as she puts it, 'the silent treatment' on her return to the US (as were Susan Sontag, David Dellinger, Daniel Berrigan and Ramsey Clark).[24] In seventeenth-century terms these people had exposed themselves to wilderness contaminants. In New England, the greatest single threat to the moral and political order came not from the Indians but from those who, in the words of Cotton Mather, ran the risk of '*Criolian Degeneracy*'[25] by entering the woods unaccompanied. Settlers who went into the wilderness of their own volition and Indianized themselves were always liable to be denounced as treacherous, for they revived the memory of what Richard Slotkin calls, 'intimacy with the Indians' and had become 'tainted'.[26] One thinks of Joshua Tift, who married an Indian woman and was wounded, captured and hung for treachery, or Thomas Pellow, who converted to Islam (with much embarrassment to English society) after Moroccan corsairs seized him in 1715.

The possibility that the forest might eventually prove more attractive than the errand to civilize it lies at the heart of Puritan paranoia in the United States and in recent wars and wilderness crusades it has become, once again, a resurgent force. Puritan abhorrence at what James Axtell calls 'Indianization'[27] overwhelmed John Walker Lindh, the American Taliban who, in the late 1990s, abandoned his comfortable, middle-class life in Marin County, California, and went to the Yemen to learn Arabic in the religious school of San'a. In the winter of 2001, Lindh was dragged, wounded and bedraggled from the wreckage of a fort near Mazar-I-Sharif in northern Afghanistan. Bearded, filthy, unwashed, covered in scabs and sores, Lindh seemed the direct descendant of Joshua Tift, his moral and physical state an apt symbol of the ruined Qala-e-Janghi fort in which he had taken refuge. Lindh was charged by the US government of fighting for the Taliban. In the coverage of his trial we are continually reminded of those 'white Indians' who integrated with the native population on the early frontier and were considered to be, says James Axtell, 'converts to . . . "savagery" '.[28] Lindh's treatment by the military, the media and the US courts reveals the extent to which 'Indianization' remains a feature of the hatred provoked by those who go on unsanctioned errands into an uncleansed wilderness. With no substantive evidence available that Lindh had had any military involvement with al Qaeda or the Taliban or that he had fired a single shot at the American forces, he was doused in oil, submerged in freezing water, blood and waste, wounded, beaten up, stripped naked, bound with duct tape, blindfolded, placed inside a metal shipping container in a coffin position, interrogated, shipped to the US where he was threatened with the death penalty and loss of citizenship, and then given a twenty-year prison sentence. It is also worth noting that the oil company, Unocal, who continued to do business with the Taliban long after the President had signed an executive order, escaped prosecution. In Afghanistan, the oil monopolies violated the law with impunity since their drive to reap profits was deemed to be in the 'national interest'. Lacking the connections to the Bush administration enjoyed by the executives and their supporters in the Republican Party, Lindh was condemned to imprisonment.[29]

America's fear of the barbarous other was a key feature of Iraqi propaganda in the lead-up to the American invasion of 2003. Mohammed Saeed al Sahaf, the Iraqi information minister under Saddam Hussein, declared that American troops would be lured into 'swamps' from which they would never return. Like most Iraqi strategists, Sahaf had studied America's wilderness adventures in detail. He prophezied that Iraq would quickly be 'another Indochina', with Baghdad a Ho Chi Minh Trail of tunnels and souks. Saddam Hussein's closest adviser, Tariq Aziz, used a similar refrain. 'Let our cities be our swamps and our buildings our jungles', he told the Institute of Strategic Studies in Baghdad, as if to emphasize the historic importance of the marsh as a metaphor for Iraqi resistance. Even Saddam Hussein – notwithstanding his opposition to the Marsh Arabs – had re-affirmed his credentials as an Iraqi nationalist and renounced his role as an American puppet prior to the first Gulf War by flooding the oil wells and the marshes to block the progress of American troops.[30]

Aziz and Sahaf would have been clearly understood in New England where the Puritan divines made a firm distinction between those who journeyed toward spiritual illumination and those who embraced the 'habitations of darkness'.[31] The same applies to Donald Rumsfeld, whose swamp metaphors, in 2003, resonate with all the commemorative energy of a Puritan magistrate driven to celebrate the draining of the swamps at the end of King Philip's War in 1676. Rumsfeld's philosophy, as illustrated during the attacks on Fallujah in April and October 2004, was to turn the city, quite literally, into a swamp. According to Patrick J. McDonnell of the *Los Angeles Times*, the streets were full of 'shattered water and sewage pipes' that left pools of 'sewage-filled water, sometimes knee-deep'.[32] The October assault was deliberately designed to create 'a shattered landscape of gutted build-ings crushed cars and charred bodies'. The journalists Kim Sengupta and Michael Gregory describe how their drive 'through the city revealed a picture of utter destruction, with concrete houses and mosques in ruins, telegraph poles down, power and phone lines hanging slack and rubble and human remains littering the empty streets'. The place, we are told, had been left 'lifeless'.[33]

New environments

'Shock and awe' was a specific attempt to rehabilitate the scorched earth policies of the Vietnam War and the attrition strategy of General William Westmoreland. In Iraq, the battle for Fallujah offered the US military a chance to bury the Vietnam Syndrome and to cleanse a polluted habitat with the purifying fire of the righteous. Fears of entrapment and insurgent rankness underpinned the technology of attrition. When Tim Collins of the Royal Irish called for 'more Malaya and less Vietnam' he was pointedly referring to 'the needless brutality' of the attacks on Fallujah and those eve of battle speeches in which American commanders instructed their troops to think of Hue and the Ia Drang.[34]

The battle plan at Fallujah – in effect, the creation of a free-fire zone in the city – reaffirmed the importance attached to the role of firepower during Vietnam. The virtue of making the city into another Hue and the architectural disasters visited on the old Viet-namese imperial capital were seen as having strategic merit. Those who were – as American commanders put it – in the process of 'making history' had unfinished business to attend to. The levelling of Iraqi towns and cities, like Fallujah, became a central precondition for corporate reconstruction and the building of a society of effi-cient consumers.[35] This was the vision of Westernization that had so appalled Mohammed Atta during the time he lived in Aleppo, Syria. His despair at the violation of the souk and the presence of 'shame-less and greedy kufr intruders' testified to his deep aversion, to what Jonathan Raban calls, the 'tireless self-reinvention' of the modern.[36] This is a common complaint of Islamic militants, including Osama Bin Laden. Speaking on an al Jazeera tape, Bin Laden describes how

Bush embroiled himself in the 'swamps of Iraq' the moment the sight of 'black gold (oil) blurred his vision' and forced him to give 'priority' to corporate agendas over the 'public interests' of his country.[37]

The policy of creating new customized environments as a strategy of social and industrial control was the business mantra that led to the creation of structured environments in South Vietnam. Here, the preferred way of encouraging social behavior was to design environments that contained most of the facilities necessary for their material well-being. The destruction of native habitat was a way of eradicating an unknown landscape. Whether it was the bar, the hotel, the fire support base, the PX store, the hospital, the airport, the metalled road, the strategic hamlet, Cam Ranh Bay, or Saigon itself, South Vietnam came to be regarded by the United States as an insular or self-contained text best understood through familiar products: armed services radio, American television, popular magazines, transistor radios, IBM 1430 computers, M-48 Patton tanks, Coca-Cola bottles, Dial soap, shaving foam. Here we see the secular legacy of what Puritan poet Edward Taylor described as 'beauty in the sanctuary'.[38] Traveling in a C-130, Mary McCarthy overhears the pilot and the co-pilot discuss their 'personal war aim . . . to make a killing, as soon as the war is over, in Vietnamese real estate'.

> From the air, while they kept an eye out for V.C., they had surveyed the possibilities and had decided on Nha Trang – 'beautiful sand beaches' – better than Cam Ranh Bay – a 'desert.' They disagreed as to the kind of development that would make the most money: the pilot wanted to build a high-class hotel and villas, while the copilot thought that the future lay with low-cost housing.

Technology provides a panorama: it gives the pilot a chance to observe the world not as he knows it but as he hopes his clients might come to know it; and to imagine the metamorphosis of wartime killing into a peacetime 'killing' in real estate.[39]

The idea of relating social reconstruction to ecological imperialism is deeply rooted in seventeenth-century colonial life. In the aftermath of King Philip's War the draining of the swamps was seen as a way of controlling the wastelands of Satan and thereby enlarging, what Cotton Mather called, 'the pleasant gardens of Christ'.[40] Jill Lepore describes this war as 'not only the most fatal war in all of American history but also one of the most merciless'. It was, she argues, 'a holy war against barbarism, and a war that never really ended'. 'There is something about King Philip's War that hints of allegory', she adds. 'In other times, in other places, its painful wounds would be reopened, its vicious words spoken again.' Philip's war culminated in The Great Swamp Fight, an event of crucial importance in the making of the American colonial character. It was, claims Lepore, particularly crucial in shaping attitudes to burial and death and in creating a legacy of 'cultural anxieties' that we now associate with wilderness experience and missionary life.[41]

Body parts

The eviction of the Narragansett Indians from the swamps and their deportation to the West Indies typify the anxiety we associate with forced resettlement and the reinvention of local place. In New England, clearance was considered necessary as a pre-condition for physical and spiritual cultivation. This was the reason why, in 1676, King Philip's son was 'sold' into slavery and taken to Tangier. There, he was 'punished to the public's satisfaction' as a terrorist threat, says Jill Lepore, and deported to a place that had long been associated, through the actions of the Barbary Corsairs, with abduction and hijack. For the Puritans there was a delicious irony in having the Indians 'shipped all the way to Africa' and 'sold into captivity' where, as Cotton Mather puts it, no one 'would offer to take them off'. Africa was considered a 'scripturally appropriate' place for a people of 'bloody and dangerous inclination' to experience captivity and a way of life that they, like the Moors, had learned to perfect.[42] Deportation was also synonymous with wilderness clearance; it anticipated the draining of the swamps and the cultivation of wilderness habitat: the very things that lie behind the modern-day practice of 'extraordinary rendition'.

In seventeenth-century New England the idea of embarking on a physical project to overcome public concern grew out of a crisis of confidence in the inability of the state to eliminate the enemy within. In early North America, says Linda Colley, fear of the Indian produced 'captivity panics'.[43] These panic attacks were inflamed when the Indians skinned the settlers 'alive', and mounted their body on totem poles 'as symbols' of victory. If death through stripping, skinning and scalping was a horrific prospect, so was the absence of a decent burial, with bodies left to rot on the ground. A local commentator tells us that after destroying one Englishman, 'the Algonquins strip'd the body of him whom they had slain in the first Onset, and then cutting off his Head, fixed it upon a Pole looking towards his own Land. The Corpse of the Man slain the week before, they dug up out of his Grave, they cut off his Head and one leg, and set them upon Poles, and strip'd off his Winding-sheet.'[44] 'Think upon the miserable captives now in the hands of that brutish adversary', thundered Boston's most prominent clergyman, Cotton Mather, in 1691:

> *Captives* that are every minute looking when they shall be roasted alive, to make a sport and a feast, for the most execrable cannibals; *Captives*, that must endure the most bitter frost and cold, without rags enough to cover their nakedness; *Captives*, that have scarce a bit of meat allow'd them to put into their mouths, but what a dog would hardly meddle with; *Captives*, that must see their nearest relations butchered before their eyes, and yet be afraid of letting those eyes drop a tear.[45]

We are reminded of Cotton Mather's concerns in an article that appeared in the *Guardian* newspaper on 4 March 2005. Sergeant David Phillips, a US soldier from Bravo Company, an infantry unit on patrol in Mosul, is asked to reveal his deepest anxieties about guerrilla warfare. 'I just want to stay alive and go home with all my body parts', says Phillips. In Iraq, Phillips is fearful of death by mutilation – death from suicide bombers and booby traps – a fate visited on American soldiers who find themselves 'in swamps', bogged down in a quagmire from which they fear they cannot break free. Phillips, says the interviewer, speaks for the '150,000 American soldiers in Iraq', each of whom fears death by dismemberment, the same fate that befell the settlers in the Indian Wars.[46]

Iraq brings to life the subliminal fears of Indian warfare. The kidnaps, mutilations and decapitations of aid workers, businessmen, contractors and journalists – Daniel Pearl, Ken Bigley, Margaret Hassan – grotesquely complement the deaths of soldiers who have been blown up and abducted at check points; the gruesome discovery in 2005 at Suwayrah, on the Tigris river, of dozens of bodies without limbs and heads, bloated and badly decomposed. Iraq has been a war against the human body and the sacredness of the human form, as if the Suni and Shia militias and the followers of al Zakarwi feel the need to remind the West of the knowledge they have gained from imperialist conflict.[47]

Fear of swamp entrapment has been a long-standing inspiration for Jihadi warriors in the Middle East. Indeed, there is clear evidence to suggest that guerilla resistance among Sunni Muslims modeled itself to a credible extent on the nationalist tactics of the Vietnamese. During the battle for Fallujah, Abdullah Janabi, the insurgent Sunni leader, could almost have been a Viet Cong guerilla in the battle for Hue. In November 2004 he said of the American forces: 'We have succeeded in drawing them into the quagmire of Fallujah, into the alleys and small pathways. They have fallen into the trap of explosive charges, land mines and, now, the defenders' short supply lines inside the neighborhoods.'[48] In Vietnam, constant exposure to bodily injury and the presence of mines and booby traps – of the kind we have seen on a daily basis in Iraq – severely demoralized US soldiers. 'Dudes got legs shot off and shit, got half their face and gone and shit', notes Charles Strong, US Army machine gunner, while combat paratrooper Arthur E. 'Gere' Woodley Jr says, 'I had never experienced anything quite as horrible as seeing a human being with his face blown apart.' Walter T. Davies describes the soldiers' responses to bodily injury and mutilation as a form of 'abjection', something which 'begins with a terrifying experience of defilement that produces repulsion, repugnance and disgust; a skin-tingling loathing that causes fear, spasms, vomiting, retching, trembling'. In Vietnam, exposure to traumatic injury could trigger a reaction of both profound disorder and aggressive need.[49]

The attempt to counterbalance this heightened sense of vulnerability, says Paloma MacMullen, led many US soldiers to become fixated with 'the body count' (the number of enemy soldiers killed) as a way of creating a semblance of order. The acceptance of the body count and the practice of mutilating enemy bodies, agrees William J. Broyles, were ways of creating artificial targets, of disavowing the vulnerability of the American body by projecting it onto the enemy self. Killings that involved ritualistic practices and extravagant reactions may have been prompted, says Robert Jay Lifton, by the soldiers' desire to 'put their world back in order' especially in a conflict where 'order', such as it was, made little 'sense'.[50] Extravagant violence, as

I have noted elsewhere, was a way of discharging an accumulated surplus of capital. In a war where military engagements were often inconclusive or 'anticlimactic' and the soldiers' energies reduced to a state of constant suspension, the disposal of a reservoir of personal energy took the form of technological demonstrations or shoot-outs. Here, the soldier released his unexpended energies through the use of a 'sacrificial machine' and the igniting of 'excess' need.[51]

In Vietnam the logic of production led to a surfeit of power in which the search for confrontation and climax underpinned expectant needs. The war in Iraq, post-Saddam, resembles this in so far as the military conflict is episodic and characterized by random killing and sporadic violence. The absence of satisfactory resolution, the 'inability to tell friend from foe',[52] the frequency of firefights and ambushes in the alleyways and bazaars, the number of hit-and-run incidents and tactical skirmishes directly contribute to 'the needless brutality' of the American response and the 'thrill of destruction' that young Marines experience when they run amok. As in Vietnam, 'most will harbor within themselves', notes Chris Hedges, 'corrosive feelings of self-loathing and regret' and, in later life, 'an unbridgeable' feeling of 'alienation'.[53] This is the lesson of Vietnam which military theorists and war managers like Donald Rumsfeld refused to heed. Where the enemy is vague and the search for confrontation is thwarted, the 'desire to strike back at somebody, anybody', as W. D. Ehrhart tells us, proves overwhelming.[54]

Donald Rumsfeld takes us on a journey beyond Vietnam and back to New England. In the colonies death by dismemberment was a practice indulged in by settlers and Indians alike, as is witnessed by the practice of decapitation, the collecting of human trophies and the public exhibition of 'butchered flesh'. What came to haunt the colonists more than anything else was the possibility that they were copying the Indians and, over time, degenerating into a form of savagery that no amount of Indian provocation could exonerate. King Philip's War gave rise to a plethora of anxieties about the moral conduct of the Puritan militias, especially their behavior during The Great Swamp Fight and the hacking to pieces of Philip's body. The indiscriminate brutality visited on the Narragansett and the attack on innocent women and children who had 'hidden in the swamp for protection during the war' undoubtedly 'violated', says Jill Lepore, all the known and accepted 'codes of just conduct during warfare'.

Military victory was accompanied by feelings of moral collapse and a loss of 'moorings'. Soldiers failed to discipline themselves in the 'holy war' to which they were committed. So did theologians like William Hubbard and Cotton Mather. Their use of words like 'barbarous' to describe the personality of their enemies inflamed tensions in the field and directly lead to an atmosphere in which 'retributive justice'[55] was regarded as acceptable military practice.

'People who die bad don't stay in the ground'

The genies that came out of the historical bottle in the aftermath of Rumsfeld's vision of a swamp-infested Iraq indicate a lack of closure on the Indian question and raise feelings of self-doubt among those who have questioned their role in the American military. Staff Sergeant Jimmy Massy is a good example. As a twelve-year veteran in the US Marines, Massy was diagnosed with post-traumatic stress and depression after his role in the invasion of Iraq as a member of the 7th Marines Weapons Company. In an interview he talks of the random shooting of Iraqi, including women and children, and the way that US soldiers debased the dead 'all the time'. Massy describes how soldiers 'would be around with charred bodies and sticking cigarettes in their mouths'. Disillusioned, he charged the American military with 'committing genocide', only to be accused by a superior officer of being 'a conscientious objector . . . a wimp'.[56] Massy's accusation was made before the massacre at Haditha on 19 November 2005 when American Marines, in a frenzy of reprisal at the loss of comrades, appeared to have 'suffered', as Sarah Baxter puts it, a 'total breakdown in morality and leadership'.[57] The shooting of innocent civilians at Haditha illustrates the ease with which indiscriminate acts of reprisal can occur in insurgent theatres. Like the siege of Fallujah, Haditha represents a moment in time when the anxiety of errand proved overwhelming for the American military. These atrocities contain echoes of My Lai, an event where the link between frustration and reprisal brings to mind all the horrors of The Great Swamp Fight.[58]

The Bush administration's willingness to re-create fundamentalist war in the belief that they are doing, as Eric Hobsbawm puts it, 'humanity a favour' is redolent with echoes from the colonial era.[59] Brian Jarvis has pointed out that 'when George Bush refers to the

US offensive against terrorism as a "war of Good against Evil", his Manichean metaphors can be traced back . . . to the Puritan crusade against the wonders of the invisible world'. Wars fought under the imprint 'of the Puritan imagination', argues Jarvis, or against un-American or immoral environments run the risk of adding to that cluster of historical anxieties unresolved from previous disputes. The recycling of anxiety through a 'tradition' of metaphor and allegory 'has always been prominent in American cultural history'. It 'derives its force from its appeals to that Calvinistic sense of Innate Depravity and Original Sin'.[60] It is because of the belief in evil and depravity that the Bush administration considers it a legitimate tactic to cast aside the Geneva Convention governing prisoners of wars and to make torture, as Jim Pfiffner has observed, an instrument of public policy.[61] In the so-called 'war on terror' the actions of the state allow for a variety of human rights abuses, from massive encroachments into civil liberties and widespread pre-emptive arrests to the abandonment of due process as an affordable luxury. In a country which legitimates the use of torture as an interrogation technique it becomes almost impossible to supervise, except on a purely symbolic basis, the actions of the military in pursuit of their larger public task.

Fallujah is again a case in point. The military's use of phosphorous on the civilian population in November 2004 was based on what the Bush administration like to call 'anticipatory self-defense'.[62] This resulted in an unofficial death toll of 2000 largely unarmed civilians, the destruction of 36,000 houses, 8400 shops, 60 children's nurseries and schools and 65 mosques and religious sanctuaries. In the siege of Fallujah the dead were buried in the gardens because people could not leave their home, while in some cases, says Jonathan Steele, 'corpses were tied to US tanks and paraded around like trophies'. 'This decade's unforgettable monument to brutality and overkill', he continues, is 'a text book case of how not to handle an insurgency and a reminder that unpopular occupations will always degenerate into desperation and atrocity'.[63] On the few occasions it was willing to investigate the allegation of human rights abuse and war crimes the attitude of the military establishment was very relaxed. The President, in particular, never 'acknowledged his own responsibility for the atrocities committed by Americans on his watch'.[64] On the contrary, he viewed the misdemeanors of his soldiers as simply anomalous, the work of a few 'bad apples' or rogue elements in an otherwise exemplary fighting machine.[65]

In spite of the testimony of soldiers and journalists who have witnessed 'widespread' atrocities and cold-blooded killing, only a handful of American servicemen have been put on trial for acts of murder and actions that have resulted in civilian death. Nor is it likely they will be. The murder of civilians at Haditha and Ishaqi, the abuse and torture of prisoners at Abu Ghraib and Guantanamo, the regular air-strikes by helicopters and F-15 fighters aircraft against civilian targest are, for a significant number of government officials, part and parcel of the normal process of war. Excess is considered acceptable. When abuses do come to light Presidential moralism is an illustration of the level of denial. It 'misses', says Andrew Sullivan, the basic Christian truth 'that even good people can do bad things' when pushed to their limits.[66] Bush's desire to embrace Old Testament thought legitimates torture as a practice that accords with the will of God. It ignores the price that soldiers must pay, as well as their victims, in carrying out the glorious errand that He has willed. James M. Skelly, for example, notes 'an increase in suicides and psychiatric problems' among soldiers in Iraq; that rate of suicide being 'nearly a third higher than the US army's historical average'. This high rate of suicide is matched by the disproportionately high number of soldiers evacuated 'for psychiatric reasons': suicide attempts, post-traumatic stress and self-inflicted injury. His evidence suggests that stress and deprivation are a direct result of 'the significant number of Iraqi civilians that have been killed in questionable circumstances'.[67]

In her book *The National Uncanny: Indian Ghosts and American Subjects* (2000), Renée Bergland relates the fear of physical death and mutilation to what she calls 'spectralization' and its origin in seventeenth-century acts of plunder: especially the violation of native sites such as rivers, forests, swamps and graves. In the aftermath of the Indian wars, she argues, the failure of the ghost to 'rest quiet' in the emerging literature points to an 'incredible discomfort' in the minds of writers at the morality of conquest. For imperialist nations like the US, 'cultural haunting' and the beginning of a process of 'psychic struggle' points to a 'dynamic of unsuccessful repression', one that persists throughout the history of the Republic. What the national literature increasingly tells us is that 'ghosts cannot be buried or evaded, and the spectre of their forced disappearance' will long haunt 'the American nation and the American imagination'.[68]

The idea that ghosts walk abroad to visit on the living the terrors and torments inflicted on the dead is brought home in an article published in *The Observer* newspaper in which a Vietnam veteran, Jack Bissell, returns to Vietnam in 2005 in the company of his son. Bissell was a believer in 'holy war', and, as he puts it, 'the virtue' of bringing 'democracy' to South Vietnam. Injured by a booby trap and the delayed effect of My Lai – the brain remnants, the fragments of skull, the torn bodies 'cut in two by machine-gun fire', the scattered parts strewn on the ground – his life falls apart. The photographs seen by Bissell when he visits the My Lai museum seem to possess a spectral quality: the 'huge blow-ups' a haunting reminder of the destruction for which he has been responsible. It is the son who tries to articulate the grief that is felt by the father. 'I am 29, six years older than my father was when he was wounded', he says. 'Can I really know the young man who went flying through the air, ripped apart by a booby trap? Can I even know this man, still flying, and in some ways still ripped apart? One day my father will be gone, but for *the parts* of him I remember.'[69]

In the work of writers such as Larry Heinemann (*Paco's Story*) and David Rabe (*Sticks and Bones*) the presence of the ghostly is an acute reminder that the Indian wars have yet to be concluded for a nation that refuses to publicly atone for the sins of Vietnam. In Michael Herr's *Dispatches* (1977) the sins of the forest are alive in the jungle. In the Western Highlands Vietnam is suffused with the presence of the 'ghostly' and the horror stories of the New England woods. As Herr puts it: 'the Puritan belief that Satan dwelt in Nature could have been born here, where even on the coldest, freshest mountaintops you could smell jungle and that tension between rot and genesis that all jungles give off'. In *Dispatches*, the power of blackness is projected onto an invisible enemy, one that sees but cannot be seen in a 'ghostly' terrain.[70] Toni Morrison, whose work is profoundly influenced by the Vietnam War, develops the idea of the ghostly as the lietmotif of a culture whose history is riddled with denial. As Ella tells Stamp Paid in the novel, *Beloved* (1987): 'you know as well as I do, people who die bad don't stay in the ground'.[71]

Notes

1. E. Showalter, *Hystories: Hysterical Epidemics and Modern Culture* (London: Picador, 1997), pp. 5, 204.
2. G. W. Bush, 'President Bush on Pearl Harbor', http://rightwingnews.com/speeches/pearl. PLP, April 25, 2005.
3. R. Jensen and R. Mahajan, 'Draining the Swamp of Terrorists', http://www.counterpunch.org/jensen4html, September 24, 2001, and T. Englehardt, 'Tomgram: On "Iraqifying" the Quagmire', http://www.tomdispatch.com2004.
4. 'What are the Consequences of Vietnam?' *Harpers*, April 1985, p. 37.
5. R. Drayton, 'Shock, Awe and Hobbes Have Backfired on America's Neocons', *The Guardian*, December 28, 2005, p. 26.
6. Ibid.
7. J. W. Gibson, *The Perfect War: Technowar in Vietnam* (Boston: The Atlantic Monthly Press, 1986), p. 434.
8. Drayton, 'Shock, Awe and Hobbes', p. 26.
9. C. Krauthammer, 'Let Us Divide and Rule', *The Guardian*, April 21, 2004, p. 23.
10. M. Jacques, 'Iraq Shows the West and its New Liberal Imperialists Have Forgotten the Lessons of History', *The Guardian*, April 19, 2004, p. 15.
11. K. J. Hagan, 'The Counter-Revolutionary Impact of the Vietnam War on American Strategic Thinking, 1973–2005: Clausewitz Reborn', Conference paper, *The Vietnam War, Thirty Years On: Memories, Legacies and Echoes*, The University of Newcastle, NSW, April 2005, p. 8.
12. Enghehardt, 'On "Iraqifying" the Quagmire'.
13. Hagan, 'The Counter-Revolutionary Impact', p. 1.
14. M. Hastings, 'Iraq: The Fatal Divide at the Heart of the Coalition', *The Telegraph*, March 12, 2006, p. 6.
15. W. D. Ehrhart, 'War and Deceit', *New Hampshire Gazette*, April 22, 2005, p. 2; J. Swain, 'Under US fire from Hue to Baghdad', *The Sunday Times*, March 30, 2003, pp. 2–3; M. Woollacott, 'The Region will Wrest Back Control when the US Stumbles out of Iraq', *The Guardian*, December 13, 2005, p. 28; R. McCarthy, 'Go Kick Some Butt and Make History, Vietnam-style, US troops Urged', *The Guardian*, November 9, 2004, p. 3; James Fox, 'Hearts, Minds and Bodybags', *The Guardian*, April 5, 2003, p. 19.
16. G. Monbiot, 'Puritanism of the Rich', *The Guardian*, November 9, 2004.
17. L. Colley, *Captives: Britain, Empire and the World, 1600–1850* (London: Jonathan Cape, 2002), pp. 141, 73, 63.
18. J. Lepore, *The Name of War: King Philip's War and The Origins of American Identity* (New York: Knopf, 1999), p. 85.
19. Ibid., p. 86.
20. Colley, *Captives*, p. 40.
21. S. Wright, *Meditations in Green* (London: Abacus, Sphere books, 1985), p. 278.

22. P. Caputo, *A Rumour of War* (New York: Ballantine, 1977), p. 79.
23. W. Eastlake, *The Bamboo Bed* (New York: Simon and Schuster, 1969), pp. 24–5.
24. M. McCarthy, 'How it Went', *The Seventeenth Degree* (London: Weidenfeld and Nicholson, 1974), p. 4.
25. J. Axtell, *The European and the Indian: Essays in the Ethnohistory of Colonial North America* (Oxford: Oxford University Press, 1982), p. 160.
26. R. Slotkin, *Regeneration through Violence: The Mythology of the American Frontier: 1600–1860* (Middletown, Conn: Wesleyan University Press, 1973), p. 126.
27. Axtell, *The European and the Indian*, pp. 247–81.
28. Ibid., p. 279.
29. J. M. Spectar, 'To Ban or Not to Ban an American Taliban? Revocation of Citizenship and Statelessness in a Statecentric System', *California Western Law Review*, Vol. 39, No. 2 (Spring 2003), pp. 263–302; J. Borger, 'Bright Boy from the California Suburbs Who Turned Taliban Warrior', *The Guardian*, October 5, 2002, p. 3; A. Sullivan, 'Parallel Lives', *The Sunday Times News Review*, December 16, 2001, pp. 1–2; Timothy Bancroft-Hinchey, 'Afghanistan – Oil not Terrorism', http://English.pravda.ru/usa/2001/11/10/20560.html.
30. Fox, 'Hearts, Minds and Bodybags'.
31. Lepore, *The Name of War*, p. 86.
32. Quoted in Englehardt, 'On "Iraqifying the Quagmire".'
33. Kim Segupta, 'A Hollow Victory', *The Independent*, November 15, 2004, p. 4.
34. J. Beattie, 'British Troops Risk New Vietnam', *Evening Standard*, October 18, 2004, p. 4.
35. J. Klein, 'The Multibillion Robber the US Calls Reconstruction', *The Guardian*, June 26, 2004, p. 22.
36. J. Raban, 'Rebels With a Cause', *The Guardian*, April 3, 2002, p. 4.
37. See http://cnn.worldnews.printthis.clickability.com. February 11, 2004.
38. P. Caldwell, *The Puritan Conversion Narrative: The Beginnings of American Expression* (Cambridge: Cambridge University Press, 1983), p. 74.
39. M. McCarthy, *Vietnam* (London: Weidenfeld and Nicholson, 1967), p. 31.
40. P. N. Caroll, *Puritanism and the Wilderness: The Intellectual Significance of the New England Frontier, 1629–1700* (New York: Columbia University Press, 1969), p. 125.
41. Lepore, *The Name of War*, pp. xiii, 175.
42. Ibid., p. 170.
43. Colley, *Captives*, p. 167.
44. Lepore, *The Name of War*, p. 81.
45. Colley, *Captives*, p. 147.
46. Rory Carroll, 'I Just Want to Go Home With All My Body Parts', *The Guardian*, March 4, 2005, p. 7.
47. Rory Carroll, 'Mystery of Iraq's Alleged Oasis of Death', *The Guardian*, April 25, 2005, p. 12.

48. A. Shadid, 'Troops Move to Quell Insurgency in Mosul', *Washington Post Foreign Service*, November 17, 2004, www.washingtonpost.com.
49. For a discussion of these issues and texts, see P. MacMullen, 'Body Wounds and Wounded Bodies', in *Corporeal Territories: The Body in American Narratives of the Vietnam War*, unpublished PhD, University of Nottingham (May 2004), pp. 98–156. I am indebted to MacMullen's analysis of 'abjection'.
50. Ibid., pp. 179, 186.
51. P. H. Melling, *Vietnam in American Literature* (Boston: Twayne, 1990), pp. 142–3.
52. J. M. Skelly, 'Iraq, Vietnam and the Dilemmas of United States Soldiers', *Open Democracy*, www.opendemocracy.net, May 25, 2006, p. 4.
53. C. Hedges, 'On War', *The New York Review*, December 16, 2004, pp. 8–9.
54. Ehrhart, 'War and Deceit', p. 2.
55. Lepore, *The Name of War*, pp. 173, 178, 179, 175 and 169. See also Slotkin, *Regeneration Through Violence*, p. 143, and Axtell, *The European and the Indian*, p. 311.
56. N. Saulnier, 'The Marine's Tale: "We killed 30 Civilians in Six Weeks. I Felt We Were Committing Genocide" ', *The Independent on Sunday*, May 23, 2004, p. 9.
57. S. Baxter, 'America's Shame', *The Sunday Times*, June 4, 2006, 2G, p. 19.
58. Quoted in Melling, *Vietnam in American Literature*, p. 22.
59. E. Hobsbawm, 'America's Imperial Delusion', *The Guardian*, June 16, 2003, p. 16.
60. B. Jarvis, *Cruel and Unusual: Punishment and US Culture* (London: Pluto, 2004), pp. 252–3.
61. J. P. Pfiffner, 'Torture as Public Policy', *Public Integrity*, Vol. 7, No. 4 (Fall 2005), pp. 313–30.
62. Jarvis, *Cruel and Unusual*, p. 252.
63. J. Steele and D. Jamail, 'This is our Guernica', *The Guardian*, April 27, 2005, p. 25.
64. A. Sullivan, 'The Horrors Really Are Your America Mr. Bush', *The Sunday Times*, June 4, 2006, p. 7.
65. R. Cornwell, 'If You Want to Find Where the Rot in the US military Begins, Go Right to the Top', *The Independent on Sunday*, June 4, 2006.
66. Sullivan, 'The Horrors Really Are Your America Mr. Bush', p. 7.
67. Skelly, 'Iraq, Vietnam, and the Dilemmas of United States Soldiers', p. 4.
68. R. Bergland, *The National Uncanny: Indian Ghosts and American Subjects* (Dartmouth: University of New England Press, 1988), pp. 1, 2, 5.
69. T. Bissell, 'Return to Tuy Phuoc', *The Observer*, April 3, 2005, p. 16.
70. M. Herr, *Dispatches* (London: Picador, Pan Books, 1982), pp. 79, 95.
71. T. Morrison, *Beloved* (New York: Knopf, 1987), p. 188.

8
After the Wars are Over: 'Lost Cause,' 'Noble Cause,' National Unity and the Presidency

Jon Roper

In February 1924, Harriet Eleanor Fay, from Savannah, Georgia, died at the age of 94 in Boston. A little over three months later, her great-grandson was born. Both he and his son, born in 1946, became President of the United States. For in 1859, the same year that John Brown launched his raid on Harper's Ferry, Fay, a Southerner, had married a Northerner, the Reverend James Smith Bush, from Rochester, New York. Ninety years and three generations of their family later, George H. W. Bush was living in Texas, at that time still racially segregated, and his son, raised there, would become Governor of the former Confederate state before moving to the White House. Indeed, George W. Bush, more so than his father, could claim to be the first representative from Abraham Lincoln's party whose political career was forged in the South and who became President.

The Civil War is a seminal event in American history. Today, at five generations distance, its impact on American politics, society and culture remains profound. It has been felt not least upon the Presidency itself. No veteran of the Confederate armies ever occupied the White House. Moreover, for almost a century, from the administrations of Andrew Johnson to Lyndon Johnson, the gene pool from which the Chief Executive was elected was restricted – apart from Woodrow Wilson – to those born outside those states which had seceded from the Union.

For the defeated South, the reconstruction of its history was as important as its preservation. Even now, naming the conflict that consumed the nation reflects a particular persuasion: to refer to the

143

war of northern aggression may be politically incorrect outside the former Confederacy, but can be acceptable to certain groups within it. How, indeed, should war be remembered? For the South, the idea of the 'Lost Cause' gained currency soon after its defeat and was further inflated after the death, in 1870, of Robert E. Lee, whose memory was preserved as its foremost exemplar. Moreover, its premise – that the war had been one in which the South had fought honourably, indeed heroically, in defence of states' rights and in which the issue of the abolition of slavery, the achievement of emancipation and the prospect racial equality might be ignored – became part of a conservative rhetoric of national reconciliation on both sides of the Mason–Dixon line, accepted by Republican and Democrat Presidents alike as the political price of re-union.

In another sense, however, the South, after Appomattox, remained a place apart within the United States. A symbol of the enduring racial divide within American society, the 'Lost Cause' also represented a refusal to engage with an alternative narrative. The Civil Rights movement, gathering momentum in the 1950s, was the expression of a competing historical memory, in which the Civil War should be interpreted as the struggle to overcome the fault-line of slavery, and emancipation should be regarded as a step towards the recognition of constitutionally protected racial equality. It was Lyndon Johnson, the first President to be elected from a former Confederate state (Woodrow Wilson, although born in the South, had made his political career in New Jersey), who understood the importance of this narrative of the Civil War in the context of Civil Rights, and who proved no longer prepared to tolerate that which his predecessors, from the time of Lincoln, had largely ignored.

At the same time, a hundred years after Appomattox, President Johnson deepened the involvement of the United States in another war: Vietnam. Longer than the Civil War, but with far fewer American casualties, it too has shaped contemporary American politics, society and culture. Thus far, since American involvement ended in 1975, for example, no Vietnam veteran has been elected to the presidency. The war remains a controversial piece of political baggage. When those among the 'Vietnam generation' have run for the White House, they have been subject to forensic questioning about what they did to avoid serving (Bill Clinton) or what they did while fighting (John Kerry).

In its aftermath, too, interpretations of the significance of the Vietnam War emerged that, like those shaping the Civil War in American memory, had implications for both national politics and Presidential power. The 'Vietnam Syndrome,' expressed in terms of a public debate that questioned whether the nation should seek military solutions to political problems, was initially a restraint on the capacity of the President to commit American forces overseas. By the 1980s, however, neoconservatives came to see it as a constraint on the President's capacity to act as Commander-in-Chief, and something that should be 'overcome.' A revisionist view of the war, reminiscent of that which took place in the South after Appomattox, placed its emphasis on the qualities of those who fought in Southeast Asia rather than the reasons why America engaged its forces there and focused on the recovery of morale and military honour as part of a process of rebuilding national prestige and Presidential power.

The moulding of historical memory in the South after the Civil War, and in the nation following the Vietnam War thus involves confrontations with a contested political terrain, in which Presidents have chosen to emphasize particular views of the conflicts. Their preferred styles of remembrance have something in common: they allow the defeated South and the defeated nation to recover self-esteem in the interests of creating national unity. Most vividly expressed after the Civil War as the South's 'Lost Cause' and after Vietnam as the nation's 'Noble Cause,' this rhetoric concentrated upon the rehabilitation of a sense of military honour at the expense of engaging with more complex, and ultimately more enduring, issues that might be drawn from these experiences of war – and defeat.

The importance of honour

In his Message on Constitutional Ratification, sent to its Congress on 29 April 1861, the Confederacy's President, Jefferson Davis, had said, 'We protest solemnly in the face of mankind, that we desire peace at any sacrifice, save that of honor.'[1] When peace came as a result of its military defeat, was the South's honour compromised? Following the initial trauma of defeat, southerners refused to accept that its armies might have suffered such ignominy. John Grammer points out: ' "We have lost all but honor," southerners told one another repeatedly in the years after the surrender: exactly what they had expected to lose, and to keep.'[2] How, then, did the former Confederacy manage to recover and to hold on to its sense of honour? The answer lay in its selective memory: preferring to focus on the conduct of its armies during the war rather than discussing why it had been necessary to fight it. Indeed, defeat could be a rallying point, creating a sense of the South as a place apart but united by its remembrance of its preferred version of its history. The nation colluded in the South's enterprise as a path to reconciliation. It suited both the former Confederacy and the Union to mould memories in ways that preserved the region's sense of its military honour. For the combatants, indeed, popular impressions of the war's conclusion at Appomattox were articulated in a way that allowed those who had experienced the trauma of defeat to salvage that which Davis had argued was essential to the South's self-respect.

A century later, Lyndon Johnson framed America's commitment to Vietnam in language that would have been familiar to his grandfather's generation. Ronnie Dugger quotes the President as arguing that 'Our course (in Vietnam) is charted always by the compass of honor,' and points out that in expressing himself in this way he 'was carrying forward his own intense regional experience of an ideal norm that is little examined, but nationally accepted.'[3] Indeed, in a similar rhetorical style, it was his successor, Richard Nixon, one of whose family died at Gettysburg, who claimed for the nation a 'peace with honor' as America withdrew its forces from Vietnam.

Yet honour, as a principle for action and as a value to be preserved, is validated by military success and threatened by failure. The reality of the Vietnam War for the United States was the experience of defeat and an initial reaction was to ignore what had happened. In its immediate aftermath, as William Gibson suggests, 'it is necessary to remember the *repression* of the war . . . its strange absence from national life.'[4] As in the South after the Civil War, the initial sense of loss of military honour and the erosion of national self-esteem contributed to a temporary sense of cultural dislocation that appeared pervasive.

For Richard Polenberg, writing in 1980, 'the war in Vietnam produced . . . fragmentation, alienation, confrontation, what the editors of *Time* would call "the loss of a working consensus, for the first time in our lives, as to what we think America means." '[5] And just as post-Civil War Reconstruction initially highlighted rather than resolved political differences between North and South, so post-Vietnam politics in America was marked by ideological polarization between liberals and conservatives. Such parallels – even affinities – that may be detected can only be pressed so far. But in this context, a common aftershock of both the Civil War and the Vietnam War was the political trauma of Presidential impeachment.

There are thus inherent difficulties in dealing with the aftermath of divisive conflicts and defeats. So how does a Civil War come to an end? This is the Confederate General James Longstreet's subsequent recollection of the surrender at Appomattox. He was one of those involved in working out the terms of capitulation and so he went to the Union Army Headquarters. There 'General Grant looked up, recognized me, rose, and with his old-time cheerful greeting gave me his hand, and after passing a few remarks offered a cigar, which was gratefully received.'[6] For Longstreet and for Grant, this had been a war of principles and values, a clash of profoundly antagonistic cultures. But it had been fought by men who had sometimes known each other as pre-war career soldiers in the regular army; who shared not only cigars but a common military heritage and who were prepared to respect one another on that basis. Longstreet's memoirs, however, in common with those of his former adversary's, have a political context. In his case they were written at a time when, to many Southerners, he had proved himself a turncoat by supporting the Republican party of his old friend, Grant. His military reputation – and in particular his conduct at the crucial battle of Gettysburg – made him a target and he was attacked as part of a campaign to absolve Lee from responsibility for that defeat in order to turn him into the paragon and symbol of the South's 'Lost Cause.' Yet Longstreet makes his own contribution to that myth by emphasizing the military camaraderie that dissipated former antagonisms.

When Longstreet saw him, Grant had already met Lee – the Confederate commander in his new dress uniform, resplendent in defeat as Grant, in his mud-spattered battle-dress was scruffy in victory – but despite such contrasting appearances, they came together as equals: a point Grant was careful to make in his remembrance of the moment of surrender. 'We spoke of old friends in the army. I remembered having seen Lee in Mexico.' The Confederate commander had been superior to Grant in rank at that time, and might not have been expected to recall him. 'But he said he remembered me very well.

We talked about old times and exchanged inquiries about friends.' The message of such recollections is clear: if both sides followed the example of their commanders in the field, the war could end without recrimination and animosity. In Grant's account of the events at Appomattox, there is also the sense of old comrades meeting and talking amicably about past and recent battles. Among the 'various officers' who came in, some 'were old friends – Longstreet and myself for instance, and we had a general talk.' In such convivial surroundings, military formalities could be forgotten. 'Lee no doubt expected me to ask for his sword, but I did not want his sword. It would only have gone to the Patent Office to be worshipped by the Washington Rebels.'[7] Grant, reminiscing after he had left the White House in 1877, saw it as important to shape this moment of southern capitulation not as an ending in itself, but instead as an opening to a future of reconciliation and national unity.

Following the surrender, Lee gave his last order to his army. They had 'been compelled to yield to overwhelming numbers and resources.' In returning home, his defeated – and depleted – forces 'will take with you the satisfaction that proceeds from the consciousness of duty faithfully performed.' His troops had done everything he might have asked of them, and he bid them all 'an affectionate farewell.'[8] Symbolic events such as Lee's meeting with Grant, the formal process of surrender, and Lee's farewell to his army, as they were couched by the participants in the language of military honour and heroic gesture, thus set the tone of a style of remembrance. They allowed defeat not to be accompanied by a sense of failure, and victory to be tempered with a sense of respect. From the moment of defeat, the South's military leaders would still interpret theirs as an honourable cause. Moreover, similar sentiments were shared among those who had spent the war on the other side of the Mason–Dixon line.

In the immediate aftermath of Appomattox, Horace Greeley, the editor of the *New York Tribune*, who, as a presidential candidate in 1872 would strongly advocate the path of national reconciliation, thus described Lee's conduct in almost lyrical terms:

> The Rebellion had failed and gone down; but the Rebel Army of Virginia and its commander had *not* failed. Fighting sternly against the Inevitable – against the irrepressible tendencies, the

generous aspirations of the age – they had been proved unable to succeed where success would have been a calamity to their children, to their country, and the human race. And, when the transient agony of defeat had been endured and had passed, they all experienced a sense of relief; as they crowded around their departing chief, who, with streaming eyes, grasped and pressed their outstretched hands, at length finding words to say, 'Men, we have fought through the War together. I have done the best that I could for you.' There were few dry eyes among those who witnessed the scene; and our soldiers hastened to divide their rations with their late enemies, now fellow-countrymen, to stay their hunger until provisions from our trains could be drawn for them.[9]

Northerners were prepared to regard their former adversaries as military equals. By 1884, Oliver Wendell Holmes Jr, who had served in the Union army throughout the conflict, gave a Memorial Day Address in which he characterised 'the generation that carried on the war' – Southerners as well as Northerners – as being 'set apart by its experience.' In his memorable phrase, 'in our youth our hearts were touched with fire.'[10] Similarly, Theodore Roosevelt, who as President appointed Holmes to the Supreme Court, saw the Civil War as an epic tale of American heroism on both sides. He emphasized that perspective in the book he co-authored with Henry Cabot Lodge, whose title, *Hero Tales from American History* (1895), made its theme explicit. Roosevelt's prose style was appropriate to his subject matter. During the Civil War, he wrote, 'countless deeds of heroism were performed by Northerner and by Southerner, by officer and by private, in every year of the great struggle. The immense majority of these deeds went unrecorded, and were known to few beyond the immediate participants. Of those that were noticed it would be impossible even to make a dry catalogue in ten such volumes as this.' Fourteen of the twenty-six chapters of the book were devoted to accounts of significant events and vignettes of important participants in the Civil War, including Roosevelt's appreciation of Stonewall Jackson – 'one of the ablest of soldiers and one of the most upright of men.'[11] For Roosevelt and for Lodge – whose grandson would become America's ambassador to South Vietnam in 1963 – the Civil War was to be remembered as the best example of American heroic military endeavour rather than a struggle over the abolition of slavery and the promotion of racial equality.

This desire to allow the Confederacy its 'peace with honour' – a phrase that would gain even greater political resonance over a century later as America sought to disengage its forces from the war in Vietnam – thus formed the context of portrayals of the ending of military hostilities and in the South the subsequent shaping of the 'Lost Cause.' As Reconstruction faltered, Northerners tacitly agreed that the recovery of honour was potentially more productive as a spur to national reconciliation than the promotion of racial equality. The significance of slavery as a cause of the War was lost from sight. Instead the conflict became an account of the struggle between Union courage and persistence and Confederate heroism and resilience. Grant, the first elected President after Lincoln, together with many of his contemporaries, as well as the generation that succeeded them, came to accept this as the price of a lasting peace: recognition that the South's sense of honour ultimately could only be recovered and expressed as part of its distinctive cultural identity. The Confederacy, which had been defeated in the war, emerged victorious in the battles over how the conflict was to be remembered. Yet this mechanism that sought to promote reconciliation paradoxically re-inforced the idea of the South as a place apart and the political consequence was that the rest of the country was largely content to let the region go its own way.

On the other hand, there were those black leaders like Frederick Douglass who realized that the myth of the 'Lost Cause' would, if accepted as the dominant interpretation of the South's ambition, deny the validity of an alternative narrative that emphasized progress from emancipation towards a national acknowledgement of the need for racial equality.

To argue against the myth of southern history was to prove a lengthy struggle. As David Blight observes, Douglass, in his speech at a banquet in 1883 to celebrate the twentieth anniversary of the Emancipation Proclamation, and at a time when the Supreme Court was about to hand down the first in a series of decisions which would legitimize segregation in the South, pointed out that 'justice and liberty for blacks . . . had lost ground from "the hour that the loyal North . . . began to shake hands over the bloody chasm." ' The phrase Douglas used echoed that of Horace Greeley in his 1872 Presidential campaign against Grant. Blight goes on to suggest that 'Douglass hoped that Union victory, black emancipation, and the Civil War amendments would be so deeply rooted in recent American experience, so central to any conception of national regeneration, so necessary to the postwar society that they would become sacred values, ritualized in memory.'[12] Yet such was the desire for national unity that Douglass would not live to see his interpretation of the significance of the Civil War and the potential of the North's victory translated into political substance. The South remained a region defined by the war and the nation felt the consequences, no more so than in terms of the impact of its influence on the Presidency.

The post-Appomattox Presidency

It is a familiar enough story. Within a week of Appomattox, President Lincoln had been assassinated. By 1868, the constitutional pendulum had swung away from the Presidency as the Congress reacted against the powers that had been assumed by Lincoln during the war. Political gridlock between the legislature and the executive culminated in the Congressional attempt to impeach his successor, Andrew Johnson. The President survived by a single vote.

Thereafter, Presidents grappled with the issues raised by re-union and Reconstruction. In the election of 1868, helped by Republican votes in the South, Grant was the first veteran from the Union Army to translate his military command into political power. After his two terms in office ended with a widespread feeling that his political acumen had not matched his military leadership – his subsequent attempt to run for a third term in 1880 would be resisted by his party – in 1876 another Republican, Rutherford B. Hayes, defeated Samuel Tilden. The outcome of this centennial election was, however, as controversial as that of the election of 2000. It was influenced decisively by the politics of Reconstruction and the influence of the South. Hayes won after an Electoral Commission established by Congress decided, on partisan lines, and with the critical support of Joseph Bradley, one of the its members from the Supreme Court, to award him disputed electoral votes in South Carolina, Louisiana and Florida – all still under military occupation at the time. Southerners in Congress threatened a filibuster that would have exacerbated the electoral crisis. But they also saw political advantages in allowing

Hayes to take office. Shortly after he became President, federal troops who had remained in Southern states were recalled.

If Douglass was ever hopeful that his alternative historical construction of the significance of the war was to predominate, from then on he fought a losing battle. As *The Nation* correctly prophesized after Hayes' election: 'the negro will disappear from the field of national politics. Henceforth, the nation, as a nation, will have nothing more to do with him.' [13] Reconstruction was effectively at an end. So too was Republican political influence in the former Confederacy. As the 'Lost Cause' gained historical traction, the region, dominated now by white conservative Democrats who would not vote for the party of Lincoln, continued to define itself in fundamentally different cultural and political terms than the nation as a whole. At the same time, just as Northerners were prepared to accept the South's interpretation of its defeat as the cost of national reconciliation, so too did they demonstrate that a cocoon of racism permeated the fabric not only of southern society. In 1896, the Supreme Court ruling in *Plessy* v. *Ferguson*, in which Joseph Bradley – from New York – concurred, legitimized practices of racial discrimination under the ironic phrase – 'separate but equal,' in which only one half of the equation was an accurate description.

By 1901, President Theodore Roosevelt, anxious for America to project its power on the world stage, was arguing not only that national reunion had been achieved, but that the veterans of those volunteer armies that had fought the Civil War were examples to the generation that might now have to fight America's foreign battles. In his first annual message to Congress he claimed:

> We are now indeed one Nation, one in fact as well as in name; we are united in our devotion to the flag which is the symbol of national greatness and unity; and the very completeness of our union enables us all in every part of the country, to glory in the valor shown alike by the sons of the North and the sons of the South in the times that tried men's souls.

Roosevelt's reference to Thomas Paine is an obvious attempt to link the Civil War with the struggle for national independence and the Revolutionary War. But he also uses his interpretation of the past as a patriotic exhortation to the nation to participate, if asked, in future military commitments:

> In any serious crisis the United States must rely for the great mass of its fighting men upon the volunteer soldiery who do not make a permanent profession of the military career; and whenever such a crisis arises the deathless memories of the Civil War will give to Americans the lift of lofty purpose which comes to those whose fathers have stood valiantly in the forefront of the battle.[14]

Despite such protestations of unity, however, the fact remained that the South, left to itself, had been effectively excluded from the office that Roosevelt held. At the time of his speech, no Southerner since Zachary Taylor in 1848 had been elected to the White House. No former Confederate soldier ever ran for executive office in the Federal Government. After 1865 it was the veterans of the Union Army who – naturally – moved into national politics. Following Grant, for over thirty years, apart from Grover Cleveland, each President until William McKinley – the last president to be elected in the nineteenth century – had served in the Union Army. In party political terms, moreover, after 1872, it soon became apparent that while Republicans could win the White House without the Electoral College votes of the South, a Democrat – and until 1912 only Grover Cleveland from New York managed the feat – could only become President if in addition to the South they could win some Northern states.

The White House was thus not a place for Southerners whether they had fought for the Confederacy or not. The exception in the century after Gettysburg was Woodrow Wilson. Born in Virginia in 1856, he grew up in the Confederacy and in states occupied by federal troops after the war, living in Georgia, then the Carolinas before going north to Princeton in 1875. His law degree was from Virginia, and he practised in Atlanta before enrolling for his doctoral degree in 1883 at the newly opened Johns Hopkins University in Baltimore. Thereafter, however, his academic and political career was forged in the north, at Princeton and as Governor of New Jersey. His southern roots helped him to the White House to the extent that in the presidential election of 1912 he gained an outright majority of the popular vote only in the eleven states of the former Confederacy. His comfortable Electoral College victory was accounted for by the fact that he won a plurality elsewhere, when the votes were shared with his two principal opponents, the incumbent, Taft, for the Republicans, and the former president, Theodore Roosevelt, running as a Progressive. Wilson thus gained the White House as a result of a unique set of political circumstances that enabled him to win the election with a minority of the popular vote. He retained it four years later in a more straightforward contest against the Republican, Charles Hughes, but even so his most decisive margins of victory in the popular vote still came from the former Confederacy.

As President, Wilson attended reunion events and gatherings of Confederate and Union veterans. On 4 July 1913, he delivered an address at Gettysburg to an audience that included survivors from both sides to mark the fiftieth anniversary of the battle. In his remarks, Wilson emphasized the themes of reconciliation, heroic sacrifice and national unity that had by then become the standard expressions of Presidential rhetoric about the Civil War:

> How wholesome and healing the peace has been! We have found one another again as brothers and comrades in arms, enemies no longer, generous friends rather, our battles long past, the quarrel forgotten – except that we shall not forget the splendid valor, the manly devotion of the men then arrayed against one another, now grasping hands and smiling into each other's eyes.... We are made by these tragic, epic things to know what it costs to make a nation – the blood and sacrifice of multitudes of unknown men lifted to a great stature in the view of all generations by knowing no limit to their manly willingness to serve.[15]

The President celebrates the battle as an event, rather than, as Frederick Douglass would have wished, reflecting on the reasons why it took place.

In 1914, on two occasions within one week, the first a service marking Memorial Day for the Grand Army of the Republic and the second, participating in the unveiling of a monument to Confederate soldiers at Arlington National Cemetery in Virginia, Wilson again talked about the Civil War. Tailoring his message to his particular audiences, he suggested to the Northern veterans that 'nobility exists in America without patent ... we have a house of fame to which we elevate those who are the noble men of our race, who, forgetful of themselves, study and serve the public interest, who have the courage to face any number and any kind of adversary.' If the veterans were noble, then so might be their cause – the expression that one of his successors, Ronald Reagan, three years old when Wilson spoke those words, would use in attempting to define America's war in Vietnam. A few days later at the ceremony for the South, the President had another message. 'My privilege is this . . . To declare this chapter in the history of the United States is now closed and ended, and I bid you turn with me your faces to the future, quickened by the memories of the past, but with nothing to do with the contests of the past, knowing, as we have shed our blood upon opposite sides, we now face and admire one another.'[16] There was, however, nothing to be admired about Jim Crow.

In 1917, speaking about the war at another meeting of former Confederate soldiers, Wilson was still using the rhetoric of noble endeavour and national unity rather than that of emancipation:

> I suppose that, as you mix with one another, you chiefly find these to be days of memory, . . . and I dare say you are thrilled as you remember the heroic things that were then done. You are glad to remember that heroic things were done on both sides, and that men in those days fought in something like the old spirit of chivalric gallantry. There are many memories of the Civil War that thrill along the blood and make one proud to have been sprung of a race that could produce such bravery and constancy. . . . I believe that one of the things that contributes satisfaction to a reunion like this, . . . is that this is also a day of oblivion. There are some things that we have thankfully buried, and among them are the great passions of division which once threatened to rend this nation in twain. . . . And one of the things that will thrill this country as it reads of this reunion is that it will read also of a rededication on the part of all of us to the great nation which we serve in common.[17]

Wilson, like Roosevelt before him, helped to establish the Presidency in the twentieth century as the fulcrum of the American political system, exercising leadership and initiative in a manner reminiscent of Lincoln's time. As a Southerner who proved electorally acceptable to the nation as a whole, he managed to transcend the sectional divide that had characterized presidential politics for the previous half century.

After Wilson, nobody born in the former Confederacy occupied the White House until Lyndon Johnson, in 1964. And it was only during his presidency that the historical narrative that Frederick Douglass had hoped would drown out the interpretation of the Civil War expressed in the 'Lost Cause' found its political voice at last answered in the President's commitment to the cause of Civil Rights. In 1965, a hundred years after Appomattox, and speaking at the White House on the anniversary of Lincoln's birthday, Johnson argued that 'Each generation of Americans stands charged, before the court of history, to answer the challenge of Lincoln to the American will and to the American heart... he challenges us to enlarge the liberties of our people... That is my goal as the leader of this Nation, and I believe it should be the goal of Lincoln's America.'[18] Yet the previous year, when Johnson had signed the Civil Rights Act as one of the landmark achievements of his administration, he had accelerated the pace of partisan political change across the South. The Democrats who had ignored the party of Lincoln now rejected the party of Johnson. A little over a quarter of a century later, the Republicans, with the Bush family as its most prominent leaders, had replaced the Democrats in Johnson's home state of Texas. At the same time, the United States was experiencing the continuing political and cultural aftershocks of the war that Johnson had pursued: Vietnam.

The legacy of Vietnam

In the aftermath of the Civil War, for Edward Alfred Pollard, 'Defeat has not made "all our sacred things profane." The war has left the South its own memories, its own heroes, its own tears, its own dead. Under these traditions, sons will grow to manhood, and lessons sink deep that are learned from the lips of widowed mothers.'[19] The South's sense of its distinctive military history, forged during the time of the Confederacy, lasted through the generations that followed and impacted upon Southern attitudes to later wars.

One of the main characters in *Fields of Fire* (1978), James Webb's novel about the Vietnam War, is a Southerner, significantly named Robert Lee Hodges. He comes from a family steeped in the South's military tradition and whose members served in the Confederate army. Each subsequent generation fought in one of America's wars. As Hodges is about to leave for Vietnam, he is thus 'offering himself on the altar of his culture . . . there was Vietnam, and so there would be honour. It was the fight, not the cause, that mattered.' It was his duty to serve 'for honour (and a whisper saying, for the South).'[20] He dies in Vietnam, but by the end of the novel, his son, living with his Japanese mother in Okinawa, has inherited this Southern sense of the importance of military duty. Webb, like his fictional character, is a Southerner and a Vietnam veteran who went on to serve in the Department of Defense during Ronald Reagan's administration.

In an article published fifteen years after the end of the war in Southeast Asia, Gaines Foster observed that 'a comparison of the South's experience with defeat and America's emerging response to its loss of the war in Vietnam may be helpful.'[21] Like the Civil War, Vietnam is a war that is a cultural reference point for the generations that live with its legacy. Observing similarities between the two conflicts, particularly in terms of the Confederacy's collapse and the nation's failure, seems an obvious way of providing a context for discussions of its impact on American society. For over thirty years the United States has had to confront the reality and the burden of its defeat in Vietnam. But unlike the ending of the Civil War, there were no remembrances of cigars being handed around as part of an attempt to salvage military honour.

In his analysis of what had gone wrong for the military in Vietnam, therefore, Colonel Harry Summers began by recounting an observation he had made to his Vietnamese military counterpart after the war. 'You know you never defeated us on the battlefield.' The Vietnamese reply was succinct: 'That is true, but it is also irrelevant.'[22] Summers went on to develop a thesis that explained how interfering politicians and lack of domestic commitment to the war had prevented the American military achieving the victory of which it was undoubtedly capable. This version of the 'stab in the back' as a way of rationalizing defeat allows the military to rebuild its morale and, as Foster Gaines points out, it 'resembles the South's interpretation of defeat in the Civil War. The South, too, insisted upon the morality, nobility, and heroism of its cause and so celebrated its efforts in the war that Southerners came to perceive their defeat almost as military victory.'[23]

The attraction of finding America's failure is America's fault is polit-ically appealing. Since Vietnam, successive American presidents have had to grapple with the need to re-establish national self-esteem and a sense of military honour if they wish once again to project American military power abroad. The 'Vietnam Syndrome' – and the under-standable public reluctance to support the commitment of American military forces overseas in the aftermath of defeat – initially could be seen as a salutary restraint on actions that might be the product of what Senator William J. Fulbright famously described as the 'arrog-ance of power.' But it could also be regarded as a constraint on America's ability to take military action in support of its foreign policy objectives and thus ultimately on presidential power itself. So the shaping of memories of Vietnam, like those drawn from the experi-ence of the Civil War, became a matter of historical re-interpretation that was part of a broader political agenda.

The post-Vietnam Presidency

In 2002, discussing the contested memories of the Vietnam War as they have been reconstructed in its aftermath, Robert McMahon pointed out the rhetorical continuities that can be seen in successive Presidential speeches about the war.[24] Like their counterparts after the Civil War, Presidents again focused on the rhetoric of national reconciliation and unity. Visiting the South, at Tulane University, on 23 April 1975, as American military helicopters were about to clatter away from the nation's embassy in Saigon for the last time, President Gerald Ford argued that: 'today, America can regain the sense of pride that existed before Vietnam. But it cannot be achieved by re-fighting a war that is finished as far as America is concerned.' Ford's 'agenda for the future' – in language he borrowed from Lincoln – was 'to unify, to bind up the nation's wounds and to restore its health and optimistic self-confidence,' but only if Americans stopped 'refighting the battles and recriminations of the past.'[25]

As his Presidency began to disintegrate, Jimmy Carter, who as a candidate had been critical of American involvement in Southeast Asia, and who early in his time in office had spoken of Vietnam as a salutary example of the dangers of American hubris, refocused national attention on those who had fought there. As McMahon observes, 'this rhetorical *volte face*, reminiscent of a similar turn that occurred following the Civil War in both North and South, paved the way for a direct and simple discourse of memorialization: a discourse wholly consistent with the language of patriotism, sacrifice and nobility traditionally employed by American leaders in remembering the veterans of previous conflicts.' In his Veterans Day remarks at Arlington National Cemetery in 1978, Carter proclaimed that those who had fought in Vietnam were 'no less brave because our Nation was divided about that war.' In this and subsequent speeches that focused upon the heroism of the troops, as McMahon argues, 'whether knowingly or not, the Southern-born Carter was employing a rhetorical approach to national memory-formation that contained some striking parallels with the post-Civil War era.'[26]

Carter, indeed, 'set the rhetorical stage for the far more radical historical revisionism' of his successor.[27] Ronald Reagan's controversial description of Vietnam while on the presidential campaign trail in Chicago in August 1980, evocative as it was of the South's 'Lost Cause,' was the overture for the historical revisionism of the following decade. His was an attempt to restore a national sense of military honour and it was, to an extent, successful. Through his speeches, as Lou Cannon points out, Reagan 'lifted the spirits of ordinary Americans, boosted military enlistment rates and roused the conservative faithful.'[28] In his first inaugural address, he paid tribute to those he held up as ordinary American heroes, buried in Arlington military cemetery, who had sacrificed their lives not only on the battlefields of the First and Second World Wars, but also in Korea and 'in a hundred rice paddies and jungles of a place called Vietnam.'[29] During the following decade, that place – Vietnam – became an abstracted space in which the war's conduct and its outcome could be interpreted in a more positive light. By the end of Reagan's presidency, therefore, as Gaines Foster suggests, Americans had 'begun to recover from their collective amnesia' with respect to Vietnam. After the Civil War, the North, seeking reconciliation, had joined the South in 'a shared, heroic interpretation of the war, thereby helping ensure that the veteran's sacrifice had purpose and meaning.' The outcome was that 'veterans on both sides de-emphasized the issues of the war, slavery and secession, and focused instead on their common wartime experience, the camaraderie and excitement of battle.'[30] During the 1980s a similar process took place. There was little reflection on the political premises that had led the nation to involve itself in a war in

Southeast Asia. Instead it became, particularly for Hollywood, another opportunity to reconstruct the spectacle of combat and to explore the human drama of its impact upon those who fought there. Memories of Vietnam and the Civil War were constructed – sometimes literally – in other similar ways. Like the South after the Civil War, after Vietnam, the nation, in rationalizing defeat, concentrated upon building memorials to its dead. During Reagan's administration, 143 monuments were proposed or built in 45 states across the Union. If Vietnam was indeed a 'Noble Cause,' then it could be absorbed within a military tradition in which heroic endeavour was valued, and the unsuccessful outcome could be more or less ignored. As President, Reagan, whose own lifetime spanned a third of America's history as an independent republic, repeatedly told the story of the nation's past as a dramatic historical narrative of success into which memories of Vietnam might now be absorbed. Speaking at the dedication of the Vietnam War memorial statue in Washington in 1984, he connected the Wall explicitly with the surrounding monuments:

> The memorial reflects as a mirror reflects, so that when you find the name you're searching for you find it in your own reflection. And as you touch it, from certain angles, you're touching, too, the reflection of the Washington Monument or the chair in which great Abe Lincoln sits. Those who fought in Vietnam are part of us, part of our history. They reflected the best in us. No number of wreaths, no amount of music and memorializing will ever do them justice but it is good for us that we honor them and their sacrifice. And it's good that we do it in the reflected glow of the enduring symbols of our Republic.[31]

Yet the success of Reagan's rhetorical efforts might be measured against the familiar concern voiced in 1989, by President George Bush in his inaugural address. Appealing for a restoration of a bi-partisan spirit between Executive and Legislature, he argued that the political antagonism between President and Congress caused by the War had endured long beyond it. Vietnam 'cleaves us still. But . . . surely the statute of limitations has been reached. This is a fact: the final lesson of Vietnam is that no great nation can long afford to be sundered by a memory.'[32] Bush's acknowledgement of the continuing divisions caused by Vietnam demonstrated the limitations of the revisionist project.

As President, Bush would undertake the biggest military commitment overseas that the US had made since Vietnam, and throughout his conduct of the Gulf War of 1991, he confronted memories of America's involvement in Southeast Asia. In a radio address on the crisis in January 1991, he was concerned to point out that this time around the military's 'morale is sky high. True, if they are called upon to fight the aggressors, they will do their job courageously, professionally, and, in the end, decisively. There will be no more Vietnams.' Announcing the commencement of military action against Iraq, like Theodore Roosevelt before him, he connected America's contemporary action with a symbolic historical memory: 'Thomas Paine wrote many years ago: "These are the times that try men's souls". Those well-known words are so very true today.' After the war was over, the President used it as an opportunity to shape the historical memory of the earlier conflict. In a speech on 4 July 1991, he forged the connection between his military success and the nation's earlier defeat: 'Desert Storm has at last brought the recognition and honor to our sons and daughters who served in Vietnam. We finally have had a chance to tell them thank you, and we're proud of them. And welcome home. A little late, but welcome home.' The Americans who were initially representative of America's defeat might be rehabilitated in popular esteem, swept up in the President's euphoric rhetoric.[33]

Bush's decision to end the first Gulf War rapidly and ultimately inconclusively could nevertheless be taken as evidence that he had achieved but a Pyhrric victory over the Vietnam Syndrome. Six weeks after the war had ended, the President repeated that America was not going to be drawn into another similar conflict, although in a slightly different context. 'All along I have said that the United States is not going to intervene militarily in Iraq's internal affairs and risk being drawn into a Vietnam-style quagmire. This remains the case. Nor will we become an occupying power with US troops patrolling the streets of Baghdad.' As the neoconservative Charles Krauthammer pointed out, George Bush had become the 'chief purveyor' of the Vietnam Syndrome. In his actions after Iraq's withdrawal from Kuwait, Bush had 'simply raised the specter of Vietnam, an analogy without substance, and let its signal power, the power of fear and defeatism, do the rest. Bush did not just prove that the Vietnam syndrome lives. He gave it new life.'[34] And despite an initial surge of popularity the political capital Bush accumulated as a result of the Gulf War largely evaporated during its aftermath and proved insufficient to help him gain a second term.

Twenty years after the war in Southeast Asia, the continuities in the style of presidential rhetoric adopted initially by Gerald Ford could be seen still when Bill Clinton, whose own conduct during Vietnam had sparked political controversy, once more appropriated the language of Lincoln, and proclaimed in 1995, in announcing the normaliz-ation of US–Vietnamese relations, that 'this moment offers us the opportunity to bind up our own wounds.... Whatever divided us before let us consign to the past.'[35] But as George Bush had found, the capacity of the Chief Executive to use military force was still influ-enced by the memories of Vietnam that were not shaped by rhetoric alone. When President Clinton deployed forces in support of a UN peacekeeping effort in Somalia, Americans had only to witness a very public military set-back on the streets of Mogadishu for the commit-ment to be abandoned. It was, according to David Halberstam:

> a major tragedy for anyone who believed that America had an increased role to play in humanitarian peacekeeping missions. For the vulnerable of the world in places like Rwanda, Bosnia and Kosovo, American help, it came at all, would come later rather than sooner, and it would come smaller rather than larger.[36]

In the United States, neoconservatives, whose influence within the Republican party was increasing, were confirmed in their view that not much had changed since the end of the Vietnam War. America remained weak to the extent that its President did not enjoy complete freedom of political action backed by potential use of military force.

Conclusion

In *Made in Texas* (2003), Michael Lind argues that George W. Bush's political attitudes were moulded by the distinctive culture of the South – more specifically the region of west Texas where he spent his childhood. As Lind observes, 'George W. Bush is a product of

the Deep South tradition of the cotton plantation country, trans-
planted to the West Texas oil region.' Yet the forty-third President
of the United States also symbolises a contemporary reconfiguration
that has occurred in American politics. Having 'emerged from the
same Southern tradition that produced Strom Thurmond and George
Wallace,' rather than joining the Dixiecrats, Bush was able to pursue a
successful career in southern and national politics as a Republican.[37]
His predecessor as President from Texas, Lyndon Johnson, is usually
held responsible: championing the cause of Civil Rights came at the
political cost of eroding the basis of Democrat support in the 'solid
south.' But the Republican's electoral success – in winning major-
ities in Congress, and in holding the presidency for all but twelve of
the past thirty-five years – is the product of a more complex mix of
factors, and not least the continuing reaction to military defeat. The
South lost the Civil War, and the nation lost the war in Vietnam.
Those who see such defeats as involving a loss of honour re-interpret
them instead as a 'Lost' or a 'Noble' Cause. In so doing, they seek
to colour the map of contemporary national politics by using the
palette of particular historical memory.

Yet despite the hopes of successive Presidents – Republican and
Democrat – the rhetoric of the 'Noble Cause' has not drowned out
the voices of those who promoted an alternative narrative, expressed
in the Vietnam Syndrome, in quite the same way as the 'Lost Cause'
eviscerated the Civil War's story of emancipation. In the first presidential election campaign of the twenty-first century, John McCain
challenged George W. Bush for the Republican presidential nomination. His candidacy revolved around the central image of what *Time*
magazine called 'the story': McCain's capacity to come to terms with
and ultimately to transcend his time spent as a prisoner of war in
Hanoi. It was this experience that authenticated his claim to have
the necessary qualities – the character – to be president. From the
wreckage of what Stanley Karnow famously called 'the war nobody
won'[38] – not even, apparently, the Vietnamese – an American hero
could now step forward to claim the political inheritance of the 'baby
boomer' generation. One reason for McCain's presidential flame-out
in 2000 was that 'the story' ultimately did not have the resonance
which he and his supporters might have imagined.

For those who fought, what happened in the war still produced
controversy that impacted upon political careers. In 2001, the

Democrat Senator Bob Kerrey from Nebraska, a veteran, and talked of as a possible presidential candidate, was implicated in accounts of a massacre that had happened during his time in Vietnam. The moral ambiguities of America's mission in Southeast Asia became a matter of public debate once more and effectively ended Kerrey's presidential prospects. In 2004, John Kerry became the first combat veteran of the Vietnam War to be nominated as a presidential candidate, but his campaign faltered not least because of Republican attacks on his war record. His defeat was symbolic. Unlike John McCain, whose service in the air force and whose time as a prisoner of war removed him from direct participation in hostilities on the ground, Kerry's conduct in the military and towards the Vietnamese became a litmus test of his suitability to graduate to the role of Commander-in-Chief. His war-record, instead of being an asset, became part of his political baggage, attacked by his opponents, as was his anti-Vietnam war activity after he returned from Southeast Asia. During the campaign, attempts to shift the focus of attention to George W. Bush's military conduct in the Texas National Guard during the Vietnam War failed to gain political traction. It was what happened in Vietnam that mattered. Like Southerners, thirty years after the Civil War, a Vietnam veteran found the executive office remained still closed to him: the divisions caused by the war apparently part of an enduring political liability.

The legacy of failure in Vietnam may last as long as that of the defeated South. As Tony Horwitz discovered in *Confederates in the Attic* (1998), at the end of the twentieth century, memories expressed in the language of the 'Lost Cause' still pervade not only the South, but especially the states of the former Confederacy. Symbolic gestures are still seen as important: on Memorial Day 2001, President George W. Bush resumed a tradition that his father had abandoned when he was in the White House and sent a wreath to be laid at the Confederate Monument in Arlington National Cemetery that had been dedicated by his fellow southerner, President Wilson. It remains to be seen if in succession to Bush, John McCain can win the Republican nomination and the White House in 2008: if so he may be the first and last of the generation who fought in Vietnam so to do. If he unites the nation in support of his candidacy, moreover his achievement may be reminiscent of that of Wilson himself almost a century ago.

Memories of war and defeat thus shape electoral prospects. It is still the case that contemporary Southern politics are filtered largely through the prism of the attitudes that define the region to itself and which were formed in the aftermath of its defeat. In the mid-term elections of 2002, for example, Sonny Perdue became the first Republican to be elected governor of Georgia since the Civil War, defeating the incumbent Democrat, Roy Barnes. The election turned on Perdue's criticism of Barnes's efforts to re-design the State Flag so that it no longer incorporated the Confederate Flag. At the same time, in Georgia's election for the United States Senate, the Republican candidate, Saxby Chambliss, defeated the incumbent Democrat, Max Cleland. Cleland was a Vietnam veteran who had lost an arm and both legs in the war. Chambliss attacked his opponent for being soft in the 'war on terror,' and his campaign ran an advertisement depicting Cleland meeting with Osama bin Laden and Saddam Hussein. It is an illustration of how political attitudes and prejudices are not only influenced and informed by memories of past military defeats but also how, as John Kerry also found, the heroism and patriotism of those who served in Vietnam is subject to partisan manipulation for electoral gain. As Karl Rove and George W. Bush demonstrated in 2004, it is still the case that political capital invested in support of certain historical myths pays electoral dividends. Yet the experience of war may impact upon political perspectives in other ways. In 2006, James Webb spurred by opposition to America's involvement in Iraq won the Democrat primary in Virginia as candidate for the Senate in the mid-term elections that again focused attention on George W. Bush's conduct of that war.

As David Blight observes, it was Frederick Douglass who appreciated that 'historical memory... was not merely an entity altered by the passage of time; it was the prize in a struggle between rival versions of the past, a question of will, of power, of persuasion. The historical memory of any transforming or controversial event emerges from cultural and political competition, from the choice to confront the past and to debate and manipulate its memory.'[39] The 'Lost Cause' and the 'Noble Cause' were moulded by a common desire to shape historical memories in a manner that allowed the reality of defeat to be accommodated within the desire to preserve a sense of military honour and to recover national unity.

Walt Whitman, writing in *Democratic Vistas* in 1871, faced up to the consequences of the social, political and cultural dislocations caused by the Civil War when he confessed that 'the fear of conflicting and irreconcilable interiors, and the lack of a common skeleton, knitting all close, continually haunts me.'[40] Despite the rhetoric of reconciliation, the political polarisation between South and North militated against the construction of that 'common skeleton' except in times of overseas military action or national emergency. So the South's reaction to America's imperial adventure in 1898, to the two World Wars, to Korea and to Vietnam was characterised by a fervent patriotic embrace of the nation's mission, and it was economic depression that helped Franklin Roosevelt to forge the coalition between northern and southern democrats that became the dominant force in national politics in the mid-twentieth century. Moreover, it was the circling of political and ideological wagons in the Cold War during Harry Truman's presidency that helped a generation to construct the cultural consensus that Whitman craved. But it was defeat in Vietnam that once again pointed to Whitman's fear.

Presidential rhetoric after Vietnam thus reflects a concern that the nation's capacity to project its power militarily overseas, and the President's ability to act as Commander-in-Chief, might be irrevocably damaged by the 'Vietnam Syndrome.' In this sense, the South's defeat in the Civil War, and the nation's defeat in Vietnam produced similar re-actions: anxiety at the loss of military honour, a sense of humiliation and vulnerability. After Vietnam, America's self-confidence and belief in itself as a nation immune to military setbacks on the world stage was open to question. Militarily, the South could never rise again, but in 1991, after the first Gulf War, Harriet Fay's great-grandson would claim that the nation had 'kicked the Vietnam syndrome once and for all.'[41] For George Bush, successful military action had restored a national sense of military honour after Vietnam. Yet one outcome of that war was to reinforce contemporary attitudes towards America in the Middle East. The presence and use of American military bases in Saudi Arabia – the location of Islamic holy sites – helped to fuel the religious fundamentalism and the development of the terrorist network of al Qaeda, and ten years later, during his son's presidency, the events of September 11, 2001 brought with it the President's declaration of a new existential 'war on terror.'

To shape historical memories of defeat in a manner that preserves and celebrates the courage and heroism of the combatants thus may help the cause of national unity but it does not allow reflection on its deeper cultural and political significance. The contemporary 'war on terror' of which Iraq is a part is another cause. Its future course is uncertain and its aftermath – if it can ever be said to be over – unpredictable. If, during this existential conflict, America has to face the fact of military defeat again, the style of remembrance it adopts will once more be critical. When the fighting is over, there are choices to be made. As Gaines Foster suggests with respect to the South after the Civil War, 'an interpretation of defeat that simply reaffirms the righteousness of the cause and the heroism of the armies, without wrestling with the implications of failure, leads only to a trivialization of the memory of the war and a failure to derive any special insight from it.'[42] Similarly, the attempt to mould memories of Vietnam as a 'Noble Cause' through the neoconservative revisionism of the 1980s needs to be set in the context of America's continuing propensity to seek military solutions to political problems. Is the shaping of memories of war and defeat simply about the recovery and preservation of military honour and national unity at the expense of alternative narratives? Or might it be better for the nation and its leaders to accept the complex challenges of contested remembrance that invite more mature consideration of meaning of war, as well as of the consequences of the unchecked use of Presidential power?

Notes

1. Jefferson Davies, 'Message on Constitutional Ratification,' *Official Records of the Union and Confederate Armies* (Washington DC: Government Printing Office, 1880–1901), Series IV, Vol. I, p. 268.
2. John Grammer, *Pastoral and Politics in the Old South* (Baton Rouge: Louisiana State University Press, 1996), p. 165.
3. Ronnie Dugger, *The Politician: The Life and Times of Lyndon Johnson* (New York: W.W. Norton & Co., 1982), pp. 146–7.
4. J. William Gibson, 'The Return of Rambo: War and Culture in the Post-Vietnam Era,' in A. Wolfe, ed., *America at Century's End* (Berkeley: University of California Press, 1991), p. 378.
5. Richard Polenberg, *One Nation Divisible* (Harmondsworth: Penguin, 1980), p. 208.

6. James Longstreet, *From Manassas to Appomattox: Memoirs of the Civil War in America* (Philadelphia: J.B. Lippincott Co., 1896), reprinted in J. Roper, ed., *The American Civil War: Literary Sources and Documents* (Mountfield: Helm Information Ltd., 2000), Vol. 2, pp. 500–9, p. 507.
7. John Russell Young, *Around the World With General Grant* (New York: The American News Co., 1879), reprinted ibid., Vol. 2, pp. 512–14, p. 513.
8. Robert E. Lee, 'Last Order,' *The War of the Rebellion: A Compilation of the Official Records of the Union and Confederate Armies* (Washington DC: Government Printing Office, 1880), reprinted ibid., pp. 510–11, p. 510.
9. Horace Greeley, *The American Conflict: A History of the Great Rebellion in the United States of America, 1860–65* (Hartford, CT: O.D. Case, 1866), Vol. 2, p. 745.
10. Oliver Wendell Holmes, 'Memorial Day Address,' May 30, 1884. See http://www.arlingtoncemetery.net/owholmes.htm.
11. Theodore Roosevelt & Henry Cabot Lodge, *Hero Tales from American History* (New York: Century Co., 1895) see online edition: http://www.worldwideschool.org/library/books/lit/historical/HeroTales-FromAmericanHistory/chap18.html, Chapter XVIII, 'The Death of Stonewall Jackson.'
12. David Blight, ' "For Something Beyond the Battlefield": Frederick Douglass and the Struggle for the Memory of the Civil War,' *Journal of American History*, Vol. 75, No. 4 (March 1989), pp. 1156–78, p. 1161.
13. Eric Foner, *Reconstruction* (New York: Harper & Row, 1989), p. 582.
14. Theodore Roosevelt, 'First Annual Message,' December 3, 1901, *A Compilation of the Messages and Papers of the Presidents* (New York: Bureau of National Literature, Inc., 1917), Vol. XIV, p. 6672.
15. Woodrow Wilson, 'Address Delivered at Gettysburg, July 4, 1913,' ibid., Vol. XVI, p. 7882.
16. Woodrow Wilson, 'Address at the Grand Army of the Republic Memorial Day Services,' May 30, 1914 and 'Address at the Unveiling of a Monument to Confederate Soldiers,' June 4, 1914, ibid., Vol. XVII, p. 7947 and pp. 7948–9.
17. Woodrow Wilson, 'Address on Memorial Day before the Grand Army of the Republic,' ibid., Vol. XXVII, p. 8265.
18. Lyndon Johnson, 'Remarks at the White House Luncheon on Lincoln's Birthday,' February 12, 1965, *Public Papers of the Presidents of the United States: Lyndon B. Johnson* (Washington DC: US Government Printing Office, 1966), Book I, 1965, p. 181.
19. Edward Alfred Pollard, *The Lost Cause: A New Southern History of the War of the Confederates* (New York: E.B. Treat & Co., 1866), p. 751.
20. James Webb, *Fields of Fire* (London: Grafton Books, 1981), pp. 44–6.
21. Gaines M. Foster, 'Coming to Terms with Defeat: Post-Vietnam America and the Post Civil War South,' *The Virginia Quarterly Review*, Winter 1990, 66, I, pp. 17–35, p. 17.
22. Harry Summers, *On Strategy: The Vietnam War in Context* (New York: Dell Publishing Co. Inc., 1984), p. 21.

23. Foster, 'Coming to Terms with Defeat,' p. 30.
24. Robert McMahon, 'Contested Memory: The Vietnam War and American Society, 1975–2001,' *Diplomatic History*, Vol. 6, No. 2, Spring 2002, pp. 159–84.
25. Gerald Ford, 'Address at a Tulane University Convocation, 23 April 1975,' http://www.fordlibrarymuseum.gov/library/speeches/750208.htm.
26. McMahon, 'Contested Memory,' pp. 166–7.
27. Ibid., p. 168.
28. Lou Cannon, *President Reagan: The Role of a Lifetime* (New York: Public Affairs, 1991), p. 293.
29. Ronald Reagan, 'First Inaugural Address,' 20 January 1981, http://www.yale.edu/lawweb/avalon/presiden/inaug/reagan1.htm.
30. Foster, 'Coming to Terms with Defeat,' p. 25.
31. Reagan, 'Remarks at Dedication Ceremonies for the Vietnam Veterans Memorial Statue,' November 11, 1984, http://www.presidency.ucsb.edu/ws/print.php?pid=39414 In 1985, an explicit connection between Vietnam and the Civil War was made when John Wheeler, a veteran and one of those involved in the building of the Vietnam Memorial on the Mall, wrote a book that borrowed its title – *Touched With Fire* – from Oliver Wendell Holmes' Memorial Day remarks.
32. George Bush, 'Inaugural Address,' January 20, 1989, http://www.yale.edu/lawweb/avalon/presiden/inaug/bush.htm.
33. George Bush, 'Radio Address to the Nation on the Persian Gulf Crisis,' January 5, 1991; 'Address to the Nation Announcing Allied Military Action in the Persian Gulf,' January 16, 1991 and 'Remarks at an Independence Day Celebration in Marshfield, Missouri,' July 4, 1991, http://bushlibrary.tamu.edu/research/papers/1991/browse_1991.html.
34. George Bush, 'Remarks on Assistance for Iraqi Refugees and a News Conference,' April 16, 1991, http://bushlibrary.tamu.edu/research/papers/1991/91041608.html. Charles Krauthammer, 'Good Morning Vietnam: The Syndrome Returns, Courtesy of George Bush,' *The Washington Post*, April 19, 1991.
35. Quoted in McMahon, 'Contested Memory,' p. 170.
36. David Halberstam, *War in a Time of Peace* (London: Bloomsbury, 2002), p. 264.
37. Michael Lind, *Made in Texas: George W. Bush and the Southern Takeover of American Politics* (New York: Basic Books, 2003), pp. 23–4.
38. Stanley Karnow, *Vietnam: A History* (Harmondsworth: Penguin, 1991).
39. Blight, ' "For Something Beyond the Battlefield" ', p. 1159.
40. Walt Whitman, 'Democratic Vistas,' in M. Van Doren, ed., *The Portable Walt Whitman* (Harmondsworth: Penguin, 1982), pp. 313–82, p. 324.
41. George Bush, 'Remarks to the American Legislative Exchange Council,' March 1, 1991, http://bushlibrary.tamu.edu/research/papers/1991/91030102.html.
42. Foster, 'Coming to Terms with Defeat,' pp. 32–3.

9

Kenny and Me: A Story of War and Friendship

W. D. Ehrhart

The weapon that got Kenny and me was an RPG, a rocket-propelled grenade. You've probably seen RPGs in news footage of Afghan mujahedeen or Taliban fighters. The launcher is a long thin tube that the gunner rests on his shoulder like a bazooka, and the projectile sticks out at the front end of the tube like a bulbous cone-shaped piece of nastiness. RPGs are light, cheap, and powerful. A guerrilla army's artillery.

We didn't call them RPGs back when Kenny and I were fighting in Vietnam. We called them B-40s. I don't recall ever hearing the term 'rocket-propelled grenade' until many years after the fact. But a rose by any other name still has thorns, and whatever you called it, one B-40 could screw up your whole day. Just ask Kenny.

Talk about irony. The North Vietnamese gunner who fired the damned thing wasn't even aiming at Kenny. He didn't even know Kenny was there. He was aiming at me. Sitting in a heavy overstuffed armchair by the window, a cup of C-ration coffee brewing at my feet, cranking rounds off now and then at the shadows in the buildings across the street, at figments of my imagination, at whatever might be over there, I was the only one that NVA gunner could see.

Kenny was sitting on the other side of the room under the canopy of a four-poster double bed cleaning his rifle. He wasn't even wearing his body armour. Hue City or not, Tet Offensive or not, after days of hard fighting, it was a slow morning in our neighbourhood.

Or seemed like a slow morning until the world exploded. Later, we figured out that the rocket came through the window on a rising trajectory, missed both the side of the window frame and my face by no more than a couple of inches either way, and detonated against the wall four-and-a-half feet above and behind me. It blew the chair apart, shattered a heavy wooden table, turned my rifle into junk, imbedded 50 or 60 pieces of jagged metal, concrete chunks, and wood splinters into the back of my flak jacket, and punched in the back of my helmet so badly that I couldn't put it back on my head, like somebody had taken a 20-pound sledgehammer to it.

I must have been knocked out momentarily; by the time Graves and Mogerdy got to me, I was conscious enough to tell them that Kenny was in the room, too, but Kenny was already gone. And by the time Graves and Mogerdy got me downstairs, Kenny was already on his way to the battalion aid station. By the time I got to the battalion aid station, Kenny was on his way to the LZ to be medevacked out.

I never saw him again. Kenny was sitting on the bed cleaning his rifle, and then the world exploded, and when the smoke cleared and the dust settled, Kenny was gone.

That is just the way it happens sometimes. Bobby Ross flew to Tam Ky one day and never came back. Gerry Gaffney headed off to the LZ at Con Thien and never got there. Mike Bylinoski got put on a chopper to Da Nang and was dead before it landed.

I knew Kenny hadn't died. The corpsman at the aid station said he would live. But he also said they would never save Kenny's arm. It was hanging by a few shreds of tissue just below the shoulder, the bone shattered and exposed. No way he could keep it.

Though I had been much closer to the blast, Kenny had gotten hit much worse than me. A doctor cleaned up my wounds, which weren't much to speak of, and gave me a couple of shots, and then I slept for a few hours. Later that same day, I went back to the war, stone-deaf but otherwise reasonably functional. A few weeks later, I made my rotation date and got out of Vietnam in one piece, and a year after that I completed my enlistment, got out of the Corps, and embarked on the rest of my life.

I always felt badly about Kenny losing his arm because that NVA gunner was aiming at me, not Kenny. Not that I lost any sleep over it. I had seen enough of war to know that is just how it happens sometimes. But I often thought about Kenny, and wondered where he was and how he was doing. He had paid a hell of a price for joining the Marines, and he wasn't even an American.

That is the thing about Kenny. He was Japanese. Not Japanese-American. Just Japanese. A card-carrying natural-born Japanese citizen. As the years passed, I wished ever more frequently that I could find him again. But I didn't know where or how to begin looking for him. Was he still in the US, or had he had enough of America and gone back to Japan? I didn't even know his full name. His last name was Takenaga, but none of us could ever remember his first name, so we just called him 'Ken.' If there's a way to find somebody when all you've got is a last name, I never discovered it in all those years.

Then in the summer of 2000, a man named William L. Myers asked if he could publish an essay of mine called 'Places and Ways to Live' in a book he was editing called *Honor the Warrior: The United States Marine Corps in Vietnam.* My essay described the combination sleeping quarters/fighting hole/reinforced bunker that Roland Maas, Kenny and I built the day after the night the VC mortared the bejesus out of us north of Quang Tri in October 1967.

At the end of every essay in his book, Myers included the full name and service number of every person mentioned in that essay. I don't know how Myers found that information about Kenny, but there it was: Cpl. Kazunori Takenaga 2320456. Now I could write to the Veterans Administration, and if Ken had ever applied for disability – which seemed highly likely, having lost his arm – the VA would forward a letter to the last address they had for Ken.

Ten days after I wrote to the VA, Kenny called me from Japan. It had been thirty-two years and seven months since we had last spoken.

Almost immediately, I apologized to Kenny for getting his arm blown off. 'Oh, no,' he replied. 'I've still got my arm. Works pretty good, too, and I've been collecting twenty per cent disability all these years. I owe you a share.' He then went on to tell me how, when he finally got out of the hospital, he had been assigned as a gate guard at the US navy base at Pearl Harbor. 'Can you imagine?' he said, the combination of wonder and mirth evident in his voice across the 8000 miles between us, 'A Japanese guy guarding Pearl Harbor!'

Over the next five years, Ken came to Philadelphia four times to visit, and I gradually began to learn what I had forgotten about him, or had never known.

Ken's mother had come to work as a fashion designer in New York City in the 1960s, and when Ken was fifteen, he joined her, finishing high school in three years and enrolling at City College of New York.

As a permanent resident, however, he was subject to US draft laws, and in 1966 Uncle Sam came knocking. Ken's father and grandfather had both served in the Japanese navy, so Ken decided he would join the navy, too, even if it was the American navy, but he discovered that he would have to enlist for four years. When he pointed out that the army only required two years' service, the recruiter told him he could join a special branch of the navy for just two years. It was called the Marine Corps. Kenny joined. When he got to Parris Island, Ken says he told the drill instructors, 'I think I'm in the wrong place. Where are the ships?'

With an introduction like that, I do not to this day understand how Ken ever got off Parris Island alive. But he did, and in April 1967 he was assigned as my fellow intelligence assistant with 1st Battalion, 1st Marines, replacing Bob Ross, who had died on a hospital ship ten days after getting shot in the lung. I had hardly gotten to know Ross before he was killed, but Kenny and I spent ten months together before that morning when the world exploded. That is a long time when people are trying to kill you.

During the first patrol Kenny ever went out on with us, the Vietnamese villagers, mostly old men and women, kept trying to talk to him. They would come up to him and start chattering away, pleading, beseeching, God only knows what they were saying, we sure didn't. When we got back to the battalion command post, Kenny was seething mad. 'Those goddamned people thought I was a gook!' he stormed. Whereupon three or four of us simultaneously chimed in, 'But Kenny, you *are* a gook!'

Kenny introduced me to *kimchi*, fiery hot fermented cabbage some relative of his used to send him in cans. I would always be right there by his side whenever another 'Care' package came for him at mail call, knowing there would be *kimchi* in it. Some years later, I learned that *kimchi* is a Korean specialty, not Japanese. I spent many more years wondering why Kenny's relatives were sending him Korean food. Only after I found Ken again was this small mystery solved: I'm sure I must have known at the time, but I had long since forgotten that Kenny was already married when he got to Vietnam – and his wife was Korean.

After Ken got out of the Marines, he stayed in the US for the next twelve years, working for Pan Am and becoming a US citizen (he has dual citizenship these days). In the early 1980s, he returned to Japan.

But he continued to work, as he does to this day, in the travel and tourism industry. Along the way, he has been married and divorced seven times – the first time he told me this, he looked at me deadpan and asked, 'Do you think I have PTSD, Bill?' – and has nine children ranging in age from the mid-thirties down to pre-school. He has a huge scar on his upper right arm, though you don't notice at first that his use of that arm is limited, and another big scar on his head.

What most amazes me, however, is how strong the bond between us has remained through all those decades when neither of us knew what had become of the other, how little effort it has taken to renew that bond, how obviously happy we both are when we have the chance to be together. But those chances have come only when Ken has reason to be in the US and time enough to detour to Philadelphia for a day or two: visits on the fly, always too brief. So when Ken asked if I wanted to visit Japan, he didn't have to ask me twice.

Ken is currently organizing a consortium of hotels in the Seto Inland Sea area of Japan. Working in conjunction with the tourism departments of Kagawa Prefecture, where Ken lives now, Kumamoto Prefecture, where Ken grew up, and the Japanese central government, Ken has spent the past few years actively trying to raise American awareness of Japanese culture, especially awareness of what he calls 'the real Japan' beyond the obvious destinations of Tokyo and Kyoto.

To that end, Ken was able to invite a delegation of six teachers to visit Japan for almost two weeks in June 2006. The group included me – which was kind of the point of the whole thing, if not the official rationale – in my capacity as a Master Teacher at the Haverford School in suburban Philadelphia; my wife Anne in her dual capacity as managing director of Voloshky Ukrainian Dance Ensemble and secretary of Svitanya Eastern European Vocal Ensemble; Chuck Yates, Professor of History and Director of the Institute for Education on Japan at Earlham College; Debra Yates, Visiting Assistant Professor of Education at Albertson College; John Baky, Director of Library Services at La Salle University; and James Brightman, La Salle's International Studies Coordinator.

As one might imagine, this was not a randomly chosen group. John and Chuck are both Vietnam veterans. John, a former army lieutenant with a Bronze Star, is the creator and curator of La Salle's 'Imaginative Representations of the Vietnam War.' The finest special collection of its kind in the world, it contains novels, poetry, plays, poster art, movies and TV shows, comic books and trading cards, games, music, just about anything at all that relates to or is in any way connected to the Vietnam War. I've known John for more than twenty years, and had introduced him to Ken during one of Ken's visits to Philadelphia.

I had first met Chuck, a navy linguist who had spent a year eavesdropping on North Vietnamese fighter pilots' radio traffic, when he invited me to Earlham in 2001 to speak in a class he was teaching about the Vietnam War. Chuck has a doctorate in East Asian Studies from Princeton, wrote his dissertation on Saigo Takamori, the last samurai, and speaks, reads, and writes Japanese fluently.

James had lived and taught in Japan for several years before coming to La Salle, and had already made use of Ken's services to bring a group of La Salle students to Japan the month before our trip. Chuck and Deb had first met during a study trip to Japan that Chuck led when Deb was a social studies teacher at an Indiana high school. Finally, as good fortune would have it, Eastern European folk music is very popular in Japan, offering Ken the opportunity to include Anne.

We spent the first few days in Tokyo and Kyoto, visiting temples, shrines, castles, palaces, and the amazing, high-speed, high-voltage Tsukiji fish market (you have to see it to believe it: acres and acres of closely-packed, crowded stalls overflowing with fish of every size and kind being sliced, diced, bent, folded, spindled, and mutilated by rubber-booted, rubber-aproned fishmongers wielding industrial band saws, four-foot long samurai swords, daggers, dirks, shivs, shanks, cleavers, and ball peen hammers while propane-powered mini-trucks zoom in and out, up and down the crowded aisles driven by men and women who are certain they are the stars of the Joey Chitwood Thrill Show).

The fish market not withstanding, however, the real fun didn't begin until we left the obvious behind and headed for some of the many places Japan has to offer that most Westerners have never seen or even heard of.

Once you leave the two cities that constitute most Americans' entire knowledge of Japan, the pace of life slows down, the crowds thin, the prices drop, the scale of everything becomes more manageable, and you discover a land of mountains (and tunnels), islands (and boats), small towns and villages, rice fields, rivers, and reasons beyond counting to be grateful you finally found your old Marine Corps buddy and he is still your pal.

In Kagawa, we stood in the midst of several hundred wild monkeys clambering after the dry soybeans we fed them at Choshikei, hiked down Kankakei Gorge, watched the awesome Goma and Wood Fire ceremonies at Emmonotaki Temple, built into a cave high up a mountainside, made our own traditional paper and bamboo fans at Marugame, and participated in a traditional tea ceremony at Ritsurin Park, each evening returning to our hotel on Shodoshima Island in time for champagne at sunset on the balcony overlooking the Inland Sea.

In Kumamoto, we ate lunch in the home of one of Amakusa Island's 'Hidden Christians,' a group of Japanese converted to Christianity by 16th-century Portuguese Jesuits, but forced to hide their faith for 250 years when the government outlawed Christianity in 1639; received a lesson in Zen meditation from the head priest of Tokoji Temple; stood on the rim of Mt Nakadake, an active volcano within the vast and ancient caldera of Mt Aso National Park; went backstage at Seiwa Bunraku Hall, where highly skilled amateur puppeteers maintain a tradition that predates Kabuki; walked Tabaruzaka Battlefield, where the Meiji emperor's army defeated Saigo's samurai rebels; and climbed to the top of Kumamoto Castle, the fortress Saigo was unable to conquer.

And food, of course: meals that went on forever, a taste of this, a bite of that, beef that melted in your mouth, fish that was swimming in the sea only hours earlier, vegetables familiar and unfamiliar, some of it raw, some of it cooked, most of it prepared right in front of us, and all of it presented as if each course were its own work of art, which it was.

And beer. Considering that beer wasn't even introduced to Japan until the 1870s, the Japanese have taken to it with an enthusiasm that any German could admire. Kirin. Asahi. Sapporo. You can't eat lunch or dinner without beer.

Or sake. Lunch, maybe. But not dinner. Dinner comes with beer *and* sake. In the summer, you drink good sake cold, not hot. And every prefecture, every town, seemingly every restaurant, makes its own sake.

All through the trip, over and over again, I would look at Ken and think, 'Jesus Christ, who would ever have imagined *this* thirty-eight

years ago?' Kenny and me in Japan. Staying in the best hotels, eating
the best meals, feeding monkeys, climbing volcanoes, watching
puppet shows, making paper fans. We used to live in the mud and
eat out of cans and wonder if we would still be alive tomorrow.

One of the coolest things Ken and I did on the trip was collaborate
on translating a poem for Morinobu Okabe, the thirty-first priest of
the 350-year-old Zen Buddhist temple of Tokoji. The priest has copies
of a poem by Shinmin Sakamura that he gives to visitors, but the
poem is in Japanese. He asked Ken to translate the poem into English,
and Ken asked me to help him. Ken gave me a literal translation, and
I adapted it. Here is what we came up with:

> The sun comes up each morning in silence;
> the moon disappears, but nobody sees.
> Flowers dance by the roadside unnoticed;
> birds twitter sweetly, but nobody hears.
> People don't stop to consider what matters.
> People work hard all their lives to achieve
> a dream of success that will make them happy:
> position or power, fortune or fame –
> until they are old and they realize too late
> that the beauty of living has passed them by
> while the river travels alone to the ocean,
> the wind sings alone in the tops of the trees.

If you visit the temple of Tokoji on Amakusa Island, Morinobu Okabe
will be happy to give you a copy of the poem – in Japanese or in
English.

The day we left Japan, Ken flew to Australia to visit his two youngest
children, daughters aged nine and five. The girls don't like his mous-
tache and made him shave it off, but they liked spending a week
with Dad.

A few days after I got home, I got an e-mail from Chuck. 'It was
especially wonderful,' he wrote,

> to see you and Ken interact, verbally and non-verbally, and
> imagine the furious rate at which both of you were stitching
> together the widely separated episodes of your relationship into a
> whole. Only the two of you were in that room in Hue, and that

puts the two of you in a place where none of the rest of us can go, a place the rest of us can't even imagine, let alone understand.

Every time the two of you stepped out for a smoke, it was easy for me to imagine the two of you going back to that place in some sense, and I couldn't help feeling really good every time I saw you and Ken off to the side lighting up because I found myself thinking, 'If these two guys can come out of what they were in together and still be this okay, then everything is going to be okay in the end.'

I'm not as confident as Chuck that *everything* is going to be okay in the end. One need only pick up the latest newspaper or turn on CNN to notice that the world doesn't seem to be doing any better today than it was when Kenny and I were saving Vietnam from the Communists. But it was great fun – one might almost say profound fun, if such a phrase can be – to share Japan with Kenny, to be able to have his company for a few weeks instead of a few hours, to understand a little better who he is and where he comes from. And although I'm not sure it's quite as mystical as Chuck makes it seem, only Kenny and I *were* in that room in Hue, and both of us came out alive, and we were both still as much each other's buddy as we were when we were two scared kids in a world of hurt. We were brothers then in no figurative sense, and we still are, and always will be. Ken calls us 'comrades.' He's right. Look it up.

Bibliography

Aaron, D., *The Unwritten War: American Writers and the Civil War* (New York: Alfred A. Knopf, 1973).

Aho, J., *Religious Mythology and the Art of War* (London: Aldwych, 1981).

Andrew, M., *The Three Things* (New York: Charles Scribner's Sons, 1915).

Appy, C., *Working-Class War: American Combat Soldiers and Vietnam* (Chapel Hill: University of North Carolina Press, 1993).

Axtell, J., *The European and The Indian: Essays in the Ethnohistory of Colonial North America* (Oxford: Oxford University Press, 1982).

Balaban, J., *Locusts at the Edge of Summer: New and Selected Poems* (Washington: Copper Canyon Press, 1997).

Beattie, K., *The Scar that Binds: American Culture and the Vietnam War* (New York: New York University Press, 2000).

Beidler, P., *American Literature and the Experience of Vietnam* (Athens, Georgia: University of Georgia Press, 1982).

Bellah, R., *Habits of the Heart: Individualism and Commitment in American Life* (New York: Perennial, 1986).

Bergland, R., *The National Uncanny: Indian Ghosts and American Subjects* (Dartmouth: University of New England Press, 1988).

Berkhofer, R. E., *The White Man's Indian* (New York: Vintage, 1979).

Berman, L., *Perfect Spy: The Incredible Double Life of Pham Xuan An, Time Reporter and Vietnamese Communist Agent* (Washington DC: Smithsonian Institution Press/HarperCollins, 2007).

Blakey, G., *Historians on the Homefront: American Propagandists for the Great War* (Lexington, KY: University Press of Kentucky, 1970).

Briley, J., *The Traitors* (New York: G.P. Putnam, 1969).

Brownmiller, S., *Against Our Will: Men, Women and Rape* (New York: Simon & Schuster, 1975).

Caldwell, P., *The Puritan Conversion Narrative* (Cambridge: Cambridge University Press, 1983).

Cannon, L., *President Reagan: The Role of a Lifetime* (New York: Public Affairs, 1991).

Capps, W., ed., *The Vietnam Reader* (New York and London: Routledge, 1990).

Caputo, P., *A Rumour of War* (New York: Ballantine, 1977).

Carroll, P. N., *Puritanism and the Wilderness* (New York: Columbia University Press, 1969).

Chattarji, S., *Memories of a Lost War: American Poetic Responses to the Vietnam War* (Oxford: Clarendon Press, 2001).

Coffman, E., *The War To End All Wars* (New York: Oxford University Press, 1968).

Colley, L., *Captives: Britain, Empire and the World, 1600–1850* (London: Jonathan Cape, 2002).

Conrad, J., *Heart of Darkness* (Oxford: Oxford University Press, 2002 edition).

Coontz, S., *The Way We Never Were: American Families and the Nostalgia Trap* (New York: Basic Books, 1992).

Cooperman, S., *World War I and the American Novel* (Baltimore: John's Hopkins University Press, 1967).

Cowley, M., *The Literary Situation* (New York: Vintage, 1958; 1969).

Creel, G., *How We Advertised America* (New York: Harper & Brothers, 1920).

Del Vecchio, J., *The 13th Valley* (New York: Bantam Books, 1982).

Doherty, T., *Projections of War: Hollywood, American Culture and World War II* (New York: Columbia University Press, 1999).

Doren, M. Van, ed., *The Portable Walt Whitman* (Harmondsworth: Penguin, 1982).

Dorrien, G., *Imperial Designs: Neoconservatism and the New Pax Americana* (New York: Routledge, 2004).

Dugger, R., *The Politician: The Life and Times of Lyndon Johnson* (New York: W.W. Norton & Co., 1982).

Eastlake, W., *The Bamboo Bed* (New York: Simon and Schuster, 1969).

Ehrenreich, B., *The Hearts of Men: American Dreams and the Flight from Commitment* (New York: Anchor, 1983).

Ehrhart, W. D., *Sleeping With The Dead* (Easthampton, MA: Adastra Press, 2006).

Emerson, G., *Winners and Losers* (New York: W.W. Norton & Co., 1976).

Fall, B., *The Two Vietnams* (New York: Praeger, 1963).

Fliegelman, J., *Prodigals and Pilgrims* (New York: Cambridge University Press, 1982).

Fluck, W., Peper, J. and Adams, W. P., eds, *Forms and Functions of History in American Literature* (Berlin: Schmidt, 1981).

Foner, E., *Reconstruction* (New York: Harper & Row, 1989).

Franklin, H. *M.I.A or Mythmaking in America* (New Brunswick, NJ: Rutgers University Press, 1993).

——, *War Stars: The Superweapon and the American Imagination* (New York: Oxford University Press, 1988).

——, *Bruce, Vietnam & Other American Fantasies* (Amherst: University of Massachusetts Press, 2000).

Freedman, L., *Kennedy's Wars* (Oxford: Oxford University Press, 2000).

French, K., *Karl French on Apocalypse Now* (New York: Bloomsbury, 1998).

Gelb, L., with Betts, R. K., *The Irony of Vietnam: The System Worked* (Washington: Brookings, 1979).

Gerould, D., *American Melodrama* (New York: Performing Arts Journal Publication, 1983).

Gettleman, M., Franklin, J., Young, M. and Franklin, H. Bruce, eds, *Vietnam and America: A Documented History, Revised and Enlarged Second Edition* (New York: Grove Press, 1995).

Gibson, J. W., *The Perfect War: Technowar in Vietnam* (Boston: The Atlantic Monthly Press, 1986).

Grammer, J., *Pastoral and Politics in the Old South* (Baton Rouge: Louisiana State University Press, 1996).

Gravel, M. (Senator), *Pentagon Papers* (Boston: Beacon, 1971).

Grey, C. G., *Bombers* (London: Faber & Faber, 1941).

Greene, G., *The Quiet American* (New York: Viking Press, 1956).

Gruening, E. and Beaser, H. W., Vietnam Folly (Washington DC: National Press, 1968).

Halberstam, D., *The Best and the Brightest* (London: Pan Books Ltd., 1973).

Halberstam, D., *War in a Time of Peace* (London: Bloomsbury, 2002).

Heilman, R. B., *The Iceman, the Arsonist and the Troubled Agent* (Seattle: University of Washington Press, 1973).

Hellmann, J., *American Myth and the Legacy of Vietnam* (New York: Columbia University Press, 1986).

Herr, M., *Dispatches* (London: Picador, Pan Books, 1978).

Herring, G., *America's Longest War: The United States and Vietnam, 1950–1975*, 2nd edn (New York: Knopf, 1986).

Herzog, T. C., *Tim O'Brien* (New York: Twayne Publishers, 1997).

Hilsman, R., *To Move a Nation: The Politics of Foreign Policy in the Administration of John F. Kennedy* (New York: Delta, 1967).

Hoffman, F., *The Mortal No: Death and the Modern Imagination* (Princeton: Princeton University Press, 1964).

Hölbling, W., *Fiktionen vom Krieg* (Tübingen: Narr, 1987).

Horwitz, T., *Confederates in the Attic* (New York: Vintage, 1998).

Greeley, H., *The American Conflict* (Hartford, CT., O.D. Case, 1866).

Isaacs, A. R., *Vietnam Shadows: The War, Its Ghosts, and Its Legacy* (Baltimore: Johns Hopkins University Press, 1997).

Jameson, F., *The Political Unconscious* (London: Methuen & Co. Ltd., 1987).

Jason, P. K. and Graves, M. A., eds, *Encyclopedia of American War Literature* (Westport, CT: Greenwood, 2001).

Jeffords, S., *The Remasculinization of America: Gender and the Vietnam War* (Bloomington: Indiana University Press, 1989).

Jenkins, P., *Decade of Nightmares: The End of the Sixties and the Making of Eighties America* (Oxford: Oxford University Press, 2006).

Johnson, L., *The Vantage Point: Perspectives of the Presidency 1963–1969* (New York: Holt, Rinehart and Winston, 1971).

Just, W., *Military Men* (New York: Knopf, 1970).

Kaplan, S., *Understanding Tim O'Brien* (Columbia, SC: University of South Carolina Press, 1995).

Karnow, S., *Vietnam: A History* (Harmondsworth: Penguin, 1991).

Kattenburg, P., *The Vietnam Trauma in American Foreign Policy, 1945–75* (New Brunswick, NJ: Transaction Books, 1980).

Kennedy, D., *Over Here* (New York: Oxford University Press, 1980).

Kennedy, R., *To Seek a Newer World* (London: Michael Joseph, 1967).

Killen, A., *1973 Nervous Breakdown: Watergate, Warhol, and the Birth of Post-Sixties America* (New York: Bloomsbury, 2006).

Lasswell, H., *Propaganda Technique in the World War* (New York: Peter Smith, 1938).

Lembcke, J., *The Spitting Image* (New York: New York University Press, 1998).

Lepore, J., *The Name of War: King Philip's War and The Origins of American Identity* (New York: Knopf, 1999).

Leverner, J. and Cohen, H., eds, *The Indians and Their Captives* (Westport,CT: Greenwood, 1977).

Lewy, G., *America in Vietnam* (New York: Oxford, 1978).

Lifton, R. J., *Home From the War* (New York: Simon & Schuster, 1973).

Lind, M., *Vietnam: The Necessary War* (New York: Free Press, 1999).

Lind, M., *Made in Texas: George W. Bush and the Southern Takeover of American Politics* (New York: Basic Books, 2003).

Lindqvist, S., *A History of Bombing* (New York: New Press, 2001).

Lomperis, T., *'Reading the Wind': The Literature of the Vietnam War* (Durham, NC: Duke University Press, 1987).

Longstreet, J., *From Manassas to Appomattox: Memoirs of the Civil War in America* (Philadelphia: J.B. Lippincott Co., 1896).

Louvre, A. and Walsh, J., eds, *Tell Me Lies About Vietnam* (Milton Keynes & Philadelphia: Open University Press, 1988).

Luhmann, N., *Soziologische Aufklärung. Aufsätze zur Theorie sozialer Systeme* (Cologne: Westdeutscher Verlag, 1970).

Martini, E., *Invisible Enemies: The American War on Vietnam, 1975–2000* (Amherst: University of Massachusetts Press, 2007).

McCarthy, M., *Vietnam* (London: Weidenfeld and Nicholson, 1967).

McCarthy, M., *The Seventeenth Degree* (London: Weidenfeld and Nicholson, 1974).

McMahon, R., ed., *Major Problems in the History of the Vietnam War* (Lexington, Mass.: D.C. Heath & Co., 1990).

McNamara, R., *In Retrospect: The Tragedy and Lessons of Vietnam* (New York: Times Books, 1995).

Mailer, N., *The Naked and the Dead* (New York: Holt, Reinhart & Wilson, 1948).

Mailer, N., *Why are We in Vietnam?* (London: Weidenfeld and Nicolson, 1969).

Matthews, L. and Brown, D., eds, *Assessing the Vietnam War* (Washington DC: Pergamon Group, 1987).

Melling, P. H., *Vietnam in American Literature: The Puritan Heritage* (Boston: Twayne, 1990).

Melling, P. H. and Roper, J., eds, *America, France and Vietnam: Cultural History and Ideas of Conflict* (Aldershot: Avebury, 1991).

Mock, J. R. and Larson, C., *Words That Won the War* (Princeton: Princeton University Press, 1939).

Moore, J., ed., *The Vietnam Debate: A Fresh Look at the Arguments* (Maryland: University Press of America, 1990).

Moore, R., *The Green Berets* (New York: Crown, 1965).

Morrison, T., *Beloved* (New York: Knopf, 1987).

Myers, T., *Walking Point* (Oxford: Oxford University Press, 1988).

Myers, W., *Honor the Warrior: The United States Marine Corps in Vietnam* (Lafayette, LA: Redoubt Press, 2000).

Nielson, J., *Warring Fictions: Cultural Politics and the Vietnam War* (Mississippi: University Press of Mississippi, 1998).

Nixon, R., *No More Vietnams* (London: W.H. Allen edition, 1986).

O'Brien, T., *The Things They Carried* (New York: Broadway Books edition, 1998).

O'Brien, T., *Going After Cacciato* (New York: Doubleday, 1978).

O'Neill, J. and Corsi, J., *Unfit for Command* (Washington DC: Regnery Publishing, 2004).

Pearce, R. H., *Savagism and Civilization* (Baltimore: Johns Hopkins Press, 1965).

Podhoretz, N., *Why We Were in Vietnam* (New York: Simon & Schuster, 1982).

Polenberg, R., *One Nation Divisible* (Harmondsworth: Penguin, 1980).

Pollard, E. A., *The Lost Cause; a New Southern History of the War of the Confederates* (New York: E. B. Treat & Co., 1866).

Raeithel, G., Ennslen, K., Ickstadt, H. and Keil, H., eds, Vietnamkrieg und Literature (Munich: Fink, 1972).

Rebuilding America's Defenses (New York: Project for the New American Century, September, 2000).

Rochester, S., *American War Narratives, 1917–1978: A Study and Bibliography* (NewYork: David Lewis, 1969).

Roosevelt, T. and Lodge, H. C., *Hero Tales from American History* (New York: Century Co., 1895).

Roper, J., *The American Presidents: Heroic Leadership from Kennedy to Clinton* (Edinburgh: Edinburgh University Press, 2000).

Roper, J., ed., *The American Civil War: Literary Sources and Documents* (Sussex: Helm, 2000).

Sandel, M. J., *Democracy's Discontent: America in Search of a Public Philosophy* (Cambridge: Harvard University Press, 1996).

Schell, J., *The Real War* (New York: Random House, 1988).

Schlesinger, A., Jr, *The Vital Center* (Boston: Houghton Mifflin, 1949).

Schlesinger, A. Jr, *The Bitter Heritage: Vietnam and American Democracy, 1941–1966* (Greenwich: Fawcett, 1968 edition).

Sheehan, N., *A Bright Shining Lie* (London: Jonathan Cape, 1989).

Showalter, E., *Hystories: Hysterical Epidemics and Modern Culture* (London: Picador, 1997).

Slotkin, R., *Regeneration Through Violence* (Middleton, CT: Wesleyan University Press, 1973).

——, *The Fatal Environment* (Middleton, CT: Wesleyan University Press, 1985).

——, *Gunfighter Nation* (New York: Harper Perennial, 1993).

Smith, H. N., *Mark Twain: A Collection of Essays* (Englewood Cliffs, NY: Prentice Hall, 1963).

Smith, J., *Looking Away: Hollywood and Vietnam* (New York: Scribner's, 1975).

Suid, L., *Guts and Glory: Great American War Movies* (Reading, Mass.: Addison-Wesley, 1978).

Summers, H., *On Strategy: The Vietnam War in Context* (New York: Dell Publishing Co. Inc., 1984).

Tuchman, B., *The March of Folly: From Troy to Vietnam* (New York: Knopf, 1984).

Turner, F., *Echoes of Combat: The Vietnam War in American Memory* (New York: Anchor Books, 1996).

Twain, M., *The Adventures of Huckleberry Finn* (New York: Penguin Books edition, 1986).

Van der Beets, R., ed., *Held Captive by Indians: Selected Narratives 1642–1836* (Knoxville: University of Tennessee Press, 1973).

Webb, J., *Fields of Fire* (London: Grafton Books, 1981).

Wells, T., *The War Within: America's Battle Over Vietnam* (New York: Henry Holt, 1994).

Wheeler, J., *Touched With Fire* (New York: Franklin Watts, 1984).

Wilson, J. C., *Vietnam in Prose and Film* (Jefferson, NC: McFarland, 1982).

Wolfe, A., ed., *America at Century's End* (Berkeley: University of California Press, 1991).

Woodward, B. and Bernstein, C., *All The Presidents Men* (New York: Simon & Schuster, 1974).

Wright, S., *Meditations in Green* (London: Abacus, Sphere Books, 1985).

Young, J. R., *Around the World With General Grant* (New York: The American News Co., 1879).

Index